SOCIAL + COMMUNICATION SKILLS & EMOTIONAL INTELLIGENCE (EQ) MASTERY (4 IN 1)

LEVEL-UP YOUR PEOPLE SKILLS, CONQUER CONSERVATIONS & BOOST YOUR CHARISMA BY DEVELOPING CRITICAL THINKING & LEADERSHIP SKILLS

STEWART HUNTER

DEVON HOUSE
PRESS

© **Copyright 2021 - All rights reserved.**

The contents of this book may not be reproduced, duplicated or transmitted without direct written permission from the author.

Under no circumstances will any legal responsibility or blame be held against the publisher for any reparation, damages, or monetary loss due to the information herein, either directly or indirectly.

Legal Notice:

This book is copyright protected. This is only for personal use. You cannot amend, distribute, sell, use, quote or paraphrase any part or the content within this book without the consent of the author.

Disclaimer Notice:

Please note the information contained within this document is for educational and entertainment purposes only. Every attempt has been made to provide accurate, up to date and reliable complete information. No warranties of any kind are expressed or implied. Readers acknowledge that the author is not engaging in the rendering of legal, financial, medical or professional advice. The content of this book has been derived from various sources. Please consult a licensed professional before attempting any techniques outlined in this book.

By reading this document, the reader agrees that under no circumstances is the author responsible for any losses, direct or indirect, which are incurred as a result of the use of information contained within this document, including, but not limited to, —errors, omissions, or inaccuracies.

CONTENTS

SOCIAL SKILLS & COMMUNICATION MASTERY (2 IN 1)

Introduction — 3

Part I
TAKING THE FIRST STEPS: BEING AWARE OF YOURSELF

1. What You Need to Know About Emotional Intelligence — 11
2. Social Skills Are Important for Life Success — 26
3. The Challenges Encountered – What Blocks You from Socializing? — 37
4. Analyze Your Current Toxic Social Habits & Behaviors, Then Revolutionize Them! — 49

Part II
PRACTICAL STEPS YOU CAN TAKE TO CONQUER SOCIALIZING

5. Make the Best First Impressions Possible — 65
6. How to Develop Rapport with Absolutely Anyone — 77
7. The Life-Changing Ability to Develop Friendships with Ease — 88
8. Going Beyond Basic Small Talk by Not Running Out of Things to Say — 100
9. Talking Isn't Everything – Learning to Become an Effective Listener — 110
10. Body Language is the Key to Successful Interactions — 121

11. Make Awkward Silences Your Best Friend &   131
Effortlessly Move Past Them Unaffected
12. It Has Ended – Wrapping up Your Conversation   139

Part III
KEEPING YOUR RELATIONSHIPS AND MAKING THEM LAST

13. How to Nurture Your Newly Formed Friendships   149
14. Conflicts Arising and How to Handle Them   162
15. Deepening Current Relationships in Your Life   179

Conclusion   191
References   197

EMOTIONAL INTELLIGENCE & CRITICAL THINKING SKILLS FOR LEADERSHIP (2 IN 1)

Introduction   203

Part I
SELF-CHECK: WHAT KIND OF LEADER ARE YOU RIGHT NOW?

1. Are You a True Leader?   209
2. The Building Blocks of a Great Leader   234

Part II
EMOTIONAL INTELLIGENCE

3. Understanding Emotional Intelligence   249
4. The 20 Must-Know Strategies That Can Boost Your EQ   263
5. Going Beyond Sympathy   273
6. Emotion Regulation is One of the Most Important Skills You Can Develop   282

Part III
SECTION 3: COGNITIVE ABILITIES

7. Our Parents Helped Us Develop It, We're Now Old Enough to Develop it Ourselves — 311
8. Deepening Your Cognitive Abilities — 322

Part IV
DEVELOP YOUR CRITICAL THINKING SKILLS AND USE THEM

9. Why Critical Thinking Skills? — 339

Part V
BUILDING BETTER RELATIONSHIPS, THRIVING IN YOUR CHOSEN PATH, & BECOMING THE BEST LEADER THAT YOU CAN BE

10. Social Skills — 355
11. The Impact of a Great Leadership in All Areas of Your Life — 368
12. Leadership and Other Skills During a Breakup — 394

Conclusion — 409

SOCIAL SKILLS & COMMUNICATION MASTERY (2 IN 1)

CONQUER CONVERSATIONS & UPGRADE YOUR CHARISMA. LEARN HOW TO ANALYZE PEOPLE, OVERCOME SHYNESS & BOOST YOUR EMOTIONAL INTELLIGENCE (EQ)

INTRODUCTION

You're in a room with several other people who are idly chatting away. You desperately want to be part of the conversation, but you find yourself frozen to the spot, unable to think of a single witty thing to say. Fear starts to creep up your spine, feeling cast out, lost, and completely inept.

Does this sound familiar?

More people struggle with socializing than you might realize. When it's happening to you, it feels like you're the only one in the world who feels that way, but in reality, it's not true. Many of the people chatting away in the room, seeming completely at ease, actually find it hard to open up and socialize with other people. The difference between you and them? They've learned the tools to completely hide their fear and show confidence in its place. They know how to respond to other people and read their body language. They get exactly what they need to do in order to make themselves feel as comfortable as possible.

You can be that person seeming at ease in a crowd. You don't know it yet, but you can.

I understand how you feel right now. You want to build relationships with those around you, you want to be able to talk and feel at ease, you don't want to worry about what people are going to think when you speak your mind, and you want to hold a conversation without always being on edge. You would love to be able to go to a party and not worry for hours beforehand about making small talk. You desperately want to build up your social circle, but the starting point of having to actually speak to people you don't know leaves you paralyzed with fear.

I understand you and I sympathize with you. However, the fact you're reading this book is the first brave step towards improving your social skills and kicking shyness and bad communication habits out of your life for good. So, pat yourself on the back for that!

You need to understand what you're doing wrong, you need to identify those bad habits and eradicate them, replacing them with good habits, and you need to learn the tools and skills to help you socialize in an easier and more free-flowing manner.

That's where this book comes in.

WHY SHOULD YOU TRUST A WORD I SAY?

You're probably reading this, rolling your eyes and wondering who on Earth I am and why I'm the authority on socializing. Well, let me tell you my story.

The reason I understand how you're feeling is that I've been where you are now. I was a shy child, and this didn't seem to change as I moved into my adolescence and early 20s. Whilst my friends at school were motoring their way through their first experiences, meeting new people, having their first relationships, going out for the first time, dreaming about what they were going to do with their career, and actually doing something about it rather than just dreaming, I was static. I had dreams, believe me, I had plenty, but acting upon them was far too much for me. I had friends, but I was always the quiet one, the one everyone thought was a little strange because I didn't say much. I blushed more than I wanted to, and I found myself stuttering over my words whenever I was put on the spot.

I berated myself every single night as I laid in bed for all the bumbling I did throughout the day. In my head, I was a confident person, I was happy, full of life, and easy in social situations. In reality, everything was the opposite. The worst thing was that I knew what I wanted to say, I could hold all of these conversations in my head and have them with ease.

You see, shyness isn't introversion. You can be introverted and not at all shy. Shyness is something else altogether. Shyness leaves you paralyzed when surrounded by people. You tell yourself that whatever you say won't be good enough, that people will laugh, or that your voice will come out all squeaky and you'll embarrass yourself. It's a fear of social situations but let me tell you something – fears can be overcome.

I overcame my shyness. How? Through hard work and focus. I had to face my fears, I had to push through those walls I'd built up around me. It was hard, it was scary at times, but it's the biggest achievement of my life to date. I worked out what I was doing wrong and I learned new habits to replace them. These days, socializing doesn't fill me with dread. I'll probably never be the world's most natural conversationalist, but I no longer worry about it, and I'm able to have easy conversations with those around me. I've met new friends because of it, I've had new relationships, and I've built up my career.

You can do all of this too.

I want to help you to achieve the same thing. I want to share what I learned and the techniques that worked for me. Then, I want you to share all of that with other people in your life who might be struggling.

The saddest part of all of this is that there are millions of people walking around, struggling with their social skills. It's holding them back; it's stopping them from living their best lives. It's stopping them from forming close relationships with other people. But, it can all be changed – the issue is that most people don't know that they can change their situation, so they simply carry on in the same way.

That's not going to be your fate.

This book will change your life. That's a bold statement, I know, but it's a true one. Being more confident in your ability to socialize will open so many doors for you, both in your professional and personal lives. You'll build those close relationships that have eluded you so far, and your fear of socializing will slowly ebb away.

Can you imagine how good that will feel?

Countless people in the world have overcome their shyness and poor social skills, creating a new life for themselves. You only have to do a quick Google search to find a whole range of such people, and they followed exactly the same advice that you're going to read in this book.

MY PROMISE TO YOU

By the end of this book, I promise that you'll be able to not only feel more confident in your future ability, but you'll be able to identify the problems that have been holding you back and overcome them. From that, you'll start to try out your new skills and you'll see the results coming your way, showing you that the progress you've made was more than worth the results.

Put simply, you will conquer your problems and you'll master socializing as a result.

So, why hang around for a second longer?

Your shyness has held you back long enough. Do not give it another second of your time or attention. Now, turn your focus towards the strategies and advice in this book, implementing them into your daily routine and looking forward to the results.

The alternative? Of course, you could simply continue as you are. You could assume that it's just too hard or that it's not going to work for you. As a result, you'll continue struggling to communicate, you'll always find it hard to build relationships with people, and you'll always be socially inept.

Is that what you want for yourself? Do you want to continue missing opportunities and watching them pass you by?

Of course, you don't, and that's why if you're smart (and I know you are), you'll turn the page and begin your journey.

I

TAKING THE FIRST STEPS: BEING AWARE OF YOURSELF

1

WHAT YOU NEED TO KNOW ABOUT EMOTIONAL INTELLIGENCE

You've made it to the first chapter, so give yourself a pat on the back. That means you've shown a willingness to start making changes in your life and begin the first step on your journey.

Whenever you want to change something in your life, you first need to acknowledge the problem. That's often the hardest part. It means admitting that something in your life just isn't working, but that is what will allow you to grow and improve.

This first chapter is going to focus on emotional intelligence, or EQ. This is important because it overlaps with every single part of what you're trying to work towards. You want to be able to socialize better, you want to communicate better, you want to connect with others. Having a higher level of EQ will allow you to do all of those things.

We'll explore what EQ is, why it is different from another very similar-sounding term, IQ, and we're going to go on to talk about the components. I'm then going to help you explore how low your EQ may be, because I'm sorry to say this – the problems you're having indicate low EQ. BUT – there is always a but – this is a fluctuant level which can be increased with some ongoing work.

First things first, let's work out exactly what EQ is.

EMOTIONAL INTELLIGENCE (EQ) - WHAT IS IT & HOW IS IT DIFFERENT FROM IQ?

There are two terms that are very often confused – EQ and IQ. This book is going to focus on EQ, because as someone who struggles in social situations and with communication generally, your EQ is low.

Now, before you panic, this doesn't mean that you're not intelligent. IQ is a measure of intelligence, EQ is not. EQ stands for emotional intelligence. It's entirely possible for you to have an extremely high IQ, to be an extremely smart person, yet to struggle to communicate with others and connecting, and as a result, your EQ is low.

Let's simplify this thing. EQ isn't about your smarts, it's about:

- How you recognize the emotions in other people
- How you connect with others
- How you communicate with others
- How you understand and manage your own range of emotions
- How you respond to stressful situations and challenges
- How you show empathy to other people
- How you handle conflict.

Emotional intelligence encompasses all of these things but it's far harder to measure than IQ. If you want to know what your IQ is, you can easily do a few cognitive tests and you'll get a pretty good idea of where you're at. With EQ, getting an actual reading is borderline impossible, instead, you need a gauge.

As someone who struggles with communication, socializing, and someone who finds it hard to build relationships with other people because of all of this, your EQ needs a little work. The good news is that working on your EQ will allow you to solve all of the socializing and communication problems that have held you back so far, but it will also help you to manage your own emotions and how you respond to stress and upsets too. You'll become more mindful, you'll be able to live in the moment rather than worrying about the past or future, and as a result, you will be much happier.

Is IQ more important than EQ? Not at all. You can be smart, but you can also be lonely. You can be the cleverest person to ever walk the earth, to be smashing tests left, right, and center, but what use is any of that if you don't have relationships with other people? If you can't speak to others and build friendships? If you can't share it all with the people in your life? For that reason, you could argue, and many people agree, that EQ is far more important in life than IQ could ever be.

WHAT IT MEANS TO HAVE HIGH EQ

So, what does it mean when you have a high EQ level? Does it mean you're always happy, you never struggle, and that everything is roses? Of course not. Life is difficult for everyone from time to time, but when your EQ is higher, it makes it easier for you to handle problems and you're able to see the more positive side of things, rather than assuming that the glass is always half empty, or always will be.

I've outlined above what EQ is in terms of how it allows you to live your life, but what clear benefits does it bring? What will come your way if you dedicate your time and effort to boosting your EQ level? How will it solve your current problems?

You Will Be Able to Handle Change More Positively

Many people struggle with change. It's no surprise, change is sometimes hard to deal with, but it happens throughout the course of life. If you find yourself often being thrown by change and it causes you to feel worried or even scared, building your EQ will help you with that. You will learn to see change as something positive, as a chance to build something new, and you will respond to it more positively in general, seeing the opportunities it could bring you.

You'll Find it Easier to Communicate and Work with Others

In terms of communication, EQ is vital. This works on many different levels, but being able to read others, empathize, and connect means that you can communicate more effectively. Your confidence grows naturally when your EQ level is higher, which certainly helps when communicating with other people, be it individually or within a group. This also means that if you are working with other people, perhaps in a collaborative session, you'll find it easier to put forth your ideas and listen more effectively to the ideas of others.

Difficult Conversations Will Be Far Easier Too

EQ allows you to read other people and gives you an almost sixth sense of what to say versus what not to say. Again, much of this comes down to confidence and self-awareness, which higher EQ will certainly help with. Whenever you're faced with a difficult conversation, either in your personal life or your professional life, building your EQ will allow you to navigate the potential pitfalls with ease, rather than bumbling, stumbling, and potentially saying the wrong thing.

You Will Recognize and Empathize with Others, Building Relationships

If you're still struggling to understand how EQ will help with communication and socializing, this next point should explain it. When you boost your EQ, you're able to understand what isn't being said. You can read body language, you listen to the words other people are saying but you also listen to what isn't being said, such as non-verbal cues, speed of speech, eye contact, etc. All of this helps you read what they really mean.

You will also notice that your natural empathy level will increase as you recognize the emotions in other people. This allows you to naturally build relationships that are built on trust, understanding, and care – the very best type of relationships!

You Will Live in The Moment

A very pleasant side-effect of higher EQ is mindfulness. You can work towards mindfulness as a route towards increasing your EQ, but it almost comes naturally. This means that you're able to allow things to occur in your life without allowing them to take you over completely. I mentioned the ability to deal with change, but it's more than that. It's about not constantly living in the past, or deeply worrying about the future. You'll live in the moment and have a sense of calm because you know that you can handle whatever life throws at you. It's a very comforting feeling.

You Will Find It Easier to Manage Your Own Emotions

You won't just recognize and read the emotions of others, you'll become more aware of your own. This increased self-awareness helps you to manage your emotions as they ebb and flow, avoiding 'in the heat of the moment' actions and also helping you to deal with problems.

People with higher EQ are better and more effective problem solvers, simply because they don't allow their emotions to get the better of them. That's not to say that they never have strong emotions, it's just that they can recognize them and deal with them far more effectively.

Now can you see why EQ is such an important part of the solution to your original problem?

THE FIVE DIFFERENT COMPONENTS OF EQ

The subject of EQ has long been of interest to researchers and five main categories of EQ have been identified. These are:

- Self-awareness
- Self-regulation
- Motivation
- Empathy
- Social skills

All of these are of great interest to you too, given that you are focused upon shedding shyness, increasing your social skills, and allowing yourself to become a better communicator.

Being more self-aware means that you can recognize your emotions and moods, but you can also read how these might be affecting other people around you. Increasing self-awareness means an ability to take yourself less seriously, to not take mistakes so harshly, and also be more aware of how other people view you.

Self-regulation links into self-awareness because you can't really have one without the other. Self-regulation means that you can control your moods and the actions that might come as a result, whilst also avoiding acting upon impulse. This can loosely be interpreted as emotional maturity, and it's also about how you respond to other people and their moods too. For instance, a person who seems short and off-handed is not necessarily upset with you, but instead, they're angry at something else that's going on in their life. Self-awareness and self-regulation allow you to see this and adjust your response correctly.

Another important element of EQ is motivation, and this is what will push you to keep learning and improving yourself throughout your life. You will see and take opportunities as they come your way, and improving your social skills, will also bring you more opportunities as a result. A person with higher EQ will take the initiative and make something happen, rather than sitting back and waiting for it to fall into their lap. It's also about identifying what drives you in life – is it the materialistic ownership of the fanciest phone, or is it success and achievement in your career or personal life?

The next component is empathy, and this is where communication really comes to the fore. When you have empathy, you're able to read other people and understand their emotions, therefore "walking a mile in their shoes". A person with high EQ understands people and situations far more effectively and it helps them to support those around them. This is a vital part of developing relationships and communicating with others.

Finally, we have social skills.

Earlier I mentioned being able to read body language, speech, listening, non-verbal cues, etc. All of this is vital in communication and socializing. It helps you to develop and maintain relationships, whilst also allowing you to have a certain ease in conversations. Empathy links into this as well, as you can find things you have in common and discuss from there. EQ boosts your communication skills, allowing you to be a good conversationalist, whilst also being a leader whenever necessary. It means you can tailor your approach to the situation you're in, and that will bring you many benefits in all areas of your life.

HOW TO IDENTIFY YOUR LEVEL OF EQ

The most natural next step from reading this chapter is going to be a keenness to learn your own EQ level. As I mentioned earlier, it's not as easy to measure EQ as it is to measure IQ. However, you can get a general idea and there are tests you can take which will allow you to get a sense of how much work you need to do in order to boost your own EQ level over time.

You don't have to take a test full of multiple choice questions to give this answer, you can be more aware of your own actions and how you interact (or how you don't interact) and that will give you a good indicator of your EQ level too. To help you with that, let's identify a few very common signs of low EQ. If you notice these on a regular basis, that's your answer!

- You struggle to communicate with those around you
- You often feel like you've failed if someone criticizes you or gives constructive guidance
- You feel embarrassed if someone points out something you've said or done
- You take your own mistakes, whether large or small, extremely to heart
- You like to be right, and struggle when someone points out that you're possibly not

- You find it hard to read other people and you're not sure where to start with body language
- You often miss signs that those around you are going through a tough time
- You're often not sure what to say to someone who is upset or angry
- You often blame other people for problems, rather than understanding your own role
- Your days are often thrown up in the air by a rising emotion
- You often overthink things and always jump to the worst-case scenario
- You find it very hard to cope with change
- You have emotional tantrums or outbursts which you later feel embarrassed or ashamed of
- You find it hard to let other people in and as a result, you find relationships very difficult.

This isn't an exhaustive list, because the scope of EQ is so large. However, if you can nod along to several of them on a regular basis, then you have some work to do. Don't worry, however, that's what the rest of this book is about! Having low EQ isn't a sign of a failure or something wrong with you, it's simply a sign that you need to focus on improving your life. By doing so, you'll gain major benefits and you'll be far happier for it.

If you do prefer to take a test, there are several you can look into. The most common is the MSCEIT, or the Mayer-Salovey-Caruso Emotional Intelligence Test. This takes just over half an hour to complete and covers 141 questions. The areas covered include perceiving emotions, understanding emotions, facilitating thoughts, and managing emotions.

Whether you want an actual score to work with or an idea that there is work to be done, the outcome will be the same. Working on your EQ is never a waste of time. It means that you will gain your overall aim – improving your communication skills, shedding shyness, and being able to socialize more easily. The content of this book will work towards raising your EQ naturally, but being aware of it and understanding that EQ is a vital component of a healthy and happy life, means that you're already on the right track.

IMPROVING YOUR EQ

So, what can you do to increase your EQ?

Often, being aware of a problem means you're more focused on fixing it. Simply being aware that you have a problem with low EQ means that you'll be more switched on when it comes to recognizing your emotions and understanding others. It turns your attention outwards, and that's a great first step.

The content of this book will help you with increasing your EQ, but if you want some specific ideas on what else you can do to raise your level, there is plenty to suggest.

Use Mindfulness to Manage Emotions

A key cornerstone of EQ is recognizing and managing emotions. Mindfulness is an ideal way to do all of that. This is a process of becoming more 'in the moment'. When you practice mindfulness, you allow change to happen without worrying about it, you don't think about what you can't change or control, and you don't worry about what is to come. It's a sense of calm and serenity that will change your life.

Mindfulness can be practiced in many different ways, but meditation is the ideal starting point. Keeping your mind in the here and now can be very difficult at first, but stick with it. By doing so, you'll be able to be more aware of your emotions, you'll be able to recognize them, understand whether they're helpful to you or not, and you'll learn to give yourself a moment to control rising emotions, before acting out of anger, upset, or jealousy, etc. This is also a great way to stop your whole day from being derailed by a short burst of intense emotion.

Try to Focus on Empathy

Communication and relationship building requires empathy. Be mindful (there's that word again) of other people and what they might be going through. Look at body language, try and read whether someone is hiding something, check whether they're making eye contact, listen to their words and try and analyze how they're speaking, rather than just allowing words to float in one ear and out of the other one.

Try and put yourself in the shoes of others and understand that everyone is fighting their own battles. By doing so, you'll increase your level of empathy and you'll find it far easier to connect with those around you as a result. This yields real, lasting relationships.

Understand Your Emotional Triggers

Everyone has a set of personal emotional triggers, but the key is to know what they are and then minimize their impact on you, avoid them altogether, or face them and overcome them. So, what are your emotional triggers? What things, people, or situations get you riled up and cause you to feel a certain way? This doesn't have to be anger, although that's the most common emotion to cause bad actions. It can be upset, sadness, jealousy, regret, basically any negative emotion.

It's a good idea to keep a journal to help you identify your triggers. Look back over the day and note down any strong emotions you felt, including what was happening around the time, what you were thinking about, or what/who you encountered. You will probably start to see patterns emerging over time and once you have that information, you can work out how best to stop that trigger from having such a stronghold over you.

Develop a Positive Attitude

Positivity will literally change your life. People with a low EQ often have a default negative attitude, but that can be changed. Try reframing. This is a cognitive behavioral therapy technique that is used for a variety of different situations.

Whenever you recognize a negative thought entering your mind, stop, acknowledge it, and then replace that thought with something positive. Repeat it and stick at it, until your brain recognizes the positive before the negative.

For instance, if you think "I hate the rain", acknowledge that as a negative thought and replace it with "the garden needs the rain". If you think "Susan always seems to be angry with me", replace that with "I need to understand Susan a little better".

It won't happen overnight, but soon you will notice the first seedlings of a more positive mindset!

Manage Your Time More Effectively

Time management and stress management work hand in hand. A person with high EQ handles stress effectively but they also don't go out of their way to put themselves in stressful situations in the first place. You can't avoid all stress, because it's a part of life, but you can do what you can to manage your time and feel more in control.

Try writing a list of goals you want to achieve that particular day and work toward ticking them off your list. Try specific techniques, such as the Pomodoro Method, which allows you to work in short, sharp bursts, along with short breaks to refresh your mind. Have a list of prioritized tasks you need to complete every day and work towards achieving them. The more in control and organized you feel, the less stress you'll encounter.

CHAPTER THOUGHTS

This first chapter has been an introduction to the rather complicated yet fascinating world of EQ. You are trying to improve your communication skills and become a master socializer, but you can't do any of that if you don't understand the role EQ plays in your life.

Working on improving your EQ means that you're focusing upon reading other people in a more effective way. Your communication skills will improve as you develop a more empathic view towards others, and you'll feel more confident with each small success.

Changing something about you on a deep level often means delving into areas of life that you don't think have that much of a connection to one another. However, EQ and your overall future aims are so closely linked that understanding the subject is vital.

Think carefully about your own level of EQ and if you want to take a formal test, go for it. The bottom line is that test or no test, you need to work on your EQ if you want to become a better communicator. It's not just about the things you say, it's about how you read others and how you react to them – conversations are two ways things and by connecting with others more deeply, you'll find it far easier to learn more about them and communicate with them more naturally as a result.

2

SOCIAL SKILLS ARE IMPORTANT FOR LIFE SUCCESS

Throughout every situation you encounter in life, you'll need to use your social skills.

You'll need to communicate with people, you'll need to assess situations, read body languages and you'll also need to tap into the other aspects of EQ, which we talked about in our last chapter. Everyone has social skills, you're not born with a zero capacity to communicate in some way with other people, but the quality varies from case to case.

For example, you might meet someone who's fantastic at communicating. They don't care if they've never met the person, they have no issues with shyness, they're pretty confident in themselves, and they're loud and proud. That is someone with highly tuned social skills, perhaps a little too far towards the end of the scale if they're super-loud or a little too confident.

You'll also meet people who use their social skills well but feel they also need to improve. Nobody is perfect and we can all do better.

You might place yourself in that category, or you might feel that your social skills need some serious work. It doesn't matter what your starting point is, it's about putting forth the effort to make things better. Part of that is about understanding why social skills are such a staple part of life.

Yes, it's about communicating with other people but it's not just about hearing the words and taking them at face value. It's also not about just speaking. People say things they don't mean when they're trying to hide their true emotions, you included. Well-tuned social skills allow you to delve a little deeper and find out what's really going on. It's also about voicing your needs and concerns and being able to read other people effectively.

Of course, social skills are also about non-verbal cues, such as facial expressions and body language. Having good social skills means that you get your point over in the right way, without misunderstandings or concerns.

If you think back to the last chapter on emotional intelligence, you'll see how this all links into one giant circle. Being a good communicator means that your EQ is higher automatically, having high EQ gives you the confidence to be able to speak your mind, look for the real meaning in someone's words, by being able to read them properly, and it allows you to control your emotions and avoid those emotional outbursts that would otherwise threaten your day and potentially put you at loggerheads with someone close to you.

In this chapter, I'm going to press home the importance of social skills a little more. You can't be successful or totally happy in life without having good quality social skills. Without them, you'll miss out in such a big way. The hope is that by showing you how important these skills are, you'll gain even more motivation to push through and improve your own situation.

WHY ARE SOCIAL SKILLS IMPORTANT? THE 3 STARTLING TRUTHS

The startling truth is actually this statement – without good quality social skills, you cannot succeed in life, either professionally or personally. There will always be more you could have done, things you wish you'd said, a problem that totally escaped you, or something which was a major blockage for you to go on and achieve what you dreamed of. You'll live your life in regret, with the "what if" looming large. Life with a question like that is no fun.

So, what are the three startling truths about social skills?

#1 Employers are always on the lookout for employees who have good social skills

No matter how qualified you are for the job, if you're going up against someone who has excellent social skills and can communicate more articulately and clearly, they're probably going to get the job over you. You could have smashed the interview, done a fantastic presentation, but their superior social skills will give them an edge that you can't overcome.

Every single day in the workplace you're going to come up against problems, complaints, collaboration opportunities, and possibly even conflicts. Good social skills allow you to traverse every single one of those situations.

For me, speaking up in a meeting has always been something that filled me with dread. I had a vision in my mind of speaking up, and my voice sounding quiet and squeaky, or even croaky. People would laugh and ask me to repeat myself, and upon doing so, they would simply demand "louder girl!" I can feel the humiliation, even though the situation never actually happened to me. That is a prime example of poor social skills and although I've certainly gone on to improve since then, I still stop for a second when in a meeting and allow that fear to show itself, before realizing that if I'm going to keep winning, I have to push it away.

It doesn't matter if you have more talent in your little finger than the other people in your office; if you find it hard to communicate, if you have low EQ and you struggle with collaboration and you can't express yourself in a way you would like, you're never going to hit the career high notes. All of that studying and training will have been for nothing because, at the end of the day, the basics matter the most. Employers will always look for someone who has great communication skills – it's often on the job description.

#2 Good social skills expand your network

It stands to reason that if you're able to socialize and communicate well, you're going to have more friends, more connections, and great opportunities for networking. Business opportunities can appear at any time; you could be at a party and a close friend introduces you to someone they know. Before you know it, you're discussing a joint venture that could bring you great wealth and future growth opportunities. It really is that simple much of the time.

However, if you lack confidence and your social skills need work, these types of opportunities will often evade you.

Networking is often thought of as something you do with business cards in hand, but every day you speak to someone new, you're basically networking. If you tell them about what you do for a living, you're networking without even realizing it. Having the social skills to get out there and make opportunities means that your overall personal success, whatever that is to you, will be achieved. If you lack social skills, you're always going to be wishing for more.

From a personal point of view, having good social skills means you'll have a larger circle, or you'll develop closer relationships with those around you. The people you laugh with and socialize with might not be your very best friends, but you're able to talk, chat, laugh, joke, and basically spend time of value. This requires social skills.

Can you see how almost everything you do in life needs social skills to some degree? Even sending an email requires social skills; you might not be talking to them, but you're expressing yourself in words, which need to be carefully crafted to ensure that you get the right message over, without offending, sounding off-hand, or perhaps unknowledgeable. Everything requires social skills to some degree and when you lack them, or you have a lower level of them, everything is going to miss the mark, leaving you feeling unfulfilled and downright frustrated.

#3 Social skills give you a better quality of life

Feeling free to speak up, confident enough to speak your mind, and not having to worry about saying the wrong thing, it feels fantastic. It's not just about having those connections I've just mentioned, it's about your life generally being better.

A good social circle means more fun. Close relationships mean you're supported and safe. Being able to be there for those around you makes you feel good. The confidence to speak your mind and put your views across helps to build your self-esteem and when that is high, almost anything is possible!

When you have high class social skills, when your EQ is high, you will have a much better quality of life overall. No more crippling anxiety, no more shyness, no more turning down dates and parties because you're worried about walking into the room alone, and no more struggling to find your voice. All of that is a thing of the past and what is left is a relaxed, easy, free, and happy canvas on which you can draw the life you really want – then go ahead and create it.

CONQUER SOCIALIZING WITH THESE 4 SKILLS

In our next chapter, I'm going to go into some real depth on the skills you can use to build up your EQ and therefore the quality of your social skills, however, in this section, I'm going to briefly introduce you to them. By understanding why social skills are important you can move forward to start building up your own levels, but you need to know the work that is ahead of you.

There are certain things you can do every day, skills you can use in your daily life, which will give you a great head start. Soon enough, these things will become second nature to you, and you'll perform them almost without any thought whatsoever. When you reach that point, you'll also be able to pat yourself on the back because that's real progress right there!

So, what four skills can you use in your everyday life that will take you a long way towards conquering the art of socializing?

Empathy

In our last chapter, we talked about EQ and mentioned the ability to put yourself in the place of someone else. This is called empathy and by learning the art of empathy and pushing it forward into your everyday routine, you'll be able to understand other people far more effectively.

This is about knowing what someone needs to feel comfortable enough to open up, knowing that you should treat others as you would want to be treated, and it allows you to listen properly and really understand them at their very core. As you can see, socializing isn't just about talking, it's about understanding too.

Listening

You might think that listening is a super-easy thing to do. You just literally listen, however, it's a skill that most people fail to do effectively. Listening isn't just hearing the words and allowing them to float into one ear, spend a small amount of time in your brain, and then float back out the other side. It's about *really* listening. It's about tuning into what is said and what isn't said. It's about reading body language, assessing the way someone speaks, and it's about other people knowing that you're really listening because this will encourage them to open up.

Co-operation

It's very rare in the modern world that we work alone, and it's far more likely that you're going to be asked to work as part of a team at some point. This takes specific types of skills and it also means fully understanding what is expected of you and what your role is within that team.

Teams have a common goal to achieve and in order to achieve those goals, people need to work together well, be able to overcome misunderstandings and problems and focus upon that common goal above everything else. Again, don't worry too much at this point about the specifics of how to develop these skills right now, as we're going to explore that in far more detail shortly. For now, simply understand that these skills are very useful in your everyday life and will help you become a better communicator and socializer, whilst reaching your aims in life.

Positivity

How does positivity help you with socialization? EQ and positivity work hand in hand, but let's be honest, most people would rather be around positive people compared to negative people. This can be as simple as basic manners, remembering to say "please", "thank you", "good morning", etc.

The basics really do get you far and never underestimate the power of manners. Most people determine whether they like someone based firmly on how polite they are and how they use their manners, it's a sign of their decency, and when you remember this fact, whilst also pushing forward with a positive attitude, you'll be amazed at how much easier it is to work with people. Again, people respond far better to positivity!

We're going to delve into these skills in our next chapter but you can see that developing your social skills isn't really anything totally mind-blowing and it's more about knowing the basics and pushing forward, whilst building your confidence to the point where you feel much more comfortable going past your current comfort zone. Shyness doesn't have to be a barrier that holds you back throughout your life, it can be something that you overcome and allow to lead you forward to greater things in life.

EXPERT'S THOUGHTS ON SOCIAL SKILLS

Don't just take my word for it, the experts all agree that social skills are a key and integral part of life.

Humans are social beings. We crave togetherness and comfort, and in order to achieve that, we need to ask for what we need, and we need to give those things to other people. How do you do that? Via your social skills.

However, we live in a digital age and a lot of the time people, especially young adults, are communicating via social media and messaging apps, rather than actually speaking to people in person. That can be extremely detrimental and we're seeing rising levels of anxiety and depression amongst younger people, thought to be linked to this lower amount of socialization going on.

When we socialize with others on a regular basis, we increase our level of EQ, we show our empathy and develop this skill to a higher level, and we understand far more. We understand the views of other people and they understand ours; we can have constructive conversations about points which might be contentious, and develop a deeper understanding whilst also opening our minds to new approaches and different ideas. Having a high level of EQ and high-quality social skills means that you are more open-minded and agreeable to other people's views and that can never be a bad thing.

Experts also agree that social skills can literally make a business deal or break one. In the business world, it often comes down to the small things as to whether a deal is going to go ahead or not. A small misunderstanding can totally ruin a fantastic deal, and when your social skills aren't up to par, it's very easy to say the wrong thing without meaning to, perhaps not understanding how the other person might perceive what you're saying.

At the end of the day, humans need those key social interactions in life, whether on a personal basis or a professional. When your social skills are high quality, it's far easier to go out and meet new people, explain your needs to those around you, and deepen friendships and relationships with people already in your life. This simply makes life better and happier. It really is as simple as that.

Without those close connections, your life will always be on the fringes and your personal relationships will always be lacking something. Developing close relationships with other people hinges on social skills and that is something that all experts agree on, after years of research and studies.

For these reasons alone, and many more besides, focusing upon overcoming your self-limiting thoughts, on understanding your weaknesses and overcoming them, whilst kicking shyness to the curb, is something you should certainly focus your time and attention upon.

CHAPTER THOUGHTS

Social skills are so important for life, not only in terms of your success but also in how you develop relationships with other people. When you connect with others, life is more fulfilling, and you have that all-important circle of support around you. You cannot meet other people and create those connections without using your social skills at the start.

In this chapter we've really driven home the importance of social skills and why you need them for your personal and professional life. Use this information as a springboard towards your own success in mastering communication and improving your skills. Now you know why they're important and the basics to build on, you should be feeling motivated to make all-important changes.

3

THE CHALLENGES ENCOUNTERED – WHAT BLOCKS YOU FROM SOCIALIZING?

Your personal reasons for struggling with socializing might be completely different from everyone else who picks up this book, but it's important that you identify what they are. Without really knowing what you need to do, you're working in the dark!

For me, it was a fear of saying the wrong thing, of embarrassing myself, and of failing. Of course, that all came down to shyness, but maybe shyness isn't your issue.

In this chapter I'm going to talk about your own blockades, the walls you subconsciously put up to stop you from reaching out to others and socializing. You might think that's a harsh statement because you're not doing any of this on purpose, but without even realizing it, you're allowing your fears and your limiting beliefs to get in the way. The key is to know what they are and learn to overcome them. Handily, the advice in this book is going to give you plenty of tips on how to do that!

WHAT ARE YOUR PERSONAL MENTAL BARRICADES?

Shyness and social anxiety are two possible barricades that are stopping you from socializing, but these aren't the only two options. It could be that you have a very different mental blockage that simply needs to be knocked down in order to make a major improvement in your life.

Let's look at a few common barriers that may be in your way to socializing:

- **Jumping to conclusions** – If someone has a tendency to jump to conclusions without fully listening to what the other person is saying, this is a huge barrier to communication. Forming early judgments means that you're not present in the moment and the other person is going to feel not listened to and not taken seriously.
- **Poor focus and low attention span** – The inability to pay attention for too long can also be a barrier to communication and can be something that affects a person's ability to use their social skills to the best of their ability. This can be due to a number of reasons, but someone who suffers from ADHD may struggle to pay attention for too long; therefore, if a person is taking too long to get to the point,

they won't be able to listen for quite as long as they would like.

- **Language barriers** – A language barrier is a huge problem in itself because this opens up the possibility of misunderstandings and a huge wall coming down between either party. It can also be the case that when a message is communicated, it loses its credibility and meaning and therefore, erodes away at its quality.
- **A lack of trust** – Communication has no space for distrust and if one of the people communicating doesn't trust the other one, there is going to be a huge barrier in the way. This basically means that one party pays very little attention to what the other person is saying and could also mean that they don't believe what they're saying. As a result, there is zero credibility to the conversation.
- **Emotions on the day** – How a person is feeling on any given day can greatly affect how they respond to others and how they communicate in general. If someone is feeling angry about something which happened earlier in the day, they can easily be short with the person they're speaking to, although completely unrelated in a topic. That can cause a higher chance of misunderstandings or the other person feeling that maybe they're angry at them. That's just one example, but how someone is feeling, and their general emotional state can cause a huge communication blockage. Great communicators try not to let their emotions get in the way of how they speak to people, but this is sometimes easier

said than done! Of course, this is also where EQ comes into the equation.

As you can see, it's not always shyness or social anxiety that causes a person to struggle with communication and their social skills in general. A person who is struggling with their mental health, in general, will no doubt find that their ability to socialize is reduced, simply because their focus is affected. If someone is struggling with anxiety, that could cause them to become fearful or even paranoid about the intentions of those they're speaking to, which leads to the distrust mentioned earlier.

It's important to pinpoint what your particular barricade is. If it's social anxiety or shyness, that's something we're going to explore in more detail shortly, but give it some thought because these aren't always the only two options available to you. When you know what the problem is, you have more information to use in terms of knocking that barricade down.

SHYNESS VS SOCIAL ANXIETY – WHAT MAKES THEM DIFFERENT?

Many people lump social anxiety and shyness into the same category, but they're actually two distinctly different situations and deserve to be separated.

Many people with social anxiety go through life thinking they're shy, but it's actually a step up on the ladder and is actually considered to be a psychiatric disorder. The good news is that if you do suffer from social anxiety, it can be treated with cognitive behavioral therapy, however, recognizing the condition is the first step.

Shyness is feeling worried and fearful in social situations. Social anxiety is panicking and being fearful to another level. The conditions are so similar that it's hard to explain them with any real separation, but it really comes down to the severity of the effects that pull them apart.

The best way to explain shyness is a personality trait. Most people who are shy don't like having the spotlight on them and if they have to attend a social event when there is going to be any amount of attention on them, they become fearful and worried. However, shyness isn't usually debilitating, although it can hold you back in life if you allow it to do so.

On the other hand, social anxiety is a far more serious deal. A person with social anxiety will have distress on a completely different level to shyness when faced with a situation that causes them to be in the spotlight, and even when they're not in the spotlight. This could mean that they completely avoid social situations altogether, in order to try and feel better. You can understand why this would be damaging because we've already established that humans need to have social interactions in order to thrive, but also to have any amount of personal or professional success in life. In addition, social anxiety can cause a person to think that they're being judged at all times, or even watched. This can erode away not only their confidence but also their mental health.

The main symptoms of social anxiety include:

- Fast heart rate
- Feeling nauseous
- Shaking
- Sweating excessively
- Facial blushing
- Difficulty getting words out
- Extreme self-consciousness
- A fear of being judged
- Avoiding any type of social situation.

Shyness shouldn't be downplayed, however. Yes, it's less severe than social anxiety, but it can still play a major role in causing a person to avoid any type of socialization and to severely damage their quality of life.

3 TRICKS TO OVERCOME ANXIETY & SHYNESS

Overcoming anxiety and shyness certainly takes time and effort. No matter what you try, it's not going to work overnight. That's something you need to be prepared for. It's easy to start something and assume that you're going to see change overnight, but you'll be disappointed here. The key to overcoming anxiety and shyness is pushing yourself out of your comfort zone, facing fears rather than running away from them, and all of this takes time to build up. However, it's time well spent, that's for sure.

In this section, we're going to talk about three specific tricks you can try on a regular basis, building up your new-found immunity to anxiety and shyness.

Don't Run Away from Fear, Face It

When you're scared of something, the first instinct you have is to run away from it. This is a normal reaction because you just don't want to have to deal with it. Why should you want to? It's painful and it makes you feel bad. However, if you run away from your fears on a constant basis, you're going to find that they start to own you. How can you overcome something if you simply run away from it every time it rears its ugly head?

The problem with shyness and social anxiety is that the fear you have isn't actually rational. To you it's very real, it was to me, but in reality, when you look back on it, you wonder why you were scared. I often feel that way now. Back in the day, I was terrified of speaking in meetings. I'd do everything I could to avoid it, even trying to busy myself taking notes and trying to look busy, but did hiding away help me overcome that fear? Not at all. If anything, it just caused it to grow. I look back now and I can't believe I was so scared. Sure, I still don't love speaking up at meetings, it's not my most favorite thing in the world, but I'm not scared anymore. If I say the wrong thing I don't shrink back in embarrassment, I just laugh at myself.

If I can do it, so can you.

Facing your fears isn't easy, but the more you expose yourself to them, the less power they have over you and the less fearful you'll be.

Step 1 - Acknowledgment

The first thing you need to do is acknowledge it. What are you fearful of? What is it exactly? Give it a name. Be as specific as you can when you acknowledge it to yourself and if it helps, write it down.

"I am fearful of standing up in front of a group of people and speaking"

Then say why you're fearful.

"I'm scared my voice will crack and they'll laugh at me".

Whatever it is, name it.

Step 2 – Challenge Your Ideas

Why do you think that someone will laugh at you if your voice cracks? Why do you think that you should be scared when you stand up and speak in front of people? Do you think everyone else in the room is super-confident and nobody else has the same worry?

Challenging your ideas means pulling apart your fear and questioning it. Fear doesn't like to be questioned because when it is, it doesn't have the answers. Then, it loses its power because you realize it's nothing more than a very clever ruse.

If you're fearful of being rejected by a group of people, ask yourself why you're automatically going to be rejected. What is so terrible about you that every person you meet is going to be instantly repulsed? There is no answer to that because it's not the truth.

Really analyze and pull apart your fear and you'll quickly start to see that the very thing you were fearful of is nothing more than fear itself. The problem is nothing more than an idea and ideas aren't always right.

Step 3 – Face Your Fear

This is the hardest part, but the first two steps will have prepared you well.

You're reading this book because you don't want to be held back any longer. You want to be able to socialize freely and be happy in your relationships. So, you need to do the work and that means ripping off the Band-Aid and going for it. You can do it, don't tell yourself that you can't!

If you're scared of speaking up at a meeting, just do it. You don't have to give a speech, you can just put forth one short idea, but the more you do it, the easier it will become and the more you'll see that your fear was just imaginary. If you're fearful of being rejected by a group of people, embrace the wonderful person you are and just go in there and be yourself. You'll soon see that people are more welcoming than you're giving them credit for.

You can't just do this once. You have to keep facing your fear to pull away from its power and eventually you'll get to the point where you can't believe you were ever so scared.

Let's Play a Game

When facing fears and pushing yourself into situations that would otherwise cause you to feel anxious and allow your shyness to spike, it's a good idea to take yourself out of the situation whilst still doing it.

Confused? Let me explain a little more.

This game is going to help you do the things that you're worried about or fearful of, but you're not going to feel like it's you that's doing them. You're going to act. You're going to pretend you're someone else and dare yourself to do more. It's easier because it's not you who's doing it, it's your alias.

For this to work, you need to design your alias very carefully in order to really be in the moment. What do they look like? What are their character traits? What do they like and dislike? You're playing a character here so you need to be as detailed as possible when creating them, so you can play them to perfection. Pretend you're an actor getting ready for your latest role.

Once you know your alias well, transform yourself into them. Go on, try it! When you're not actually being yourself, it's easier. You might even find it easier to style yourself slightly differently, perhaps dress differently or do your make-up differently. Don't make it too 'out there', but do whatever you need to do in order to get into character.

Then, go for it. Do whatever it is that you're fearful of, but do it as the character you're playing, not yourself. Dare yourself to push it a little further and get your competitive spirit flowing. If you're scared to approach people you don't know and speak, dare yourself to do it twice and give yourself a pat on the back when you manage it. You could even bribe yourself with the promise of a reward later!

Practice Makes Perfect

Preparation is key when trying to overcome something. If you're getting ready to give a big presentation at work, you'd practice several times over to get it right. You need to adopt the same mindset to overcoming your socialization barriers.

Of course, practice means putting yourself out there and doing the one thing that scares you, but there are ways you can minimize the exposure and make it feel slightly less daunting to you. Here are a few suggestions.

- **Work on practicing non-verbal cues –**
  Communication isn't just about the words you say, it's also about gestures, body language, and the way you speak. You can practice those things whilst minimizing how terrifying it feels to you. If public speaking is your fear, start slowly by making sure that you're opening up your body language, keeping an eye on your facial expressions, and maintaining eye contact. Start watching the body language of other people too. This still means you're building up your social skills but you're doing so in a protected way.
- **Try to use activities along with conversation –**
  When you try to build up your social skills, you're going to be worried about holding a long conversation and you're going to be fearful of awkward silences. However, if you work towards situations that allow you to do something, e.g. you're part of an activity, you have something to busy yourself with whilst you're talking. For instance, you could

be at a sporting event. You're watching the game but you're also chatting.

- **Dare yourself on a daily basis** – Setting yourself a dare is a good way to keep on practicing. You could call this a goal if you prefer to avoid dares. All you need to do is set yourself a target of speaking to one person randomly per day. This means striking up a conversation. See how many days you can keep it up for and try and push your boundaries a little more every day.

Remember, overcoming shyness and social anxiety takes time and effort. I'm not going to lie to you and say it will be easy, but it will be the most worthwhile thing you'll ever do. Take small steps every day and before you realize it, you'll have walked more than a mile.

CHAPTER THOUGHTS

Whatever barrier is standing in the way of you improving your social skills, it's important to identify it, or the plural barriers if that's the case. Don't be down on yourself for whatever it is that you do acknowledge but use it as motivation to make changes.

In this chapter, we've talked at length about shyness and social anxiety, as well as what makes them different. Despite the fact that they certainly aren't the same thing, overcoming them uses a very similar approach. Your anxiety or your shyness does not own you. I know this myself. It feels like it does, but trust me, you're the one in control and all it takes is learning that fact to give you the courage and the strength to knock down those barriers.

4

ANALYZE YOUR CURRENT TOXIC SOCIAL HABITS & BEHAVIORS, THEN REVOLUTIONIZE THEM!

As we go through life, we pick up habits and behaviors that may not be useful to us. Of course, you pick up very positives ones too, but throughout the years you're walking on this Earth, you're going to absorb a few negative traits too.

The problem is until you address these traits and behaviors, you might have no clue that you have them. These traits and behaviors could be connected to the way in which you socialize, or don't socialize, and as a result, they could be contributing greatly to your problems. The key is to practice self-awareness and be more mindful of what you're doing when you're not actually paying attention.

Of course, from the point of view of EQ, having toxic traits is very damaging. For example, if one of your toxic traits is that you're always on your phone when you're with people you're supposed to be socializing with, you're not present in the moment. This lowers your EQ because you're not responsive to those around you or showing them the attention they deserve.

In this chapter, I want to turn your attention to the possible traits that might be dwelling within you, without your knowledge. This isn't something you should feel shameful of, but it is something you should take seriously. Once these traits are identified, you should do all you can to try and reverse them. This will have a very positive effect on your EQ and your ability to socialize with others.

I'll hold my hands up and say that I used to use my phone far too much. I'd go and meet friends and my phone would be on the table next to me. It was rude, but I didn't realize it at the time. It's only by looking at myself carefully that I identified this trait and worked to stamp it out. Now, I keep my phone in my bag and only take it out if it's a very important call. Being present in the moment is extremely important – people aren't going to want to talk to you if you're basically ignoring the time and attention they're giving to you.

So, let's look at a few of those traits and work out whether you have any work to do too.

LABELING TOXIC BEHAVIORS

When we talk about someone having toxic behaviors, that doesn't mean the person themselves is toxic, it means that they're showing behavior that isn't helpful and isn't respectful of others. If they don't realize they're doing it, you can help them to overcome their traits. However, if they know they're doing it and they simply continue, that's a whole other ball game that cannot be fixed without their will to do so.

The best gauge to know whether you've been around a person with toxic traits is to think about how you feel after you've been with them. Did you feel disappointed? Did you feel like it was a waste of time? Did you feel listened to? What did they do in particular that made you feel like the whole interaction was pointless?

Some common toxic traits include:

- Acting in a judgmental manner
- Taking up a huge amount of someone's time unnecessarily
- Refusing to take responsibility for their actions.

You might think that these aren't actually connected to communication but they're very integral to EQ, which is basically the same thing! If someone is judgmental, they're not showing empathy. If someone is taking up your time, they're not too bothered about what else you need to do and they're being disrespectful. If someone refuses to take responsibility for their actions, they're pushing the blame onto others and again, showing zero empathy.

Using your social skills links in so closely to EQ and any trait which negates that, also affects how you communicate with those around you.

Now, I'm not suggesting that you have any of these traits, but it's possible you do. Be honest with yourself. Do you do anything on a regular basis that could show other people that you're not taking them seriously? That you're not showing them empathy? That you basically don't want to give them the time of day? Again, no judgment here – perhaps you're not aware of it. However, it's easier to be aware of this in other people first and foremost and then become used to how it looks and feels. It's much easier to analyze yourself once you have a little background information as the victim, rather than the perpetrator.

THE TOXIC HABITS & BEHAVIORS THAT NOBODY WANTS

Everyone has a different idea of what toxic is, however, there are some common traits which most people would consider to be toxic. This section is going to take a good look at them in turn.

- **Focusing too much on yourself** – If you make everything about yourself, it's not only annoying but it's extremely off-putting to people around you. You want to build up your social skills, but you also need to be a person with whom others want to socialize. By making everything about you, you're not showing empathy to others.
- **Not listening to others** – Pushing your views onto other people, not listening to what they have to say, and assuming that you know what they're going to tell you without taking the time to hear them speak, these are all negative traits that have no place in the life of a person with high EQ and good relationships with those around them.
- **Being judgmental or critical** – Again, this means you're

not showing empathy. You don't have the right to judge or criticize anyone, because you're not living their life and you're not walking in their shoes. By doing so, your empathy has gone out of the window.

- **Blaming everyone for your problems** – People who push the blame onto everyone else and never take responsibility for their problems or issues aren't fun to be around. This can also be quite manipulative and border on narcissism. Let's face it, we all make mistakes and nobody's perfect – own it!
- **Not being present in the moment** – I've mentioned this one already, but if you're always off on another planet when people are speaking, distracted, or on your phone all the time, you're not present in the moment and you're not showing them respect.
- **Feeling entitled and showing it** – In this life, nobody is entitled to anything. We have to work for what we have and feeling like you're entitled to everything falling into your lap doesn't make you a great person to be around. You're not owed anything.
- **Using arrogance to hide fear or worries** – It's normal to be worried, to be fearful, or to feel inadequate but if you use arrogance to try and hide that, you're showing very negative communication styles and you're not going to endear people towards you. Be real. Show that you're not perfect, show that you're fearful sometimes. People respond far better to authenticity.
- **Being too competitive** – Being a little competitive is fine,

but pushing others out of the way to get what you want isn't. If you're going to be competitive with anyone, be competitive with yourself by pushing yourself to meet your own goals. Don't make everyone your rival otherwise you run the risk of alienating people.

- **Jealousy** – Do you regularly allow the green-eyed monster into your life? If so, it's not going to endear you to anyone. Feeling envious is normal but allowing that to turn into jealousy is nothing short of damaging.
- **Being stubborn** – Refusing to do something out of pride or out of a so-called cause isn't cute. If anything, it will cause other people to become frustrated with you and that becomes a huge barrier to communication.
- **Holding on to grudges** – Do you hold onto grudges long after the initial problem is over? Everyone makes mistakes and that sometimes means that we say or do things we don't mean. By holding onto those issues and punishing those around you, you're just going to push them away. In the end, the only person who suffers is you.
- **Regularly playing the victim** – I'm going to talk about the victim mentality in greater detail later in the book but if you're someone who is always playing the victim, those around you are going to quickly become tired of it. You're in control of your life and whilst negative things happen in life, allowing them to make you feel and act like the victim on a constant basis isn't going to help you develop strong relationships.
- **Always being about the drama** – Do you gossip

regularly? Do you love drama? It's not a good thing to admit to. Being around someone who is always in the middle of a drama or someone who is always gossiping and trying to be into everyone else's business doesn't allow you to build up trust. Relationships will always be less than they could be because of that huge barrier between you. If you want people to trust you, you have to just be yourself and stop judging and talking about others. Drama is nothing but stressful anyway!

You can probably come up with a few other negative traits and behaviors that are on your list of things you dislike. However, these are some of the most common and some of the most damaging when it comes to the relationships and connections we have with those around us.

I should point out that everyone has bad days and that means that sometimes you might show one or two of the above traits. There is no issue when something happens just once or twice, but when it becomes a habit, you need to address it to stop it from turning into a major barrier.

EVALUATING SELF: DO I POSSESS THESE HABITS & BEHAVIORS?

We've talked about some negative traits and behaviors and you're probably building up a picture in your mind of what all of this looks like, but now it's time to be real. I've encouraged you to think about whether you have any of these, but now you really need to dig deep.

Don't be scared and don't be hard on yourself. The fact you're reading this book willingly shows that you want to improve. We all make mistakes, we all have traits we wish we didn't, and we all catch habits that don't help us. What sets you apart is that you're willing to change them.

So, how can you tell if you're exhibiting these toxic traits or qualities without really knowing about it? Let's look at a few signs to help you out. If you can nod along to several, that's a good indicator that perhaps you need to do some work. It's important to be honest with yourself when reading these signs also; don't push something aside just because it's uncomfortable. This entire journey is going to revolutionize your life, but you have to be willing to do the work, some of which won't be pleasant to you.

Signs You've Developed Toxic Habits or Behaviors

- Your friendships and relationships don't last long
- People seem to be distracted or show negative body language after spending any time with you
- Friends don't always share their good news with you
- You always have some drama going on in your life
- You've been described as a perfectionist or competitive
- You've been accused of being jealous more than once
- You often gossip about other people
- You don't say 'sorry' too often
- You bond with others by talking about people you both know
- You often consider yourself to be the victim in situations

- You're often quite needy and find it difficult to spend time alone
- You lose your temper quite easily
- You have a negative and pessimistic attitude
- In honesty, you take from people more than you give to them
- You use social media as a way to fish for attention
- You rarely see how your problems are caused by you, and you blame everyone else
- You always like to be right
- You find it hard to accept someone else's opinion as just as valid as yours
- You take everything quite personally
- You often need validation in order to feel good or as though you've succeeded

You might have one or two traits to work on, or you might have a whole bunch. The number doesn't matter right now, but your attitude towards it does.

LET'S GO FROM TOXIC TO HEALTHY

You might be feeling pretty down after reading the above list, depending upon how many traits you can tick off. It's time to plaster on a smile because there is plenty you can do about it. Moving from toxic to healthy is entirely possible and the more you try, the easier it will become.

Many people who struggle with social skills and communication are bogged down with not only possible shyness or social anxiety, but also several barriers that they place in front of themselves. In order to make life a little easier, they develop negative traits as a coping mechanism but these work against them, rather than for them. By identifying these traits, you can work out what you need to stop doing and then focus on the right kinds of techniques instead.

So, how can you turn your toxic traits into something totally healthy? Here are a few ideas.

Fake a Smile

Go on, try it. It's not possible to smile and not feel slightly more uplifted than you did before. When you smile more often, you'll also see that those around you respond to you differently too. We're far more likely to talk to people who smile and look approachable than someone who is frowning and looks troubled. So, plaster on that smile, even if you don't feel like it, and wait for the good vibes to spread.

Keep a Gratitude Diary

This is a very useful technique for a variety of different problems, but it helps you to avoid negativity and that annoying victim mentality. By being grateful for what you have, you feel uplifted, happier, and comforted within yourself. All you need to do is write down one or two things you're grateful for out of any particular day, every evening. You'll soon see that there are more positive in your life than you're aware of.

Avoid Being Sucked into Gossip

You have a choice whether you gossip about someone else or not – nobody is making you backchat. You have the power to excuse yourself from any conversations that feels negative and that are characterized by talking about other people.

Learn to be aware of when you're gossiping, stop yourself, and mindfully change the subject. Remember, talking about other people says more about you than it does about them.

Do a Good or Kind Deed Every Day

The more good we do, the more we want to do. In addition, when you do a good deed for someone or you show kindness that makes them smile, it makes you feel good too, increasing your confidence and your empathy. Every single day, aim to do something good for another person, even if it's just complimenting them on their sweater. However, make sure that whatever you say or do is done with the best intentions and not simply to tick an item off a list.

Learn to Laugh at Yourself

Taking yourself too seriously isn't going to make your life very happy or fulfilling. We all make mistakes and do silly things occasionally, but that doesn't mean we should beat ourselves up about them. Learn to laugh at yourself and your mistakes, and you'll be less overcome with self-hatred and upset whenever something doesn't go your way.

Take a Break from Social Media

The very thought of logging off your social media accounts for a week might fill you with dread but trust me, it's a very useful tool. We are all far too obsessed with what everyone else is doing, thinking, and the validation we seek from our followers. It's time to focus on yourself, those around you, and learn to only look for validation from within. Taking a break from social media will allow you the chance to reconnect with yourself. Let's be honest, social media is nothing but drama anyway.

Stop Trying to Take Control of Everything

Perfectionism isn't a good thing, no matter what you might have taught yourself to believe. By trying to control everything, you're not allowing yourself to live in the moment or to experience the joy of spending time with those close to you. Stop, slow down, take your hands off the wheel, and just allow yourself the chance to drift for a while. If you find yourself going off course too much, you can easily correct your direction. Chill out and go with the flow a little!

Learn to Use Positive Affirmations

Never underestimate the power of positive affirmations. They might feel a little odd at first, but they are one of the best tools to help you develop a positive mindset. Choose an affirmation that really resonates with you and repeat it several times a day, when you wake up, when you go to bed, and at any point in the day when you feel your resolve shaking.

Your affirmation can be anything. "I am able to do whatever I set my mind to", "I am a strong and kind person", "I am willing to deal with whatever comes my way with positivity and success" are just a few suggestions but you can choose whatever you want. Head online for plenty of inspiration or just make up your own.

Stop Blaming Everyone Else for Your Problems

There may be some problems in your life that really aren't your fault, but they're not anyone else's either. Stop pushing the blame onto others because by doing so, you're creating a toxic energy that causes people to steer clear of you. Instead, accept your problem and create a plan to overcome them, using your new positive affirmation to stay on the right track.

Be Mindful of How You Speak to Others

For a while, be very mindful of the verbal and nonverbal language you use when speaking to other people. You might have picked up a habit of using closed body language, avoiding eye contact, or being sarcastic, without even realizing it. The only way to identify it is to be mindful and observe yourself. Once you recognize a negative communication trait, be even more mindful to stamp it out. If you catch yourself doing it again, stop, change course, and over time, it will become second nature to avoid it.

Keep Your Complaints to Yourself

A little earlier I suggested keeping a gratitude diary and that should help a lot with this particular suggestion too, but you need to stop complaining! It's very likely that people are avoiding spending time with you if you're constantly complaining about everything that's going wrong in your life. It literally sucks the energy out of people! Reframe those complaints and remember that there is always someone worse off than you.

None of these action points are hard to do and you can start working on all of them right now. Even if you don't have a huge number of toxic traits to stamp out of your life, using these techniques can really help you to increase your EQ level, which will of course help to boost your social skills too.

CHAPTER THOUGHTS

As we move through life, it's easy to pick up habits that are perhaps more negative than they are positive. Whilst it's never a good thing to just carry on using them willy-nilly, it's sometimes difficult to stop and take stock of what you're doing without being extremely mindful in the process.

Using toxic habits and behaviors will not help you to become a better communicator and it won't allow you to build relationships and the social circle you crave. However, you can quickly identify the problem, or problems, and work to eradicate the issue. Rather than becoming down or having these traits, pat yourself on the back for admitting it and get to work.

II

PRACTICAL STEPS YOU CAN TAKE TO CONQUER SOCIALIZING

5

MAKE THE BEST FIRST IMPRESSIONS POSSIBLE

Welcome to the second part of our book!

The first part was all about emotional intelligence, why social skills matter, and really raising awareness of the journey you need to take. This next part is going to be practical, action pointed, and it's going to give you lots to work on in order to really start seeing major improvements in your relationships with those around you, your confidence levels, and how you interact with other people.

In this chapter, I want to talk about a very important aspect of communication – the first impression.

THE FIRST IMPRESSION LASTS

Think of the last time you developed a first impression of something or someone. Did you find it easy to shake that first impression, even if you were proven incorrect in your assumption later down the line? Probably not.

First impressions stick. We make them quickly, we assume they're correct, and they're very hard to overcome once they're solidified in your mind. Even if that thing or person does something to make you think that perhaps you were wrong about them, you still have a niggling doubt in your mind afterward, simply because of the impression you made right at the start. It's for this reason that businesses place such a huge amount of importance on marketing strategies that really hit the right mark. If you allow your customers to think the wrong thing about you, they're just going to go to one of your competitors instead.

In terms of your personal communication style and social skills, first impressions matter just as much. This is vital in both your personal life and your professional life.

The psychology of first impressions is quite interesting to learn about.

It is thought that you have just a few seconds to make your impression on someone. In this time, you're being judged for your trustworthiness, your integrity, your attitude, and unfortunately, also your attractiveness. After that, a deeper conclusion is formed, more about personality traits than anything else at this stage. This happens over just 3 seconds.

All of this occurs because of something called cognitive bias and that forces someone to make a quick-based judgment upon you. That judgment may be entirely correct, or it might be very far from the mark. It's worth noting that these judgments can also be affected by a person's stereotypical thoughts, so sometimes it's not entirely your fault if someone gets the wrong first impression of you. However, if the judgment is negative and incorrect, changing it takes far longer than the time it took to make the judgment in the first place.

Cognitive bias is what happens when you're quickly processing and coming to a conclusion about what is happening around you, but that conclusion can be affected to a large degree by your confidence levels, whether you're a positive or negative person and situations you've encountered before. Basically, it can't be relied upon entirely, but we do so because we believe what we tell ourselves.

To throw another term into the mix, we also have the primacy effect. This is the reason why a negative first impression lasts. The brain remembers things in sequence order, so when you encounter a person or a thing for the first time, that's the first step in your sequence, however, you'll always remember the first step more than any of the others. It's easy when you think about it – we remember our first love, the first time we tried out our favorite food, the first time we went to a certain place, etc. That means if someone meets you for the first time and they gain a negative first impression, rightly or wrongly, that's the first thing they'll remember about you when they come into contact with you again.

Of course, by making a snap judgment such as this, it also affects whether that person wants to be around you again in the future and how they treat you. On the flip side, if you make snap judgments about others incorrectly because you gained a bad first impression of them, it will affect how you communicate and interact with them too.

Can you see how important first impressions are? They're a very easy way to be misunderstood or misunderstand someone else and they affect so much more than just that one moment.

Your journey towards mastering communication and social skills has to incorporate first impressions. If you avoid this or ignore it and assume it's not important, you're not going to get very far with your journey.

The impression someone has of you isn't always about what you say, but also about how you present yourself. As humans, we focus a lot on faces, and that's likely to be because when we're very young, we watch the facial expressions of our parents to work out whether we're about to be fed, etc.! That habit tends to stick with us throughout life, so it's definitely worthwhile remembering that it's not all about what you say but often how you show yourself to the world. It can also be about how you do things, e.g. your choices and your competencies.

Let's look at a few examples.

- A person who is scowling will probably be considered unfriendly and unapproachable, but someone who is smiling and has a soft facial expression will be considered warm and approachable
- A person who runs up the stairs will be considered active and healthy, but a person who takes the elevator might be considered lazy
- A person whose hair is a little unkempt may be considered lazy or even dirty, but a person whose hair is neat and tidy,

presenting themselves in clean clothes will be considered professional and clean

Can you see how your habits and how you show yourself to the world is part of the deal too? It might seem like a lot to remember, but much of it comes down to common sense. Simply focus on being well turned out every day, clean, tidy, and be mindful of how your facial expression may be judged by others.

LEAVING THE BEST FIRST IMPRESSION

In order to build up professional connections and personal relationships, you need to know how to make those positive first impressions. This will make your social life so much easier and you won't be constantly backtracking, trying to correct an incorrect opinion someone has gained of you. You'll also find that you are successful in opportunities without failing and having to learn what you did wrong the first time.

There are countless times when you'll need to make a first impression, in fact, you might even have a few in the space of a day. For instance, a job interview is one of the most common and most terrifying times you need to make a good first impression, but how about if you attend a party? Whilst you might not relish the idea of speaking to new people at a party, by the end of this book you'll be doing it more than ever before! However, you'll need to make a good first impression on those people for your efforts to work.

So, how can you make sure that you're leaving the best first impression when you're socializing? Let's look at five important steps.

Be Mindful of How You Speak

The words you say and how you say them are two of the most important aspects of making a good first impression. It sounds complicated but it actually comes down to the basics more than anything else.

For instance:

- Remembering someone's name shows that you're taking them seriously and you value their input, and you're not passing them off as someone unimportant.
- Manners are vital – most people will form a very poor impression of someone who doesn't use 'please' and 'thank you' and who doesn't treat people with respect so always be mindful of this. Remember, manners cost nothing!
- Using too much slang and not speaking correctly can also work against you. Whilst nobody expects you to speak the Queen's English, you should avoid talking as though you're a grumpy teenager. You've never met this person before, so you need to show that you're someone who is interesting enough to strike up a conversation with.
- Try not to say 'erm', 'um' and 'ah' too much. Whilst it's normal to use in the odd occasion, saying these too often will just show that you're nervous, you're not sure what to say, and could even tell the other person that you don't really know what you're talking about. Try and appear confident, even if you're not.

- Try not to speak too fast or too quietly. Again, this shows that you're not confident or at ease. Slow things down and give yourself the time to think as you're speaking. That will automatically give you more confidence and also avoid the other person not being able to really understand what you're saying.
- Avoid using words that are overly complicated and that the other person might not understand. For instance, if you're speaking to someone about your job or another area of expertise that you're familiar with and they're not, don't litter the conversation with technical jargon. You're alienating them by doing this because they can't be expected to understand this subject as well as you, and they'll feel annoyed about it too. That is going to show them that you're not on the same level as them and they'll form a poor impression because of their experiences.

Put Your Phone Down!

I've mentioned this one several times before and we're all guilty of it occasionally, but keep your phone in your pocket or in your bag. In this digital age, we're constantly connected and switched on and it's extremely easy to lose yourself in the virtual world, whilst completely missing the real world around you. By doing so, you're letting people know that you're not interested in what they have to say and that you're quite rude and ignorant of their presence.

If you're waiting for an important call, just keep your phone in your pocket and put it on vibrate. That way you'll know when the phone is ringing, and you can excuse yourself outside to answer it. Constantly checking your social media accounts, emails, or generally scrolling through the news is not going to endear you to anyone and it's just going to make you look plain rude. Nobody likes rudeness.

Be Punctual

A positive first impression can be as easy as showing up on time. If you make someone wait for you, they're going to assume that you don't respect their time and that you deem them unimportant enough to show up when you're supposed to. Again, it's rude and it's one of the biggest bug-bears for most people.

A little earlier I mentioned manners and being punctual really ties in with this. For many people, bad manners are a deal-breaker, and they are for me too. I know if someone turns up late and then just doesn't seem to be very polite, I'm not going to like them very much and it's going to take a lot to change my mind. It doesn't take a huge effort to be on time, and if you do find that you're running late and you can't do anything about it, have the respect to call the person and explain, so they're not hanging around waiting for you.

Dress Comfortably Yet Impressively

I'm a big believer that you should dress for yourself but there is a very big difference between wearing slouchy, unkempt clothes at home when there is no-one around, and wearing them outdoors when people are unfortunately going to judge you. Such clothes will inevitably lead people to the wrong first impression of you, assuming you don't really care much about how you look.

For that reason, dress for comfort but also dress for style. Make sure that what you wear is suitable for the place you're going to and make sure that you feel good within it. If you feel good, you'll be more confident and that will help you to speak and socialize with fewer barriers between you.

I don't have to tell you about clothes that aren't the best idea versus ones that are, I'm pretty sure you know how to dress yourself appropriately, however, do be mindful in professional situations. There are no rules that women have to wear skirts and men have to wear suits but do make sure that you always look very well put together and you're not overstepping any imaginary lines, e.g. wearing skirts that are too short, or wearing suits that are too tight. Just make sure that you look professional and you feel comfortable within it.

If you're attending a party or a social gathering and you want to try out your social skills, what you wear does matter. People do notice these things almost instantly, probably as you walk into the room. So again, wear something comfortable but also something which shows you in your best light and doesn't place unnecessary negative attention upon you.

It goes without saying that you should always be clean and tidy, but again, I don't have to tell you that.

Be Aware of Your Body Language

The final step to making the best first impression possible is your body language. I'm going to cover all the do's and don'ts of body language in a later chapter, so I'm not going to dwell on it too much here. However, be aware that your body language does cause a person to decide upon their judgment of you very quickly indeed.

People with high EQ can read body language almost instantly. For instance, a person who is avoiding eye contact, crossing their arms over their body and fidgeting looks nervous and as though they're either trying to avoid something or they're lying. That's not the best first impression.

All you need to do is make sure that your body language is open and relaxed. That means making eye contact regularly (although, don't try and stare them out), you keep your arms relaxed by your sides and not over your body, you smile, nod along to what they're saying, and you avoid being too stiff or tense. Just relax into the moment and avoid fidgeting.

THE FIRST ISN'T THE LAST

Despite the fact that first impressions are very important, don't worry too much if someone does form a negative first impression of you. There are still chances for you to change that perception of yourself, although it's always better to get it right the first time!

Of course, this depends upon you knowing what you did wrong; they're unlikely to simply tell you, so being aware of how you come across to other people is key. Using the tips in the last section will allow you to do that and you'll become more self-aware as a result. Once you know what you did wrong, work to change it by showing them what you can do right and showing them a different side. For instance, if you appeared unkempt and tired the first time they met you, make sure that you are better turned out the second time and that you're more energetic and friendly. Once won't be enough, however, so you'll need to keep showing that positive side of your character to the point where their first impression is challenged enough in their minds.

Most researchers agree that it takes around eight positive situations to change a negative one. So, if you gave someone the wrong first impression, you'll need to show them around eight times (it's not an exact number) that their first impression was a little off-key.

That simply means being polite, using your manners, being friendly, smiling, making eye contact, watching your body language, and making sure it's positive, and being well turned out. These things aren't difficult but for someone who is struggling with their social skills, trying to remember it all can be difficult. My advice is to just focus on treating people in the way you would like to be treated. If you do that, you can't go wrong.

However, there may be situations when you really got off to a bad start with someone and something needs to be explained in order to push the metaphorical elephant out of the room. If you really feel like you need to explain why you came over so negatively, e.g. you were very snappy and rude, ask the person if you can have a quick word and apologize for your negativity and explain that you were caught off guard due to a personal issue. You don't have to go into more detail than that, you don't have to explain, and you only need to apologize once. Let it go after that and carry on being a positive and happy person that they want to spend time with.

Whilst first impressions are undeniably important, it's not a case of sudden death if you get it wrong. You can redeem yourself, although it's always better to not have to.

CHAPTER THOUGHTS

Making a good first impression on someone helps to build up a positive interaction and could lead towards friendship. However, if you give off a bad vibe during a first impression, you're going to have to work harder to put it right. It's far better to be aware of how you come over to other people and avoid this from happening.

A lot of the work that goes into making a good first impression is about the basics. Be polite, be on time, make sure your body language isn't going against the words you're saying, and simply be aware of the fact that on some level, whether they're aware of it or not, you are being judged.

6

HOW TO DEVELOP RAPPORT WITH ABSOLUTELY ANYONE

Our last chapter served as the first practical step towards actually going out there and having fulfilling conversations with other people. That first impression is very important but to have a good conversation and to be able to use your social skills to their highest level, you need to build up something else – a rapport.

A rapport is an understanding or connection that two people, or a group of people, have with each other. This enables them to read the other person, to understand what they're thinking and feeling, and to be able to converse in an easy and friendly way. When you have a rapport with someone, communication is easy and smooth, and whilst there might be the odd awkward silence (inevitable, even for the most high-quality communicators) they won't faze you or cause the discussion to be disjointed or thrown off track.

Building up a rapport with someone doesn't always mean that you need to have a lot in common, but it is important. Let's explore why in this next chapter.

CONNECT WITH OTHERS: THE IMPORTANCE OF RAPPORT

We know that rapport is a connection of some kind, but how deep does that connection need to be? Not very. Colleagues can have a rapport simply because they work in the same place, they have something to talk about and they have a common goal to work towards. Friends have a rapport because they have a pre-existing connection, but strangers can also develop a rapport. It can be something as simple as commenting on the weather, "raining again, I hate rain!" and the other person says "yes, I really don't like it too" – the starting blocks of a rapport!

Rapport can happen without really much effort. If you've ever met someone and just instantly clicked, or "hit it off", that's an instant rapport. However, it's not like that for everyone and sometimes you have to work a little harder. It's likely to be the case that some people you just click with and others you don't, but that doesn't mean you can't build up a rapport with those people and look forward to fulfilling conversations and interactions.

Rapport is important not only in your personal life, with friends, family members, and strangers you strike up a conversation with on the street, but also in your working life too. An employer is far more likely to employ a person who they believe will fit in well with their current staff. Again, that harks back to the importance of social skills because being able to fit in and build up a rapport basically means you have strong social skills.

Rapport will also help you when working as part of a team when you're brainstorming and collaborating or simply when you're in the office or workplace in general. Rapport means that you have an understanding with someone or with a group of people and that can begin as small talk.

You might be someone who hates small talk, in fact, the chances of that are high. I used to hate small talk to the point where I used to avoid going to the hairdressers for as long as possible. However, small talk doesn't have to be excruciating and over time, it can actually be fun. Small talk allows you to search for the common ground you have with someone, such as hating the rain or being a big fan of chocolate. It can be absolutely anything, but the more you have in common with someone, the greater your rapport will be.

However, not having a huge amount in common with someone doesn't mean you can't build up that rapport, it just means you'll need to try harder.

Now we know what rapport is and why it is important, let's look at a few ways you can look to build up a rapport with people you meet.

EVERYONE IS ADMIRABLE, AND YOU SHOULD TELL THEM HOW

Everyone loves a compliment, whether they want to admit it or not! The single best way to build up a rapport with someone is to pick out something you admire about them and tell them. You don't have to gush about their amazing personality or how much you admire their work ethic; you can just tell them that you like their hair color or say you like their t-shirt and ask where they got it from.

The point here is that you're moving towards starting a conversation but you're doing so on a positive footing. You're not walking in there and complaining about something and then building a rapport based on something completely negative (never a good thing), and instead, you're moving towards building up that rapport from a positive point of view. The conversation obviously won't be all about whatever it is you admire about them, but it's a starting point and from there you will both feed off of one another to keep things going.

Before you panic, yes I know, small talk and keeping a conversation going is terrifying when you're not the greatest communicator in the world but practice really does make perfect. Not all conversations are going to be stilted and difficult. Some will flow and move from the topic with ease. The more you build your social skills, the more of the latter type of conversation you'll have in your life.

The key to giving compliments to start a rapport is to not make it sound like you're being over the top, that you're sugarcoating it, or that you're trying to suck up to them. You don't want to sound false and you want to make your compliment sound genuine. For that reason, only choose something which you genuinely admire. If you really detest their coat, you're not going to compliment them on it because your facial expression or your tone of voice is probably going to give you away.

If you really can't think of anything you want to compliment them on without it sounding false, you can rely on one other subject – the weather. "It's a lovely day, isn't it?" As with the comment about the rain earlier, it's a great way to connect but it's always better to focus on a positive comment, rather than a negative one, i.e. avoid "I don't like", "it's horrible", it's bad". These types of phrases will get the job done but they could hamper the first impression that the other person has of you – you're going in with a negative comment, so does that mean you're quite negative yourself?

YOU, ME, AND OUR HUMANITY

Common ground is vital if you want to not only start a conversation but also keep it going. When we have something in common, it's almost like a small light is ignited inside us and we become excited. We want to talk, we want to connect – we're humans, we're social beings whether we realize it or not!

A little earlier I mentioned that some people you meet will be supremely easy to speak to and others a little more difficult. This is because some people you have more in common with than others. It might be that you don't have a lot in common personality-wise but maybe you have a shared experience you can base the conversation on or a set of circumstances that you both share.

Again, we're going back to small talk. This helps you find that common ground by doing a little gentle digging but you're best sticking to non-contentious subjects. Don't go straight in there and ask their opinion about politics, religion, money-related subjects, or a very controversial subject on the news. Keep it light and non-inflammatory. You don't know this person yet and they might have very strong views which can be ignited very easily!

The most important thing to remember is that you're a human speaking to another human. They're not a monster, they're not a superhero, they're a human being just like you. It might scare you to start having conversations with people you don't know, but how do you know they're not thinking the same thing as you? Someone has to make the first move if a conversation is going to start and that might as well be you. It's entirely possible that the other person is waiting for you to go ahead and say something, so they know that you actually want to talk to them.

Rely upon your humanity and look towards theirs. If all else fails, inject a little humor to lighten the moment.

TALK ABOUT THEM (NO, NOT BEHIND THEIR BACKS!)

Finding common ground is easier if you ask questions of the person, but that doesn't mean firing question after question at them and making them feel like they're in an interrogation.

By shifting the focus of the conversation away from you, you'll probably feel a lot calmer and find it easier to talk, and by turning the focus on the person, they'll feel like you're genuinely interested in them and learning more about them.

Of course, in the moment it can be hard to come up with questions and your mind is likely to go blank. For that reason, having a few easy go-to questions in your armory will help you and will give you confidence.

Here are a few generic questions you can save to the back of your mind when you're in need of a quick conversation starter.

- The weather is great today, don't you think?
- I love animals, do you have any pets?
- Do you have any plans for the weekend?
- Have you been busy at work today?
- What kind of music do you like to listen to?
- Do you enjoy your job?

As you can see, finding common ground means asking very simple and generic questions that allow you to learn more about the person. From there, you can work out whether you have any common ground you can use to move the conversation forward and build up that important rapport.

There is one thing to be aware of here. When asking questions make sure that you separate questions by using filler. This means giving your own answer to the question and using that dreaded small talk.

For instance, let's look at asking "do you have any plans for the weekend?"

Your conversation partner will answer and say yes or no and probably elaborate on what those plans are to some degree. Rather than going straight to another related question, make sure that you give a little information about your own plans. Don't go into huge detail, but simply say "that sounds great, I think I'm going to have a relaxing one with my partner", as one example. By doing that, you're not firing question after question at them and probably scaring them somewhat!

ADJUST THE CONVERSATION

A little earlier I mentioned that some conversation topics can be a little difficult for some people and topics such as religion, culture, and politics, in particular, can be quite sensitive for many people. It's best to avoid these if at all possible but you might hit upon a difficult topic without realizing it. For instance, you might accidentally speak about an experience you've had which the other person finds distressing because of their own personal experiences. You have no way of knowing about that because you don't know the person.

In that situation, you need to stay calm and simply adjust the conversation slightly, diverting attention away from the sensitive subject and moving it towards something more mainstream. The weather is a great option here, but you have to do it in a way that is seamless and doesn't make it look like you're working towards damage limitation.

You'll understand that you've hit upon a difficult topic by reading the other person. This is where empathy comes to the fore. Watch the person's body language – if they tense up, if they don't make eye contact, or simply seem uncomfortable, the likelihood is that they're not entirely comfortable with the topic you've ventured towards.

Be receptive to the differences in their body language and their general stance and be ready to adjust the conversation accordingly. You don't have to do a quick U-turn, but you can simply redirect your chat towards something less contentious. A good reroute here is a compliment, just as you started the conversation. This may shake them out of their "moment" and put the chat back on course. Either way, simply changing the conversation is enough because by doing that, you're showing the other person that you've recognized their discomfort and you want to help them move past it. They'll be grateful and they'll no doubt do their part to keep the conversation flowing on, past that particular subject.

OPEN MINDEDNESS IS THE KEY

The most important thing to remember when conversing with anyone is that you should not judge, you should not allow your perceived ideas to cloud your mind, and you should certainly place stereotypes to one side. Put simply, you should be open-minded.

Being open-minded is the key to quality conversations that help to build connections. By being more open to talking to people you probably wouldn't otherwise speak to, you might learn something new, you might find a new friend that you can build up a fantastic rapport with, and you will be able to increase your social skills and build your EQ.

As humans, we tend to judge people very harshly and very quickly, especially in today's society. This does nothing for our connections with other people because we're too busy assuming that someone isn't going to be our type of person, so therefore we shouldn't try to speak to them. We might also become fearful of them because they look a certain way or belong to a certain culture or religion. These are all thoughts and ideas which need to be cleared from your head.

Every single person is worth getting to know. You don't know who you might connect with until you've attempted to look for common ground and build up a rapport. Avoid close-mindedness by simply seeing a person as a human being and blank canvas of stories, experiences, and fun that you might really enjoy getting to know.

Once you start to see people in that way, life becomes more fun because who knows who you could meet. You could meet the love of your life, your new best friend, or simply someone with who you have a really great conversation. You might learn something, you might not, but either way, being open-minded allows you to become a better person and allows you to connect with those around you more easily.

CHAPTER THOUGHTS

Building up rapport not only gives you the confidence to take conversations further, but it's the first step towards building relationships with people, either professionally or personally. We all have some amount of common ground, it's simply that in some cases you have to dig a little deeper to find it.

Practice using small talk, complimenting people, and using questions to try and find out what you may have in common and once you hit gold, use that subject to deepen the connection.

7

THE LIFE-CHANGING ABILITY TO DEVELOP FRIENDSHIPS WITH EASE

Friendships really do make life easier, more fun, and generally more rewarding. A life without friends is dull and you'll probably feel like you have to take on the world yourself, without any support.

However, meeting new friends can be a huge challenge for someone who lacks social skills and who finds communication difficult. The good news is that like all the topics in this book, this can be overcome, and you can look forward to meeting plenty of new friends, provided you open yourself up to the possibility.

Not everyone is going to end up being your friend, but that doesn't mean that you can't have great connections with them in the short-term, even if it is just one conversation. However, knowing how to move towards making connections with friendship potential is important and it's easier than you might think. That's what we're going to focus on in this chapter.

GETTING THE SOCIAL LIFE YOU'VE ALWAYS DREAMED OF

I used to regularly watch the TV show "Friends". I used to long to have that kind of close-knit group of friends who backed each other up through thick and thin, who never laughed at one another, who always supported each other, and who could always be depended upon to be there for either a good night out or a quick chat on the phone.

Whilst this type of social circle doesn't happen for many people, even those who are great socializers, it is possible to have a social life that is fulfilling, surrounded by people you really do call friends. It's important to remember that not everyone you meet will turn out to be who you think they are, and that sometimes you might find yourself led astray by someone with ill intentions, but these are all lessons you will learn as you start to navigate life with an active social element. For every bad one you meet, there are several good ones in their place and it's better to place the focus on experience and enjoyment, than trying to collect a set number of friends in your life.

It can be very hard to meet friends as someone who struggles with socializing. You put yourself into your own little bubble and close yourself off to some degree, I know I did. This doesn't make it easy to meet people and it makes it almost impossible for other people to see you for the warm and friendly person you really are.

The more you build up your social skills, the easier you'll find it to socialize for fun and as you do this, you'll find that you meet new people who end up being your friends. Whether they remain friends for life or for just a season remains to be seen but building up your social life will certainly become easier as you put in a little more effort.

FRIENDS, AND WHERE TO FIND THEM

If you want to meet new friends, you have to get out there and go to places where potential fits might be mingling themselves. Of course, it's better to try and meet people who have the same kinds of interests as you and in that case, think carefully about how your key interests can take you out of the house and into situations where other people are likely to be.

It's easy to think that you should sit at home and live your life online because it seems easier and safer, but by doing that you're not actually getting out and testing your social skills at all. Hiding behind a keyboard isn't fun and it's not going to help you build up emotional connections – the connections you have with people you meet online aren't going to give you the same fulfillment unless those connections translate to the outside world. Even then, safety has to be a concern.

For that reason, where can you go to meet people who have the same kinds of interest as you? If you enjoy crafts, can you go to a night class to learn more about a potential craft you might enjoy and meet other like-minded people? If you enjoy dancing and keeping fit, how about joining a Zumba class and meeting other dancer types? If you enjoy trivia, why not go to the local pub quiz? There are many places you can go to combine your interests and meeting other people, you just need to think outside of the box.

If you want to meet people generally, there are countless places you can start to go for yourself and socialize with new people. The more you do this, the more confident you'll feel at striking up conversations and trying to build up a rapport. It's far easier to find people than you might think. Let's look at a few potential spots.

- Coffee shops
- Bars
- Public transport/bus stops
- Volunteering centers or whilst doing charity work/fundraising
- Local meetups advertised online
- Whilst walking the dog in the park
- Gym
- Museums and art galleries
- Parties and family gatherings
- Sports and fitness classes, e.g. yoga, dance classes, etc.
- Evening or weekend classes
- Pub quizzes
- Sporting events
- Weddings
- Joining a sports team
- Workplace
- Religious groups
- Wine clubs/book clubs, etc.
- Music festivals.

The list goes on. By choosing something that actually interests you, you're more likely to meet people with whom you have common ground. That means it will be easier to build up a rapport from the start and you won't need to work quite so hard.

THE HABITS OF PEOPLE WHO CAN EASILY MAKE FRIENDS

Some people find it very easy to meet new people and strike up a friendship. The best way to emulate their efforts is to find out what their habits are and to start incorporating them into your own life. You can start working on these habits right now!

Be Your Own Best Friend First

You can't expect other people to want to spend time with you and genuinely like you if you don't really like yourself much. You need to work on your relationship with yourself before you try and make friendships with others. Many people are scared of spending time alone, but this is actually one of the most nourishing things you can do. It's not about being lonely, it's about choosing to spend time in your own company.

This means you're more self-assured, you don't need the company of others and instead, you want it, which is altogether different.

So, how can you work on your relationship with yourself? Nourish your soul, do things you really enjoy, give yourself compliments, keep a list of your positive traits and add a new one to it every day, learn more about who you are and what makes you tick, and don't be afraid to do things on your own, such as going to the movies or going out for dinner. The more assured you are in your own company, the better company you'll be for others.

Focus on Experiences

Friendly people don't chase people for the sake of it, they focus upon the experience. This means they target where they spend their time and as a result, they meet people with who they're likely to get on well with.

In our last section, I talked about where you should go to meet new people and that if you want to meet people with whom you share common ground, you should go to places that bring you joy and interest first and foremost. This is what friendly people do; not to meet people, but to enjoy an experience. Meeting people is a pleasant side effect.

You'll be far more relaxed and, in your element, when you're in a location that you enjoy or doing an activity that brings you happiness. That makes you a better version of yourself and someone who others will want to connect with.

Be Positive

Positive people radiate joy and they're far more approachable too. Would you rather spend time around someone who is upbeat or someone who is more akin to Eeyore from Winnie The Pooh? People will go for the Tigger character time after time.

Developing a positive attitude will bring many benefits into your life, not least in helping you become a more comfortably sociable person.

Positivity radiates from you and it will make you more approachable, it will naturally make you smile more, and these are all qualities and elements which make a person friendlier and more likely to strike up friendships with new people.

Start Saying 'Yes'

Do you often say 'no' when you're invited out somewhere or when a new opportunity comes your way? It's time to start saying 'yes'. You need to start pushing yourself a little and moving beyond that little zone that is so comfortable to you. If you want to meet new people, you have to go where they're likely to be and they're certainly not going to be in your living room!

Whether you're fearful of trying something new or going out when you really don't want to, push yourself to do so and you'll be far more likely to meet people who may become your new best friends.

DON'T BE AFRAID TO TAKE THE FIRST STEP!

A particular habit of friendly people is the ability and willingness to take the first step and be the one to break the ice. Terrifying? The first few times, yes, but after that, it becomes surprisingly easy.

Someone has to be the one to take that first step otherwise nothing will happen. There will be zero conversations, and zero friendships as a result of those conversations. In some situations, another person might be the one to take that first step, but in many situations, it is going to have to be you.

When you're a child, making friends is much easier. You're thrown together into a school situation and you form a bond. You might also bond over how much you like someone's toy or their hair, and it's as simple as that. It's easy to assume that building friendships when you're an adult is much harder, but the mechanics are actually the same as when you first went to kindergarten! The only difference is that you have many years of life that have forced you to build up walls around you, fears, and worries. Those are the things that hold you back and stop you from using your social skills to go out there and meet new people.

It's time to tap into the spirit of the young child you used to be and take that first step.

A little earlier I mentioned that giving someone a compliment is a great way to break the ice and start a conversation but how do you actually get to that point and prepare for it? You don't want to open your mouth and your voice comes out quivering with fear! Preparation is key.

- **Don't prepare for rejection** – The fear of being rejected will stop you from reaching out to people and taking the first step. So, rather than preparing for rejection, prepare for being accepted instead. Assume that this person is going to like you, because why wouldn't they? There is nothing wrong with you, you're wonderful!
- **Forget what happens in the movies** – In the movies, friendships are drawn together by destiny but in real life, most friendships need a little work. Know that it's not going

to fall into your lap and prepare for the need to take that first step before doing it. Take a deep breath!

- **Remember that you have nothing to lose** – You have everything to gain, however. Trying to build up a connection with someone isn't a negative thing and there is nothing you could say or do which would cause anyone to think otherwise. Of course, you need to make sure that you make a positive impression and say the right things, but we've already covered how to do that. Throw away any thoughts that cause you to think everything hinges on this conversation – it doesn't, it's just a chat.

- **Prepare to keep doing what you're doing** – Once you've made the first move and build up a connection with someone, a friendship isn't going to happen overnight. You're going to need to keep showing up to the place you met the person, keep that connection burning and growing. It takes work, but it's worth it.

- **Learn to be yourself** – For some people, making the first move is terrifying so they pretend to be someone they're not, in order to put on a mask of sorts. Doing that might get you through that first meeting but the person you're speaking to isn't getting to know the real you. It's also exhausting trying to be someone you're not and you're just not being genuine. Just be yourself. You're wonderful and you need to keep telling yourself that.

Unfortunately, breaking the ice, initiating the conversation, making the first move, whatever you want to call it, really does come down to taking a deep breath and just going for it.

NOT EVERYONE IS ON THE SAME PATH, SO MOVE ON

Before we end this chapter on making friends, it's important to mention one thing.

Not everyone you meet is going to be someone you connect with or even want to connect with after speaking to them for a few minutes. It's not possible to get along well with everyone in life and there are always going to be people who we just don't 'get'. That's fine, in fact, it's perfectly normal and happens to everyone. Don't think that you've failed somehow or your attempts to build up a conversation didn't work. It's simply that the two of you aren't meant to be friends and you have your own separate paths to walk on.

Focus on the positives from the situation, such as the fact that you took the initiative, you learned something new, you realized that you didn't want to be friends with this person and therefore, save yourself some time. Whatever the positive is, take it.

It might also be that someone doesn't want to be friends with you.

Rejection stings but it's inevitable in life sometimes. You have no idea what that person's reason for not wanting to be friends with you is and you really don't need to know. As long as you've done nothing wrong, i.e. you've not hurt or upset them in any way, just move on and find someone else who is worthy of your time.

It could be that they know someone you're close to and they don't want to blur the lines, it could be that they just don't vibe with you, and that's okay too.

The saying that "friends are the family we choose for ourselves" is true. If someone doesn't want to be friends with you or rejects you in some way, that's no reflection on you and it's simply something to shrug off and move on. I'm not saying it doesn't feel like you've been kicked, because it does; nobody likes to be rejected, but then you're not going to be everyone's cup of tea.

If everyone in the world got along with everyone else, it just wouldn't work. It sounds like it would be idyllic but in reality, it would be a mess. We're supposed to be close to people who we vibe with, who we have common ground with, and who we build a rapport with. It's not possible to get along with everyone because sometimes our differences in the opinion just don't gel.

If you're rejected by someone in this way, be kind to yourself. Know that you did nothing wrong, that it's not a reflection on your character, and instead hold your true friends closer to you and invest more time in them. Also, take heart in the fact that you tried to build up a friendship with someone new, using your social skills, and that shows true progress on your journey to mastering communication.

CHAPTER THOUGHTS

Friends make life better, that's a fact. However, not everyone finds it easy to go out and meet new people who may become friends. The good news is that you can practice and learn. Whilst you may never build up the rapport that Monica, Chandler, Joey, et al had, you will be able to create connections with people who enjoy the same things as you.

Be brave and make that first move, know that everyone else is probably worried about taking the first step and breaking the ice too, and simply get out there and enjoy yourself. By doing so, you'll find that people gravitate towards you naturally, because you seem like a happy and upbeat person.

8

GOING BEYOND BASIC SMALL TALK BY NOT RUNNING OUT OF THINGS TO SAY

When it comes to starting conversations with new people, one thing which strikes fear into the hearts of most people is running out of things to say.

It's awkward. You stand or sit there, no idea what to say, your mind goes blank, the other person is also floundering, not sure what to say or do, and you want the ground to open up and swallow you.

I've been in this situation a few times, but you know what? I'm still here. I survived and nothing terrible happened, and you'll survive too.

In this chapter I'm going to talk about why resorting to small talk isn't just filler or fluff, and why it can sometimes be a great way to turn the heat down on a difficult conversation or pass a little time whilst inspiration strikes you for conversation topics once more. I'm also going to give you a few ideas to use during your conversations, so you never actually run out of things to say, you might just need a minute to remember them!

STARTING WITH SMALL TALK ISN'T WRONG

There is a view that small talk isn't worthwhile. I disagree. Small talk isn't just filler, it's a way to find out more about a person, to ask questions, and to delve a little deeper. By doing that, you build up your confidence and you avoid jumping in too quickly to deep conversations. Small talk helps you to find that all-important common ground we were talking about earlier; you can't just walk over to someone and ask them what they have in common with you, you need to be more subtle than that!

Small talk is a very valuable tool to help you build rapport and whilst most people don't enjoy it, assuming that it's pointless, turning your attention away from that viewpoint and realizing that it's useful, may help you to engage in general banter more easily.

Of course, when you experience one of those momentary pauses in conversation, small talk can be your savior. This helps you to avoid the conversation ending prematurely or awkwardly – who said small talk wasn't worthwhile?

Small talk should cover general topics and not delve too deeply into specific areas or controversial subjects. I'm talking about things like the weather, a big entertainment new story, the upcoming holidays, sports, or lighthearted current events. You can usually rely upon such things. For instance, "did you see the Oscars last night? Some of those dresses were amazing!" Or, "I watched the game with my partner last night, are you into sports?"

As you can see, small talk deflects the attention away from anything too deep but allows the conversation to keep going, therefore, slowly building up that rapport.

Small talk can also be about what is going on around you, such as if you're both standing at a bus stop and a car drives by far too fast, or it suddenly rains very fast and catches everyone out.

In a work situation, small talk doesn't have to be about the actual job, but can be about things which connect you as colleagues, e.g. "Jenny thanks so much for making those cookies in the canteen, they're fantastic" or "what are everyone's plans for the weekend?"

Small talk is something you should try to see as a positive tool to help you build up conversations and rapport, rather than something which makes you cringe on the inside.

TURN YOUR FILTER DOWN A NOTCH

Everyone has a filter, but the fact that you're struggling to socialize means that maybe your filter is turned up just a little too high.

Your filter is in the internal voice that tells you not to say something because it's inappropriate, people won't like it, or maybe people will laugh at you. Through every single day, we have countless thoughts, a running inner dialogue that we use to talk to ourselves and wrestle with ideas and feelings. When you have no filter, it basically means that every single thought or idea that comes into your mind also comes out of your mouth. You basically don't screen anything that you say.

This is good and bad in equal measures.

Not thinking before you speak isn't to be recommended. You may say something which offends someone, you may say something which really isn't appropriate, or you might wish you'd just kept your mouth closed! However, having your filter turned up too high is equally as damaging.

By keeping your filter up, you're not allowing yourself to come up with free conversation topics. You're too stilted, too controlled. Some of your thoughts and ideas will be fantastic conversation starters and filler, it's just that you need to weed out the inappropriate or strange ones and use the good ones instead.

Holding yourself back from having a conversation isn't going to help you build your social skills and you're basically standing in your own way. It's better to allow your filter to be set to medium instead. Don't be afraid to allow your inner dialogue out, but screen it a little before it leaves your mouth.

YOUR INTERESTS WILL COME IN HANDY

If you're struggling with conversation topics, lean upon something which is familiar to you, such as your interests. Those will never let you down and the passion you have for them will show through to the person you're speaking with. It's even more useful if they share the same interest as you, or maybe they're keen to learn more about them.

Most people enjoy watching movies, reading, or walking in nature, so those are pretty safe topics, but if you have a different or unusual hobby/pastime, don't be afraid to talk about it. The other person will be interested in what you do and how you do it, and maybe they might decide to take it up for themselves!

When talking about your hobbies, however, don't downplay them. A lot of the time, people who struggle with social skills tend to play down anything in their life which is positive. I know I used to. I had quite a self-deprecating attitude and sense of self and this meant that I found it especially hard to take compliments. Thankfully, as my confidence has grown, this has changed, but back in the day, I was quite keen to play down anything that I was interested in or which I was good at. I guess this was because I was scared of being laughed at or that the other person wouldn't find it as interesting as me.

However, I've come to learn that's not the point of having hobbies. If you enjoy something, why hide it? Talk about it and share it with the other person. Share a little and see how they respond, and when they ask questions, answer them in-depth, asking them questions about their hobbies to bring them into the conversation too.

Hobbies can be a great way to reignite a conversation that might be starting to stilt a little or to actually start a conversation in the first place. It doesn't always have to be about the weather!

TALK ABOUT WHAT'S IN THE CURRENT NEWS

A little earlier I mentioned that it's best to avoid any subjects which are particularly sensitive, e.g. politics or religion, and I also mentioned big news stories in that too. However, if the news story isn't too problematic to talk about, e.g. it's not about something which is going to upset the other person, current news events are good ways to get a conversation started and to keep it rolling on.

There are a few things you need to remember when using news stories as conversation starters, however. Not everyone has the same opinion as you, and the news is, for the most part, multi-dimensional. For instance, if you talk about the US Presidential election, you could find that you're speaking to someone who is rooting for the other guy when you're firmly in the opposite camp. Most people find this easy to navigate, but you might be speaking to someone who is extremely passionate about this topic and as a result, their heckles rise, rather than allowing a rapport to be built.

The most important thing to remember here is that if you do experience views about certain issues that are quite strong, don't judge or push them down. The other person is allowed their opinions and views just as much as you are and by belittling them or showing the other person that you're not taking their view seriously, you're putting yourself on track towards a very negative first impression, one that may never be overcome.

Hear the other person out, let them talk about their view, nod along and show that you're listening, and be as open-minded as you can be. Remember, we can't all be the same, we can't all think and believe the same things. That's what makes life and humans so wonderful – we're a huge melting pot of differences that are as equally wonderful as one another. Judging someone for having a different view to you is closed-minded and that's a pretty negative trait. You never know, by listening to someone's view on a particular subject, you might learn something, or your own view might be changed too.

For the most part, however, when talking about current news events, it's probably best to stick to "safe" subjects. If there was an earthquake, a volcano eruption, or an adverse weather event, these are subjects that can be spoken about quite safely and you can both empathize with those involved.

Celebrity and entertainment news can also prove to be a safe subject or anything which doesn't lead towards a passionate discussion. However, you shouldn't automatically steer clear of passionate discussion because that could be the one thing that bonds you together and creates that future friendship. Always remember, however - if you need to, agree to disagree.

EVER HEARD OF THE SNOWBALL TECHNIQUE?

A good way to make sure that you never run out of things to say is to use the snowball technique.

The idea for this technique comes from a small topic which is rolled around, opinions and views added to it by various people, until it becomes a bigger conversation, involving several people or opening up both parties to expressing more opinions.

You can use this technique to keep the conversation going and to hold the other person's attention, without having to worry about them becoming bored or unsure of what to say themselves. You'll also learn a lot about the other person by using this technique, which will help you to look for common ground and hopefully build up a rapport.

Step 1 – Ask a question but wrap it in something less obvious

You need to start the technique by asking a question, but you don't want them to feel like you're interviewing them. To do that, surround the question in an observation to make it more conversational, such as "I work in the hospital too, which department do you work in?"

Step 2 – Make sure you listen carefully

Show the other person that you're listening by making eye contact, nodding along, and making agreeable noises, such as "uh-huh", "hmm", "oh". This is also ideal for getting the ball rolling with the conversation because it turns the attention away from you and helps you to build confidence.

Step 3 – Repeat back what you've learned but add something extra

The key is not to do this in a parrot fashion but to show the other person that you were listening and that to encourage them to carry on and move the conversation onto another topic or expand on the current one. The best way to do this is to give your opinion on what they've just said. "oh, you work in the x-ray department, I bet that's really interesting. How long have you worked there?"

Step 4 – Repeat the above step

The idea is to keep adding something else to the conversation and digging into it a little more deeply. So, when they tell you how long they've worked in the x-ray department, you could add another detail and then another question. "My friend used to work in the x-ray department at another hospital, they really enjoyed it, do you like it?" This also has the added bonus of helping them to open up a little more which helps you to find out whether there is that all-important common ground to build up a rapport.

Step 5 – Remember an earlier detail

The idea isn't just to keep the conversation flowing, but to ensure it's authentic and that the other person knows that you're paying attention. A good way to do that is to remember something they said earlier and use it to take the conversation even further. "You've worked in the x-ray department for six years, that's a long time! What did you do before that?"

As you can see, the conversation grows in momentum, just like a snowball rolling down a hill. The hope is that as you ask questions, they open up more to you and they also ask you questions that allow the conversation to become multi-faceted. This is a great technique to use because it gives you a general structure to follow and allows you to feel confident in the fact that you're not going to run out of things to say.

CHAPTER THOUGHTS

One of the biggest worries for people who lack social skills is that if they do strike up a conversation, they're going to run out of things to say. There are a million things to talk about, it's simply that they're evading you in the moment because you're nervous. Relax and allow yourself to use your interests or news events to strike up small talk. The idea that small talk is useless is completely wrong. It allows you to search for that all-important common ground.

Also practice using the snowball technique, even if you have to practice in the mirror to begin with. This is a great and structured way to build up the momentum of a conversation and give you more confidence to keep going too.

9

TALKING ISN'T EVERYTHING – LEARNING TO BECOME AN EFFECTIVE LISTENER

Think back to our first chapter when I explained in detail about emotional intelligence (EQ). Can you remember the elements that make up EQ? One of those was listening.

A huge part of communication has nothing to do with what you say and everything to do with how you present yourself to the other person. In addition, it's also about how you understand them, via reading their body language and also listening to what they're saying and what they're not saying.

For instance, if they're talking fast and appear a little flustered, would that tell you that they're nervous? Or maybe they're lying? If someone is fidgeting, avoiding eye contact, and stumbling over their words, what would that tell you? These are all ways you can really build up a picture of what is really going on and therefore learn to communicate in a far more effective way.

In this chapter, we're going to focus on the art of listening. You might think listening is super-easy; you literally just, well, listen. However, it's not just about hearing words, it's about putting the picture together. Not everyone says what they mean or tells you the full story. Listening will allow you to read that situation accurately. In addition, listening, and showing the other person that you're listening, will deepen the connection you're building, keep that rapport going, and help you to build up your social circle, or indeed move a little further up the ladder with your professional career.

You will get nowhere in this journey without learning how to listen. In particular, you need to learn the art of active listening. Let's explore this topic a little more.

REMEMBER, A CONVERSATION ISN'T ONE WAY

In order for a conversation to be enriching and to help you to build up a rapport, it needs to be a two-way deal. That means one person speaks whilst the other person listens, and then they swap tasks, keeping the swapping going throughout the conversation. Without this to-and-fro motion, a conversation just doesn't work.

By listening, you learn more about the person and the topic they're talking about, you build up that rapport that's so important when building connections, and you can easily find out whether you and that person have much in common.

If you search for a definition of listening, you'll find that it's more than just hearing. It's being able to understand the message someone is conveying to you with their words whilst also showing them that you're interested and paying attention. You can show you're paying attention by nodding along, by making agreeable noises, by maintaining eye contact (although not constantly, that would be nothing more than uncomfortable), and by repeating back what they've told you in a summarized version and asking questions.

These are all important steps to add to your social skills repertoire and to build up your communication level naturally.

WHY LISTENING IS SO IMPORTANT

You might wonder why listening is actually important. As long as you say the right thing at the right time and you get the general gist, surely that's enough? Not at all. People aren't stupid and they're going to get a feel if you're not paying attention. Even a glance in the opposite direction for a couple of seconds too long, an ill-timed sigh, or not quite catching the end of the sentence can tell the other person that you're far from in-tune with what they're saying. By doing that, you're not only being quite rude but you're also damaging the rapport that you might have worked hard to build up, or if it's the first time you've met them, giving them a very poor first impression of you.

Never underestimate just how important listening is and know that it goes far beyond just hearing words. Hearing is literally just that, hearing sounds, and nothing more. However, listening is hearing words, putting them together into a meaning, and interpreting how that meaning links into the rest of the information you're gathering. When you learn to become an active and effective listener, all of this is done simultaneously, within seconds, and without too much effort, but before you get to that point, you'll need to pay far more attention than you normally would.

Listening is important for many reasons:

- Quality communication is impossible without listening
- When you're effectively listening, you're showing the other person you're paying attention
- It keeps the conversation going and stops those awkward silences
- It helps you to understand the other person's point of view and therefore enhances your empathy
- It avoids misunderstandings and errors of judgment
- It helps us to connect with other people in the simplest of ways
- It helps us to pull together the real meaning of someone's words, by interpreting their non-verbal cues at the same time
- It helps you look for common ground that can help you to build up rapport and quality connections with other people
- It helps you to sort out problems and resolve issues that may be causing conflict
- It helps the other person to feel respected and understood
- It will take your career and your personal life to another level.

How many times have you been in the company of someone who just seems a little 'off'? Their body language is low, they aren't making eye contact, they seem down, and they're speaking to you in a slow and non-interested way. When you ask them what's wrong, they say "nothing, I'm fine". Do you believe them? If you're a poor listener then yes, you'll take their words at face value and you'll assume that they are indeed as fine as they say they are. However, as you learn to use active listening, you'll know that their words are being contradicted by their non-verbal cues and they're actually covering up their real emotions. When you reach that point, you'll know that your EQ level has risen because that's when you're showing real empathy.

YOUR STEP BY STEP GUIDE TO BECOMING AN EFFECTIVE LISTENER

You know why listening is important and you know that it's going to help you build up your social skills and make you a fantastic communicator, but how do you get from where you are now to being an effective listener?

Step 1 – Think of every conversation as a method of learning something

The best way to approach a conversation is with learning in mind. By thinking in this way, you'll be keener to listen and as a result, you'll find that you really tune into what is being said and how it's being said. Assume that every single person you have a conversation with has the role of a teacher in some way.

Step 2 – Slow down and stop thinking about what you're going to say next

When you're nervous about holding conversations with people you've never met before, it's easy to try and pre-empt what you're going to say next. However, by doing that you're actually hindering your efforts to listen and you're also making the whole thing appear and feel unnatural. Turn your attention towards the person who is speaking and give them your undivided attention. Push any other thoughts out of your mind.

Step 3 – Encourage dialogue with open-ended questions

You need something worthwhile to listen to and that means giving the other person a chance to speak. Encourage them by asking open-ended questions, avoiding anything which is likely to lead towards a 'yes' or 'no' answer. This is a closed-ended question and is a real conversation killer. Of course, once you ask one of these questions and the person starts to speak, tune into them completely.

Step 4 – Show the person you're listening

You need to make the other person know you're listening to them and that will keep the conversation going. You can do that by nodding along to what they're saying, mirroring their body language (more on that shortly), maintaining eye contact, and making encouraging noises sparingly, such as "uh-huh" or "mmm".

Step 5 – Give them a summary of what you heard

This doesn't only help your understanding, but it reinforces to the other person that you've listened to them. By doing this, you're also ensuring that there are no misunderstandings. You don't need to parrot everything back to them but a quick summary such as "so you went to the park because you heard the dog was on the loose?" or whatever else you understood from the conversation.

Step 6 – Be aware of your body language and facial expressions

Make sure that you're not in-avertedly doing something which might show the other person that you're not listening or that you'd rather be elsewhere. This includes pulling a strange face without realizing it or sighing at the wrong moment. I'm going to explain a lot more about body language in a later chapter but it's certainly something you need to be very aware of because it speaks volumes.

It's particularly important to be aware of your facial expressions if the person you're speaking to is talking about something which you don't agree with or which you find strange. Remember to respect the other person's point of view or opinion and be non-judgmental and open-minded. That includes showing the other person that you completely accept their view too.

5 THINGS MOST PEOPLE DO WRONG IN CONVERSATIONS, AND HOW TO LEARN FROM THEM

There are many habits and behaviors that derail a conversation and make it far less likely that a rapport will be established or that the person speaking is going to feel listened to and taken seriously. It's important to know whether you're developing any of these habits or whether you're already using them because that knowledge will help you to change your tactics and eradicate these habits from your life.

Let's look at 5 specific things that people do wrong in conversations, particularly when they're supposed to be listening. If you do notice these are things you do, pay attention to the advice on what to do instead and be more mindful when you're having conversations in the future. It's very easy to concentrate on other things when you do have a low confidence level related to your social skills but by turning your attention to the speaker, you'll be able to show them that you're listening completely.

Mistake 1 – Jumping to conclusions or making snap judgments

Let the person finish before jumping in with your view on the situation. Firstly, that means you've formed a judgment of the problem or situation and that's not something we should be doing when trying to communicate with others.

Instead, let them finish and be open-minded, remembering that everyone has their view and it's just as valid as yours. You don't have to agree with them, and you don't have to show them that you don't either.

Mistake 2 – Multi-tasking or daydreaming

If your mind isn't on what the person is saying, they're going to notice and they're going to feel pretty aggrieved that your attention isn't on them. Don't allow yourself to think about the things you need to do, or half-listen to the conversation and half-listen to the radio. Also, don't try and think about what you're going to say next either. It's understandable to do that if you're a little nervous about speaking to people you don't know, but by being distracted in this way, you're not allowing yourself to listen properly and they're going to see that.

Mistake 3 – Offering a solution

People don't always speak about things because they want advice or a solution, sometimes they're just talking and being polite. If you're always interrupting and trying to offer a solution, it means you're not showing empathy because you're not putting yourself in their shoes. Instead, you're being proactive, which is a completely different thing altogether.

You might have the best intentions at heart but it's possible that this person doesn't want your advice, they simply want to talk. If they want a solution or advice, just know that they'll ask you for it and then you're well within your rights to offer a suggestion – not before.

Mistake 4 – Interrupting

It's possible that you're excitable because you've heard something you have an experience of and you want to put your side of the story over, but interrupting is a huge no-no when someone else is speaking.

You might not be trying to end the conversation early, but it shows the other person that you're far too busy to listen and you want them to get to the point already. This isn't going to show you in the best light and it's a huge conversation killer. If you want to say something, wait until they've finished.

Mistake 5 – Changing the subject or deflecting away from the subject

Sometimes we remember something halfway through a conversation and we want to say it before we forget again. However, if you change or deflect the subject it tells the other person that you're not interested in what they were talking about and that you were bored. It might not be the case, but that's how it comes across.

If you really do want to say something which is totally unrelated to the original conversation, try and weave it in or link to it in some way. You might have to be creative, but it's better than just abruptly changing the direction of the conversation.

CHAPTER THOUGHTS

Listening is an underrated skill that can make or break your communication efforts. Even the slightest hint that you're not truly paying attention can cause someone to avoid talking to you again and can create a very poor first impression. However, by listening properly, you gain so much. Not only do you learn something new, but you also build a rapport with someone who may turn out to be someone you can socialize with, or a good professional contact.

Practice your listening skills by doing more than just hearing the words.

10

BODY LANGUAGE IS THE KEY TO SUCCESSFUL INTERACTIONS

Throughout this book so far, I've talked about body language a few times and reassured you that we're going to delve into the subject in more detail later on. Now is that time!

Body language is one of the most powerful methods of speaking you possess, and to do it, you don't even open your mouth. Being able to read the body language of other people allows you to understand them in much greater detail and it also allows you to play the role of detective in some ways too. Not everyone says exactly what they mean, but their body language will always give them away.

In this chapter, I'm going to talk about what body language is, why it's important to be able to read it and why you need to be very mindful of the type of body language you're showing to other people.

NOT EVERYTHING HAS TO BE VERBAL

Non-verbal communication is just as important as verbal and in some cases, more important. Someone can say words, but their body language can totally contradict them. I gave the example earlier of someone saying, "I'm fine", when their body language is slumped, and they won't look you in the eye. When that happens, you're more likely to believe what their body language is telling you than their words because it's so powerful.

Body language is just one type of non-verbal communication. The others include facial gestures, how you speak, whether you maintain eye contact, and hand gestures. These are all unspoken ways of communicating what we really mean and usually what we really feel.

When you're able to read body language, you get the full message and the full meaning of whatever someone is trying to tell you, or in some cases, what they're trying not to tell you. This makes you an effective communicator and it also allows you to build up a true rapport.

Someone with good levels of emotional intelligence can read non-verbal cues very quickly and tends to even get a gut feeling when something isn't quite right. This isn't a psychic ability, it's just that they're able to read signs quickly and effectively and put the picture together. That tells you just how powerful these non-verbal signs are, even more than actual verbal words. If you pit the two against each other, body language will win out every time.

USING NONVERBAL LANGUAGE TO YOUR ADVANTAGE

In your journey to become a master communicator, you have to place a huge amount of importance upon body language and being able to use these non-verbal cues to your advantage during a conversation. You can make the other person feel at ease by ensuring that your body language is soft, open, and relaxed, or you can show that you really mean business if you need to, by sitting upright and appearing professional.

Once you understand body language a little better, you can use it to show your intentions and make sure that the other person doesn't get the wrong impression of you. It also helps you to show others that you're listening to them, and it stops you from being misunderstood and misread.

The other plus point is that when you understand body language, you can read it and use it to think of interesting things to say. Body language can guide the conversation in some ways because it gives you cues about the underlying emotions of the person you're speaking to. You can use this to show empathy, to help them out even, and to encourage them to open up.

All you need to do is know what good body language looks like, versus the bad. Handily, that's something we're going to explore in our next couple of sections.

IT'S ALL GOOD: THE POSITIVE NONVERBAL CUES

In order to start working towards using positive nonverbal cues, and kicking out some of the negative ones, you need to be more aware of the body language you're showing to those around you. This is going to be quite time consuming at first because it's possible you have no idea that you're showing a poor or maybe positive example to the world.

Simply be more mindful of what you do when you're communicating, how you show yourself, what your face is doing, what your hands are doing, and how you're standing. Over time, positive body language will become a thing of habit.

Let's look at some examples of positive non-verbal communication and how you can start to weave these naturally into your socializing efforts.

- **Tilting your head to one side** – This is a very slight inflection to one side whilst someone is talking and it shows not only that you're listening, but that you're also very interested in what they have to say. However, do make sure that you don't squint your eyes or pull a face at the same time, as this could show that you don't believe them or you're not taking them seriously. Keep your face neutral, or simply raise your eyebrows in interest.
- **Quickly rubbing your hands together** – You might think this means that you're cold, but that's not the only reason! Depending upon the context, you can use this non-

verbal cue to show that you're excited or keen to do something or speak about something. It's usually accompanied by a smile to get the right meaning across.

- **Sitting with your palms facing up** – Obviously to do this your hands also need to be open and it's the same kind of thing you would do if you were worshipping at a church. In that situation, you're showing respect to God, but in a communicative situation, you're showing that you're being open and honest. This is a good move to try and build trust.
- **Sitting up straight with your shoulders pulled back** – Be careful that you're not sitting bolt upright here; the stance should be straight but relaxed and the idea is that your shoulders pulled back means you're not slouching. This shows that you're relaxed and professional at the same time. You can also practice this as you're walking too, as it shows that you're relaxed within yourself and confident.
- **Rubbing your chin** – This shows that you're interested. Think about Sherlock Holmes when he was thinking about a case and trying to solve it – that's the look you're going for! This type of body language is usually shown when someone is trying to think and decide on something, but it can also show that you're deep in thought.
- **Mirroring their body language** – You might find that you do this without thinking because most of us do when we're with someone we're talking to and we're interested, or someone we feel comfortable with. If you're mirroring someone's body language it means that you're basically copying how they're standing. So, if they're leaning against a

wall, you will do the same subconsciously. It shows that you're relaxed, but it has to be done naturally otherwise it comes over as false.

- **Gently leaning into the person** – If you're speaking to someone, lean into them very slightly to show that you're listening. Be careful not to lean in too much as this could be misconstrued, but a slight lean shows that they have your attention and your interest.
- **Maintaining eye contact** – Be careful not to stare them out, but holding someone's eye contact and being relaxed within it shows that you're listening to them, you're interested and you're comfortable. Remember to blink and look away for a couple of seconds occasionally.
- **Nodding along** – Nodding your head whilst someone is speaking shows that you're listening but also shows that you're agreeing with what they're saying. This can encourage them to carry on speaking, especially if you throw in a few "uh-huh" or "hmm" noises too.

WARNING! NEGATIVE CUES TO WATCH OUT FOR

We've talked about positive non-verbal communication and now we need to cover the negative side of things. Remember that body language happens without much thought, it's totally subconscious and it can be interpreted in different ways according to the person you're conversing with.

However, if you're speaking to someone and you see some of these negative points, it could show you that they're feeling uncomfortable or maybe not interested in what you're saying. In that case, you can adjust your conversation or simply change the topic completely. You should also be mindful that you're not showing these non-verbal cues yourself.

- **Crossing arms over the chest** – Crossed arms show defensiveness because they act as a barrier between you and the other person. It can also show that the person is displeased with the topic or that they don't agree.
- **Biting your nails** – For many people, nail-biting is a habit that is born out of nerves or stress, but it can also show that you're not interested in what someone is saying, and you're distracted. Even if it is out of nerves, you're showing the other person that they make you nervous and this could be a huge barrier to communication and rapport.
- **Furrowed brow** – This is a sign that someone is confused or they're simply not paying attention and their mind is elsewhere. If a furrowed brow is accompanied by a hand on the cheek, it can show that you're lost in thought and you've totally lost the flow of the conversation. Either way, it's a barrier you don't need.
- **Tapping fingers or tapping a pen** – Tapping something means that you're impatient and you'd rather be elsewhere. It shows that you're bored and would much rather end this conversation quickly. Of course, it can also be nerves but it's not often interpreted that way.
- **Touching the nose** – This isn't an obvious one but touching your nose can show the other person that you're

lying because it's a form of fidgeting. It can also be that you don't believe them or that you're feeling rejected.

- **Forming a tent with your fingers, or placing the tips of your fingers together** – This is a way of telling the other person that you feel superior to them or that you're in authority. It's a quick way to form a huge communication barrier and stop the other person from communicating any further.

- **Crossing your legs at the knee or ankle** – This is another form of defensiveness because it's that barrier you form between you and the other person once more. You might think it's comfortable or even demure, but it can show that you're lying, you're worried, you're nervous, or that you'd just rather be elsewhere.

- **Sitting too close to the edge of your chair** – This doesn't show that you're super-excited to hear what someone is going to say, instead it shows that you're very nervous and you're trying to make a quick getaway.

- **Putting your head in your hands** – Even if you do this for just a second, it shows that you're bored and frustrated. It might also show that you're embarrassed or ashamed of something.

- **Playing with your hairs, rings, or clothing** – Any type of fidgeting is pretty negative and shows that you're either nervous, you're bored, you're impatient, or you're feeling insecure.

YOU GIVE THEM OFF TOO ...

Everyone has body language, but you might not be aware of your own. In order to be able to use more of the positive non-verbal cues and less of the negative ones, you need to build up awareness. How can you do that?

It really comes down to being mindful of your actions during a conversation, but you could ask a trusted friend or family member to highlight any common habits that you use when you're talking. Maybe you slouch a lot, or perhaps you fidget without realizing it. The problem with body language is that it's completely subconscious, so you're not even thinking about it. For the most part, you don't even know what you're doing.

Being aware means that you can change your habits and make the positive ones your default setting. You could even try having pretend conversations with others in a full-length mirror. Practice using positive body language cues and watch how it changes your entire look and how you could be perceived by other people. The more you do this, the more aware you'll be of your body language when you're in real conversations and you'll be able to spot any negative habits quickly and reverse them.

CHAPTER THOUGHTS

Body language is extremely powerful, and it has the potential to completely change someone's words into a different meaning altogether. When you show negative non-verbal traits to the world, you're telling them a story that perhaps you don't mean to tell. It could show people that you're not listening, you're not interested, and you'd really rather be anywhere else but there. You probably don't mean that, but that's what you're telling them, and they have no reason to believe anything else.

By learning more about positive and negative body language, and by practicing being more aware of your own, you can ensure that you're showing the best possible version of yourself to other people. In addition, you can start to recognize body language in other people and use it to your own advantage when you're socializing.

MAKE AWKWARD SILENCES YOUR BEST FRIEND & EFFORTLESSLY MOVE PAST THEM UNAFFECTED

THE DREADED AWKWARD SILENCE.

Even some of the most comfortable communicators in the world seem to think that a momentarily lull in the conversation has to add up to a major disaster. It doesn't.

As you build up your social skills and start to branch out more in terms of communicating with other people, you have to be prepared for an awkward silence or two. You also need to change your view regarding these silences and see them as just a part of the deal, and not necessarily a negative event.

Many people blame themselves when an awkward silence happens, thinking that maybe they said the wrong thing, or they weren't exciting enough. However, sometimes these silences need to happen as part of a naturally evolving conversation. It could be that the topic has come to a natural end and both people need to think of a natural change of topic direction, or that someone has said something really interesting and even proud, and maybe it needs a moment to be digested. It could even be that one half of the conversation is feeling a little tired or distracted, and a silence has happened for a couple of seconds as a result.

Awkward silences aren't always negative and they're not always awkward either!

In this chapter, I'm going to talk about these so-called dreaded events, try to dispel the fear, and give you plenty of tools to help you deal with them when they do crop up.

THE SILENCE IS NOBODY'S FAULT

There are two common reactions to a silence – either panic or a need to quickly fill the silence with another conversation. Neither are necessary.

Silences are a natural part of a conversation and they're either an opportunity to end the conversation and move on or a chance to pause and readjust.

Firstly, you need to accept this as a fact and stop assuming that it's your fault alone when a silence does occur. You should also stop calling them 'awkward silences' because by labeling them in that way, you're creating a stigma and fear around them. Silence is normal and, in some ways, it's to be welcomed – a constantly flowing conversation sounds great but in reality, it's exhausting! Sometimes you need a second to gather your thoughts.

You should also know that the look on the other person's face isn't an expression of disappointment. They're not thinking "what is wrong with this person? They can't even hold a conversation", they're simply trying to come up with something to say themselves. Nobody likes these silences, but it's a stigma that needs to be broken down if you want to become a better communicator and if you want to get over your fear of socializing with new people. Silences are part of the deal. They are going to happen sometimes, and it doesn't mean that you're not a good fit, that there is no rapport, or that you've failed, it's just a natural part of socializing.

BE THE MORE CONFIDENT ONE

You might not be aware, but allowing a silence to become awkward is actually a choice you make. Silence isn't awkward naturally or by definition, it's just a lull in a conversation or a period of time when there is no speech from either person. There is nothing necessarily awkward about that unless you make it so.

Everyone experiences silence in conversations, and from this point, I'm going to stop labeling them as 'awkward' because they don't need to be. You will always believe them to be awkward until you realize something really quite important. You realize that you're to blame for making it awkward.

There will normally be one person within the conversation who is more confident than the other yet when a silence happens, each party blames themselves for the lull. Their minds are working super-fast to try and think of something to say, anything to rescue themselves from the cringe-worthy feel of the moment. However, in reality, both parties aren't to blame, only one is – the one who deems it awkward. If you both simply let the silence happen and accept it as a normal part of communication, it will pass, nobody will feel like they want the ground to open up and swallow them whole, and the conversation will either naturally end, or you'll come up with something else to say.

By acting the one in the conversation who is more confident, you're guiding the other person. Confidence really is a 'fake it until you make it' kind of deal and if you act confident, sooner or later you'll start to feel it. You'll also trick the other person into thinking that you are too and it's infectious. By going into every conversation with this confidence and understanding that silence doesn't have to be so awkward, you'll be able to side-step these moments of peril and navigate your way seamlessly through.

HOW TO GET PAST IT: BRING THE CONVERSATION BACK

If you're really keen to get the conversation back on track, you'll need a few tricks in your armory to employ whenever one of these silences takes hold. Thankfully, it's not particularly difficult to get a conversation going again, but maybe you don't actually want to continue. Think of that for a second. Maybe the conversation has come to a natural conclusion and it's time to go about your day.

In that case, all you need to do is make your excuses. "I can't believe how fast today's gone, I better get on" is enough to let the other person know that you're not at all uncomfortable with the silence but you're ready to move past it. Every conversation has to end at some point otherwise we'd all be stuck chatting forever!

If you want to revitalize a conversation that seems to have been stilted by silence, here are a few tricks you can use.

- Turn the conversation towards a story on the news
- Observe something happening around you, such as a big gust of wind or asking them where they got their pretty necklace from
- Share a highlight of your day to get the conversation moving again
- Recall something that you spoke about earlier in the conversation and turn the conversation back around to it
- Mention something that you're really looking forward to, e.g. "I can't wait for dinner, I'm cooking a huge roast"
- Ask open-ended questions rather than questions that require a 'yes' or a 'no' answer
- If all else fails, point out the silence and make a joke about it. This will take the sting from it and help the other person to feel relaxed.

Getting a conversation back on track doesn't need to be a big thing. You can simply ask a question and act like the silence never happened. Remember, it's only awkward if you make it so.

AWKWARD SILENCE CAN BE YOUR BEST FRIEND

You always have the choice over whether you deem something to be awkward or not. If you choose for it not to be, then it won't be. It's really that simple.

Even when you're not conversing verbally, you're still using communication. Remember in our last chapter that we talked about the power of body language? During these silences, your body language will be deafening if you allow it to become negative. However, if you maintain a positive stance and use the habits I mentioned as positive, you'll show the other person that you're not concerned about this brief silence and that will allow them to relax too. By doing so, the silence will end far faster. It also shows that you're relaxed within yourself, which is a very enviable trait.

Use the silence as a second to gather your thoughts. What do you want to say to this person? What do you want to find out? Whilst you're doing this, your body language will be speaking for you, so always be mindful of it, as before.

Use the silence as a tool rather than something which causes you to kick-start into fight or flight mode. You also shouldn't feel like the pressure is entirely on you. The other person can also break the silence too!

Using this silence as a positive just means being calm, poised, and using it as a way to think. When conversations are batting back and forth it's easy to forget yourself and what you want to say. Use the conversation lull to regroup.

TAKE IT AS YOUR CUE

Of course, a silence sometimes means it's time to end the conversation and you can take it as a sign that you've done well, the conversation is over, and it's time to bid them goodbye. This doesn't have to be done in a stilted, "okay, we've run out of things to say" kind of way, it can be a natural end.

Sometimes a silence happens because you literally have run out of things to say but not negatively because the conversation has exhausted itself. There is literally nothing left to say about that topic, and you don't always have to find a way to fill a silence either. It's a choice of what you want to do, and you shouldn't feel pressure to quickly come up with an interesting new topic.

As I mentioned earlier, simply let the other person know that you're finished talking now. It sounds harsh, but it doesn't have to be! "I suppose I'd better get back to work" accompanied by a good-natured shrug and a smile is enough to end the chat in a positive way. "It's been really nice to talk to you. I've got to get on because my bus is due, but we must meet up again". These are examples that allow you to signal an end to the conversation but leaving it on a positive and upbeat note.

Don't always feel the need to fill the silence, sometimes silence is a cue.

CHAPTER THOUGHTS

We're quick to label silences as awkward, but what about the saying "silence is golden"? It's a truth and one you must embrace.

You choose whether a silence becomes awkward or whether it simply means a lull. Nobody can speak constantly for the full course of a conversation, no matter how long or short it is. We have to give ourselves time to think and breathe occasionally!

Silences are nobody's fault, they're completely natural, but it is your fault if you choose to make it an awkward moment.

You get to choose whether the conversation is over or whether you want to continue it on, but learning how to use these lulls to your own advantage is key if you want to overcome your fear of these moments of silence and continue your journey towards increased communication mastery.

12

IT HAS ENDED – WRAPPING UP YOUR CONVERSATION

All conversations must come to an end.

In our last chapter, we talked about awkward silences and how these sometimes signal the end of a conversation. However, conversations don't always end with a lull or a silence, they sometimes need to be ended for another reason.

Maybe the conversation is just going round and round in circles, maybe the time is really getting on and you need to go, or maybe you're just ready to bid them goodbye. Either way, knowing how to end a conversation in a polite way and how to ensure that the conversation isn't your last, is key.

In this chapter, I'm going to talk about those very subjects. For some people, ending a conversation is difficult because they feel like they're being rude if they say, "I'm sorry but I've really got to go now", but if you don't do something, you could be standing there all day long!

Thankfully, it's not that hard to learn how to end conversations without feeling like you've just offended someone.

THE TIME HAS COME

Knowing when it's time to end a conversation is key. Allowing a conversation to go on for too long can take a good chat into bad chat territory. What starts off well starts to become stilted, you answer with monosyllabic noises and body language has started to tell you that the other person has had enough.

It's good practice to spot the signs so that you can end the chat in a friendly way and then swap details so that you can perhaps meet up again in the future. If you allow the conversation to go on for too long, especially if it's the first time you've had a conversation with someone, you might be remembered as "that one person who went on, and on, and on" and they're going to avoid wanting to talk to you again. Of course, that might seem unfair if you were pretty keen to end the conversation as well, but if you didn't show them that, how can you expect them to know? They're not mind readers!

So, what are the signs that it's time for a conversation to end?

- You're the one doing all the conversing and they're simply answering you back with 'just enough' to be polite
- You're hearing more and more monosyllabic answers, e.g. words with just one syllable, such as 'yes', 'no', 'oh', 'ah', 'okay', etc.

- The other person is avoiding eye contact, or they're starting to fidget or look around the room
- The other person yawns, glances at the clock, or looks at their watch
- Stretching
- If the other person suddenly stands up. In that case, it's a cue that they're ready to go
- They say that they better get on with work or they have to be somewhere else
- The conversation just feels heavier and harder work.

In these situations, it's time to end the conversation and go about your day. It might also be that you're the one who needs to end the conversation because you need to be somewhere perhaps. In that case, don't feel guilty – everyone has a life outside of the conversation they're currently having!

If someone is showing you signs that they want to end the conversation, be sure to notice them and take action. Dragging on a conversation is not a good idea, but you shouldn't be offended by their actions either. They may genuinely need to be somewhere, just as you may need to be too.

ANOTHER PERSON CAN HELP YOU

If you really need to end a conversation but the other person doesn't seem to be of the same opinion, how are you supposed to extract yourself politely?

You could be direct and explain that you really need to be somewhere, or you could employ a very useful tactic - bringing another person into the conversation. This tactic does rely on another person you know being close by but it's a good option to have in your mind, in case the situation does arise.

This is a very useful way to end a conversation with someone whom you don't really want to leave on their own. Maybe they look lonely or they're simply standing alone, and you feel bad to leave them there. In that case, introduce another person into the chat, stick around for a few minutes, making idle chat, and excuse yourself, leaving the other two to continue their conversation.

There are two plus points to this tactic. Firstly, you can get away from the conversation without causing offense or upset to the other person. Secondly, you can help the other two people to create a rapport and connection alongside the one you've just created. You're basically helping them out whilst helping yourself out, which is never a bad tactic to use!

It goes a little like this.

"Adam, you've been on holiday to Spain before haven't you?" Adam will say that yes, he has. "Karen here is looking to go this summer, where was it that you went?"

By doing this, you've introduced Adam into the conversation and they're talking about something which is easy-going and relevant to both parties. In that case, they've got something in common and could go on to form a rapport. You should stick around for a short while, ensuring that they keep chatting and put your input into the conversation a little too. "I'd really like to go to Spain too, I might look for this year".

Then, after a couple of minutes, you could look at your watch and say "I can't believe the time. I'm so sorry, I'm going to have to rush off and pick up the kids. Let me know where you decide to go in Spain". Then, you leave Karen chatting to Adam about Spain and you're free to go about the rest of your day.

Easy!

ENDING IT ON A GOOD NOTE

It goes without saying that you should always try to end conversations on a good note. In some ways, last impressions are as powerful as first impressions to a degree. The way you leave a person stays with them too, so you need to be sure that you end the conversation in a way that is polite, not abrupt, and that hopefully leaves them wanting to have further conversations with you in the future.

You could say something like "I'm really going to have to go in a minute but before I do, I want to tell you about this place I went to for dinner last week". That shows the other person that a) you're about to go so the conversation is coming to a natural end, but that b) you want to tell them something else first and you're keen to continue talking to them another time.

Some things to avoid include:

- Abruptly ending the conversation with "I've got to go now" and then literally just walking away
- Zero pleasantries – Always say something like "it's been great chatting to you"; avoiding this just looks rude
- Just walking away when a silence begins
- Using an excuse that is so obviously fabricated that the other person feels like you didn't enjoy talking to them

Ending on a positive note will ensure that there is a next time, and you can continue to build upon the rapport you've established.

HOW ABOUT NEXT TIME?

Assuming you want to talk to this person again, how should you go about arranging it?

Don't make them set a concrete date because that's just needy and will make them want to avoid you. However, don't be so vague that it makes them think you're just saying you want to meet up again out of politeness. You need to strike a useful piece of middle ground.

By discussing setting up a plan to meet up again it tells the other person that you had a great time talking to them and that you want to get to know them better. This can be used in a romantic situation and in a friendship situation, it works equally well regardless.

So, how can you do it without seeming too keen?

It really comes down to using your body language in the right way and choosing your words carefully. Don't allow yourself to seem desperate. By pushing your contact details onto the other person and trying to pinpoint them down to a particular date or time, you're showing that you're desperate for someone to talk to and that's not going to get you what you want.

Instead, be casual about it. You can say something like "I had a great time talking to you if you want to meet up again just let me know" and then the other person can agree, and you swap contact details. You can also agree to do something that you talked about at some point in your chat; maybe you talked about a great little coffee shop you went to and they served the best cakes or a great spot in the park for walking the dog. These ideas link back to the conversation and something you've already built up a rapport about, so they're ideal opportunities to meet up again and try and build up a deeper connection and nurture that potential new friendship.

Never just leave it cold. By doing so you're going to confuse the other person and they're not going to know whether you enjoyed the chat or not. You might not think they'll be too concerned, but you can't read their mind. How do you know they're not a little awkward in using their social skills too? Some people hide shyness or social anxiety quite well sometimes. So, don't allow an opportunity to pass and simply reach out. If they call you, great. If they don't, no problem.

CHAPTER THOUGHTS

Trying to get out of a conversation can be tricky and sometimes it's a reason why people don't want to stop and get into one in the first place! However, it doesn't always need to be difficult and you simply need to know the signs to look for that signal the conversation is naturally coming to an end.

There's no need to take offense if someone needs to be elsewhere, because there will be times you're speaking to someone and you need to go somewhere too. We all have busy lives, and we all need to expect that sometimes conversations are going to start at bad times.

Try your best to leave conversations on a positive note and swap contact numbers so you can continue to nurture the rapport you've built up. You never know, this could be a new friend to add to your growing collection!

III

KEEPING YOUR RELATIONSHIPS AND MAKING THEM LAST

13

HOW TO NURTURE YOUR NEWLY FORMED FRIENDSHIPS

Once you start to create rapport with other people, you'll also start to form connections and friendships. That means all your hard work is finally paying off!

Friendships truly make life worthwhile. However, it's also worth pointing out that nothing is 100% positive all the time. Friends have arguments, conflicts, they clash on subjects, and sometimes it's painful because you don't want to argue with someone you've grown close to. However, it's important to remember that friendships are basically two human beings trying to navigate life. That means that sometimes there are going to be problems but it's about how you get through them together that counts.

As you start to build friendships, it's normal to give your all because you're worried that they're going to go away as quickly as they came. My advice is to relax and be yourself. You do not have to force things, and you have to allow friendships to develop naturally. Yes, you need to ensure that you're spending time together and you're not doing anything which causes undue upset or concern to your friend, but you also don't need to pretend to be someone you're not and you don't have to be the one always trying to reach out. Friendships are two-way deals.

This isn't meant to be a negative overview of what a friendship is by any means. Friendships are wonderful things, but when you've struggled with your social skills for a long time and then you suddenly find yourself meeting new people who want to be your friend, it can be very easy to become fearful that as quickly as you received these people into your life, they're going to be taken away. They're not.

This is something I experienced, which is why I want to highlight it to you. I battled with shyness for so long that I had very few friends. However, once I started to overcome it and open myself up to having conversations with other people, the natural thing happened – I gained more friends. It was amazing and whilst I was embracing every second, I was fearful at the same time.

By doing this, you're actually defeating the object and you're actually working against yourself. So, my advice is to relax and enjoy the fruits of your labor. You deserve this, and it's because you've worked so hard for it. However, the hard work isn't over yet!

SPENDING QUALITY TIME IS ESSENTIAL

There are many reasons why having friendships in your life is important. Not only do they make life more worthwhile and fulfilling but having friendships is actually very important for your mental health.

The benefits of having friends include:

- Helps you to feel like you belong to something other than yourself
- Helps you to identify a purpose in life
- Helps you feel happier and more positive
- Allows you to manage and reduce any stress in your life
- Boosts self-confidence
- Boosts self-worth
- Gives you a support network during difficult times, such as the loss of a loved one, relationship problems, or job issues
- Helps you to avoid unhealthy coping mechanisms during hard times
- Encourages you to talk about your feelings rather than keeping them bottled up inside.

Of course, friendships are two-way streets. For all the benefits that having friends brings to you, you should also be providing the same level of support and happiness to another person.

In order to nourish a friendship, either newly formed or long-standing, you have to put in the work and that means spending quality time together. This is a vital part of your friendship because without it, your bond will weaken and over time you'll just grow apart. Maybe this has happened to you in the past.

It's often the case when people meet early in their lives, e.g. during high school perhaps. Once they leave school, they become so engrossed with the new parts of their life that they forget to put the effort in to keep their old friendships ticking along. Before you know it, months and years have gone by and no communication has occurred. Friendships can easily die out by not dedicating quality time to one another.

You can spend time together in many different ways. This can be hanging out in person, such as going for a coffee, going for a walk, arranging to go out for a meal, etc. It can be chatting online when you don't have the time to meet up or when circumstances don't allow it. However, it's always better to limit the amount of online interaction you have and make a priority out of meeting in person or at least speaking over the phone.

The most important thing to remember is that when you do hang out together, that you're completely present in the moment. Put away your phone! Your friendships are a deeply important part of your life and by constantly being on your phone when you're supposed to be spending quality time with a friend, you're showing them that they're not that important to you.

Think how you would feel if your friend was constantly checking their phone when you were out for dinner together. You would feel annoyed, wouldn't you? And you would be right to feel that way.

Being present in the moment means ensuring that your attention is firmly on your friend and the conversation you're having. It means you can have more in-depth chats and really build upon your rapport. It also means you can share experiences together and build memories, which is what friendship is all about. If a friend is sharing a woe with you, perhaps something which has happened in their life, and you're not really in the moment or listening properly, they're going to know. Remember, your friends know you well, even if you've not been friends for that long. This means they're going to know if you're not really listening or paying attention and they're going to feel upset that you're not concerned about what they're telling you. In some cases, this can be enough to end a friendship, and that's not something you want.

By making time for your friends, making them a priority in your life, and being present in the moment when you are spending time together, you'll nourish those connections and benefit from them in a big way.

MAKING AN EFFORT HELPS TO BUILD

We've already established that to help a friendship grow and to keep it ticking along nicely, you need to spend quality time together on a regular basis. However, that also means you need to make an effort. It's vital that this effort isn't just placed on your shoulders, and equally, you shouldn't expect the other person to do all the leg work either. This is a shared responsibility.

Nurturing a friendship does take work, but whatever you put into the friendship is going to give you more out of it. You don't have to make huge gestures or plan elaborate outings; sometimes the smallest things can show that you're making an effort and that you care. For instance, sending your friend a funny meme you've found online, or maybe you see something you know they would like, so you send them a link to it. This shows them that you're thinking about them and that small action keeps things ticking along.

Small acts of kindness in friendships are so important and they really do go such a long way. Maybe you've made a cake at home and there's some leftover; when you meet up the next day, you take a piece for them to try. Perhaps you saw their favorite beverage in the supermarket, and you thought you'd surprise them. Effort doesn't always mean gifts, but it certainly always means time and attention.

However, I want to go back to the idea of being the one doing all the work for a second. This is something you need to be very mindful of. The reason is that constantly pushing could be off-putting to your friend. Maybe they're going through a stressful time at work or they're just not feeling that great at the moment. By constantly trying to get them to meet up or bombarding them with messages, you could make them feel quite stressed or annoyed.

The best advice is to invite them to do something and then leave it in their hands. You've made the effort and they will get back to you. Busy yourself with something else. If they don't reply to you, you could send a follow-up message but not straight away – leave it a few days and enquire if they're okay. That's all you need to do. Effort doesn't mean pushing too much, it means just enough to keep things moving and nourishing the connection you have.

DON'T BE AFRAID TO BE VULNERABLE

The closest and most supportive of friendships are born out of the ability to knock down walls and allow yourself to open up. That means being vulnerable.

Being vulnerable can be a terrifying experience for some people but it's important to remember that you don't have to share anything you're not comfortable with. Set yourself boundaries and work within them. You can always adjust them whenever you feel comfortable doing so.

However, on the flip side, it's also important not to be overly vulnerable and basically over-share everything that you think and feel. Your friends are there to support you, that's the truth, but they're not there to prop up your emotions and listen to every single thing that goes wrong in your life. It's about finding a happy medium.

Being vulnerable can also be difficult because someone who has been through a hard time in the past, or someone who has struggled with social skills, is likely to have built up high walls around themselves. This is especially true if someone has betrayed and hurt you in the past. However, these walls do nothing for you. You might think they're protecting you from further hurt, but in reality, they're just holding you back and stopping you from building enriching and supportive relationships with other people.

Being vulnerable means, you need to trust the other person to listen and be there for you, but this huge gamble isn't an effort wasted because it also lets your friend trust you too. Trust is a two-way deal and with friendships, it's truly a case of share and share-alike.

If you need a little nudge in the right direction, these are some of the reasons why allowing yourself to be vulnerable creates some of the best friendships around.

- Being vulnerable shows your friends that you've placed your trust in them
- Being vulnerable also encourages your friends to open up to you
- When you're vulnerable, your friends can act as encouragement for you to overcome whatever is bothering you
- When you're vulnerable it means not only that you trust your friend but also that you value honesty and openness, which are positive traits to have and show
- Friendships built on mutual sharing of worries and concerns are authentic and usually long-lasting
- Being vulnerable with your friends also gives you the confidence to go out there and solve whatever problem you're facing, because you know you have the support of your circle.

Keeping things bottled up inside is not healthy and it does nothing for your mental health. All it does is create stress and causes you to overthink. Friendships are the ideal outlet for voicing these worries, allowing your friends to listen, support, and usually advise you too. This isn't a case of judging your problem or telling you what you should do, it's about someone who knows you well, giving you their honest opinion and guiding you, should you need extra help.

Friendships without vulnerability are quite stilted and closed. You could argue that these types of friendships aren't really genuine. Yes, you know each other and enjoy spending time together but a true friendship is about sharing and supporting one another. You can't do that if you're not willing to open up and share the things that you need support in, and vice versa. Being there for one another is what takes a friendship from just two people who know each other, to two people who care about and want the best for each other.

If you struggle to open up to your new friends, perhaps because you've built those walls around you, start slowly and small. Share one detail and see how you feel. Over time, you'll feel more confident in breaking down those barriers and opening up.

THE UPS AND DOWNS OF FRIENDSHIPS

The beauty of friendship is that you're there for each other through the good and the bad. A good friend will share your sorrows and celebrate your successes and it's through these joint experiences that a true and lasting bond is formed. However, it's important to remember that in order to enrich your friendship and really be there for one another, that means showing up during the hard times in life.

It can be easy to show up for the good and only half show up for the bad. This can be because you're not sure what to say, or you feel awkward seeing your friend emotional. However, as their friend, it's your job to put that discomfort to one side and play the role you're supposed to play – supporter.

It's being there through the hard times that helps to build up a greater level of trust and as a result, your friendship will be deeper, lasting, and truly beneficial for both of you. Being there doesn't mean offering great advice or being able to understand completely, it often just means listening, running any errands they need, and being a supportive and positive figure in their life.

If you think back to the last time you went through a hard time in your life, you probably didn't really want anyone to step in and solve the problem or offer revolutionary advice, you just wanted someone to be there and to listen to you, put their arm around you and tell you that everything's going to be alright. That's the role of a friend.

There's no judgment, no telling you what to do, they're simply focused on making sure that you're doing okay and giving you a helping hand when and if you need it.

Of course, friendships aren't all about the bad times, and there has to be a balance here too. If as friends all you're doing for each other is mopping up spills and making each other feel better, it's a supportive relationship and not an actual friendship! You need to have laughs and smiles, positive memories to draw upon and those are what will power you through the hard times.

KEEPING YOUR EXPECTATIONS REALISTIC

We've been fed images of friendships since the day we were born, mostly from TV shows and blockbuster movies. Do you remember earlier, I mentioned that I always wanted a social circle akin to the one on Friends? These images can cause you to develop unrealistic expectations of your friendships, and when those expectations are inevitably not met, you become angry, worried, and it could even cause a conflict to occur between you.

It's important to remember that friends are human beings and sometimes human beings are busy with other things, tired, stressed, unwell, or simply just being a little selfish. It's important to have realistic expectations of your friendships so that you're not causing a problem out of something which isn't worthwhile.

Whilst it's normal to have the rose garden idea of friendship in your mind, it's important to keep your view realistic. Understand that life gets in the way sometimes and that people say and do hurtful things occasionally – just like you do from time to time too. Plans may be canceled for other things sometimes, misunderstandings happen, people prioritize other things over their friendships when they need to. A realistic view of a friendship bears all of this in mind and as a result, reduces the chances of a major problem occurring.

However, that doesn't mean you should allow your friends to constantly cancel your plans, and constantly take whatever you say the wrong way. In that case, it's not a friendship! It's about balance, and it's about understanding that sometimes in life, things go wrong and plans have to change. Don't take it to heart if a friend has to do this, just as they shouldn't take it to heart if you have to do so either.

In our next chapter I'm going to talk about how to handle conflicts in friendships but for now, let's focus on those expectations. That's the single best way to avoid a problem from happening in the first place.

Realistic Friendship Expectations

- Friends treat you with respect
- Friends do their best to avoid upsetting you or hurting your feelings
- You both make time for one another
- Your friendship doesn't push you or make you feel uncomfortable
- Friends make you laugh and make you feel better in general
- Friends support you when you're going through a hard time.

Unrealistic Friendship Expectations

- Close friendships bonds occur overnight
- You share your deepest secrets almost instantly
- You expect to spend a large amount of time together, even shortly after you meet
- You expect friends to drop everything and listen to you or be there for you at a moment's notice
- You expect to be their number one priority in life.

It's important to remember that real friendships have boundaries and they move at a pace that is comfortable for both people involved. Trust takes time to build up and by throwing your all into a friendship from the very first moment you meet, you're simply putting too much pressure on the potential friendship. If anything, you might also be scaring the other person away by being too much too soon. Slow down and allow the friendship to develop naturally, but remember to spend quality time together when you both can.

CHAPTER THOUGHTS

Friendships are wonderful things, but unlike what the movies tell you, they don't happen overnight, they're not going to fall into your lap, and you do need to put some effort in.

Having friends is important for your mental health and your general happiness, but you should also put in just as much as you take too. Remember to be there for your friends as much as they're there for you and always be present in the moment when you're spending time together.

It's also vital that you allow yourself to open up and be vulnerable at a pace that's comfortable to you. This doesn't mean sharing your darkest secrets and concerns if you're not comfortable doing so, but authentic relationships need vulnerability to help build trust. This can be difficult for people who have had difficult pasts and even for those who struggle with communication in general. Just go at a pace that's comfortable for you and don't feel rushed. You'll get there as long as you keep putting one foot in front of the other.

14

CONFLICTS ARISING AND HOW TO HANDLE THEM

As someone who struggled with shyness for a long time, I know how it feels when you start to make headway and you notice that you're connecting with people and making new friends. It's like you've got a new lease of life. It can also be terrifying because you're scared that you're going to say or do something to mess it up.

You have to relax into friendships and allow them to evolve. When a misunderstanding occurs, which it will at some point, do not panic! It's easy to go from 0 to 100 in less than a second and see disaster lights in front of your eyes but misunderstandings are easily cleaned up. Whilst learning how to improve your social skills and be a better communicator you have to know that mishaps are still going to happen, they're part of life. But, mishaps don't mean the end of friendships or opportunities, they're just a part of the story.

It's not possible to 'get' each other 100% of the time and there are always going to be occasions when you don't like something they did, or maybe they take offense to something you said or did. Part and parcel of friendship is accepting that people mess up sometimes and as long as work is done to repair it, i.e. an apology if one is necessary, these things can be overcome, swept under the rug, and forgotten. Maybe there is a lesson to be learned within that problem and in that case, certainly go ahead and learn it but don't assume that your newly formed friendship is over at the sign of the first hint of trouble.

In this chapter, I want to talk about conflicts within friendships and how you can handle them calmly and in the right way. Life sometimes throws us a few road bumps to keep us on our toes, but your new communication skills will help you out, even as they continue to grow and evolve.

NOT EVERYTHING CAN GO SMOOTHLY

If I've learned anything from life, it's that things rarely go as smoothly as you plan. Sometimes you have to take your hands off the control wheel and try and see where things go naturally. I've also learned that if something doesn't go as smoothly as you hoped, that's fine, because there will always be a way to steer it back on track, or maybe find another route that is even better than the one you had planned in the first place.

When you involve more than one person in a situation, there is a chance of misunderstanding and conflict. That's two individual people, two opinions, two egos, two sets of thoughts, two brains, and two lots of pride. Understand that people can be difficult! Friendships are littered with mishaps every so often but unless it's something earth-shatteringly bad that you've done, there is always an opportunity to fix it.

The information in this chapter will help you to deal with conflicts if and when they occur but having the right mindset from the start is important. Know that misunderstandings and problems happen in any friendship and that when they do happen, it's not the end of the world. Repeat that as a mantra as and when you need it!

CONFLICTS CAN BE BENEFICIAL

Believe it or not, conflicts can actually be very useful for a friendship. It's a little like a spring clean, it allows fresh air to enter the room, gets rid of the cobwebs, and leaves the scene feeling spick and span. A friendship that never experiences a difference of opinion, a misunderstanding, or a conflict in general probably isn't genuine or completely invested within. When emotions and opinions are involved, misunderstandings are bound to happen at some point, and it is even more confusing and even hurtful when it's a friend because this is someone you care about.

However, having the right mindset towards conflict means that you can look to solve the problem far easier and save some time. A relationship can grow and develop following a conflict, but it requires honesty and reflection to do that.

Of course, any type of conflict leaves you feeling upset and sad. It's confusing and you're not sure whether you feel guilty or attacked.

How you feel initially depends upon your view of conflict, which is developed throughout your early years. If you were taught to deal with issues constructively and to communicate clearly, you won't have as much trouble as someone who has always had problems with communication, i.e. you. However, the good news is that you can turn the tide on a conflict by understanding why they're actually quite useful. Two people who have had a conflict and a good conversation afterward can grow closer as a result.

Let's look at a few reasons why conflict can be useful.

Conflict gives you an opportunity to reflect

It could be that the conflict is designed to tell you something, i.e. your priorities are in the wrong place. Once you have a conflict, step back for a minute and look at the situation. What caused it? What can you learn from it? Did it happen because you aren't placing the right amount of interest in your friendship because you're not communicating clearly? Is the problem you're clashing over really worth it? Sometimes it's better to just allow things to pass and let things go.

Conflict identifies habits and behaviors that need to change

A conflict can be a sign that something needs to change, i.e. maybe you've developed a toxic habit or maybe your friend has. In that case, the conflict can serve as a wake-up call. If you're having regular arguments or misunderstandings, that makes it all the clearer that you need to look at things and assess what may need to change.

Don't see the conflict as a potential full stop to your friendship, instead see it as an opportunity to change things and breathe new life into a situation that is clearly struggling for some reason. Pay a little more attention to what you and also what your friend does and how you communicate with one another. This should give you the answers you seek.

Conflict serves as a learning curve

Any type of conflict gives you a chance to learn, especially when you look at what you're misunderstanding each other over, or what you're fighting about. That particular subject could be a trigger that needs to be resolved. Do you need to learn to be more understanding? Do you need to listen more? What is it that you can learn from the problem and what can you change in the future? Of course, this also means that your friend needs to do the same thing, in order for the learning opportunity to work.

COMMUNICATE WHEN YOU'RE UPSET

Much of the time, conflicts happen because of a communication problem. For instance, a misunderstanding happens because one person doesn't explain an issue clearly and the other person takes it to mean a different thing. Even a full-blown argument can be the fault of a problem with communication, because one person says something in a slightly off-hand or sarcastic way, and the other person takes offense to it.

Conflict, in its basic form, always comes down to communication issues.

This entire book is about learning to be a better communicator but sometimes that means taking it back a notch and using simple and clear language. You don't always have to be fancy or make everything complicated, sometimes the best approach is the simplest.

When you're upset about something, it can be easy to let your emotions get the better of you. For someone who doesn't have the highest level of EQ, this is quite likely to be the case. However, as you build up your EQ, become more confident in your ability to communicate, and as you develop your social skills, you'll be able to handle your own emotions, manage them, and stop them from causing you to act out in a way which could cause a conflict, or worsen an existing one.

When you try to resolve a conflict, the single best approach is a simple one. Simple and clear communication means that the other person knows how you feel, they understand what they did wrong, and they know how to stop it from happening again. Or, if you're at fault, simple and clear communication shows the other person that you know what you did, you understand it was wrong, and you're going to take steps to stop it from happening in the future. When you overcomplicate things, you run the risk of making the matter worse, even if your intentions are honorable.

The most likely emotion is anger and this is also one of the strongest too. Anger is responsible for almost every conflict if you look carefully at the root cause. Anger causes you to see red, it numbs you to the reality around you and it pushes you to say and do things that are extremely inadvisable.

Part of emotional intelligence is, of course, being in the moment and mindfully aware of what you're saying and doing. This is the single best technique when handling anger. Take a moment, stop and breathe, and count to ten. By taking yourself out of the situation for just a very small amount of time, you're able to gain perspective and that will stop you from doing anything that could come back to haunt you later on.

There are also some questions you should stop and ask yourself before you attempt to communicate with a person with who you are having a conflict with.

Question 1 – What do I want to get out of this?

Rather than reacting in the moment, stop and ask yourself what you want the outcome to be. In this situation, it's likely to be that you want to solve the conflict and for your friendship to be repaired. Keeping your aim in mind will stop you from saying or doing anything which could cause another outcome to occur, e.g. saying something in the heat of the moment in anger. By stopping and asking yourself this question, you're also giving yourself the time to calm down and gain perspective – that your friendship is worth more than this conflict.

Question 2 – What do I say to get the result I want?

Now you know what you want, it's time to think about the things you should say in order to get that result. That could be 'I'm sorry', or it could be 'I don't want us to argue', as a precursor to the conversation that hopefully solves the actual problem.

This time also allows you to think about how you say the word and not just the words themselves. You could say the most heartfelt sentence ever, but if you say it in the wrong way, perhaps with a hint of sarcasm and the wrong type of body language, it's going to amount to nothing and could even make the problem worse. Be heartfelt, open, and honest.

Remember to communicate your emotions to add authenticity, e.g. "I feel sad that we are fighting", or "I was angry".

Question 3 – How should I say it?

I just mentioned that you need to be mindful of your body language and you also need to avoid being sarcastic, because that totally takes away the meaning of your words and gives you the opposite effect. Before you actually go in and speak to your friend, work out how you're going to say it. Be mindful of the type of body language that is going to speak in your favor versus the type that is going to go against you.

Avoid crossing your arms over your body when you're speaking as that's classic defensive body language. This will tell the other person that you're not actually sorry and that you're feeling attacked. Instead, keep your arms down by your sides and maintain eye contact. The simplest body language is sometimes the best in these situations.

Speak slowly, carefully, and avoid any type of joke or sarcasm, even if it's meant to be humorous. It could be taken the wrong way and that will derail your efforts. Simple is best.

Question 4 – When should you speak to your friend?

To get the outcome you want, you need to choose your time carefully. Give yourself the time to calm down and be relaxed. Make sure you approach your friend at a time you know they're feeling calmer too and not when you know they're going to be in the middle of something important, e.g. picking up the kids from school or just finishing work.

You need to choose a time when you know that your efforts to smooth things over are going to be received well, rather than a time that is going to make it worse. You know your friend better than anyone, so give this some thought and don't feel rushed – a good communicator knows that there is no need to rush, the words and the sentiment will do the job when the time is right.

DO'S AND DON'TS OF HANDLING CONFLICT

When handling conflict, there are common do's and don'ts. Knowing these can stop you from going down the wrong route and potentially making things worse. When emotions are involved it's very easy to rush, but you need to calm down before you do anything. Make that your number one rule!

Do's of Handling Conflict

- **Choose your moment carefully** – As I mentioned in the last section, make sure that you choose your moment very carefully and wait until you're calm enough to speak without your emotions rising once more. You also need to choose a time when your friend is also going to have calmed down and a time which isn't going to be particularly bad for them in general.

- **Speak in person rather than via text if possible** – You can send a text to ask if you can meet up to talk, but have the actual conversation in person. Texts are so easy to misunderstand, and you could end up worsening the situation. Speaking in person also gives you the opportunity to read their body language and gain more from the meeting.

- **Keep things simple** – Simple communication is the best when calming a conflict. Don't say too much, don't overcomplicate it, don't use long-winded sentences that never really get to the point. Just keep it simple and say what you want to say.

- **Think about what you're going to say** – Whilst you can't rehearse a script because you don't know what the other person is going to say, you should think about what you want to say and what your aim of the conversation is. By doing so, you won't forget an important point and then kick yourself later on.

- **Be firm in your beliefs but keep your mind open too** – If you truly believe that what you said or did was right, or that you acted with the best intentions, but it went a little wrong, you can stick by your beliefs. You don't have to admit you were wrong if you weren't. Adults are able to agree to disagree. However, you should be open-minded enough to listen to their side of it and how they interpreted your words or actions and acknowledge that their view is just as valid as yours.

- **Use your breath to keep emotions under control** – If you feel like you're starting to become upset, turn your attention to your breath and bring your emotions under control. This is a very easy tactic you can use in many situations but when you're trying to communicate and you don't want your voice to wobble or your eyes to start watering, focus on something that isn't moving and turn your attention to your inhale and exhale. Make sure that you slow it down and stick to deep breaths. This will ground you and pull any rising emotions back into check.

- **Listen!** – It goes without saying that the number one do of dealing with conflict is that you should listen to your friend when they're speaking and show them that you are doing so. If you need a recap, go back to our chapter on listening and revisit the points we talked about. This is such an important aspect of handling conflict and could be the difference between a resolution and a further issue.

Don'ts of Handling Conflict

- **Be defensive, this isn't a battle** – If you did something wrong, admit it and move on. Do not allow yourself to become defensive and try and deflect the blame elsewhere. Also, avoid that defensive body language we talked about earlier. You are speaking to your friend here, not a fighter from an opposite army. Even when you're misunderstanding each other and conflicts are happening regularly, you're still friends and you still want the best for each other. There is no need to raise your walls and be defensive.

- **Drag up the conflict once more** – You're trying to solve the conflict, not continue it. Don't bring up points and start to argue once more. You can address points but, in a way, that means you're keen to move past them. By dragging up things that you don't agree with, you're just going to end up with round two.
- **Allow yourself to become emotional** – In the 'do' section we talked about using your breath to bring your emotions under control and that is very important. By becoming emotional, you're going to potentially say something you regret and not really get the outcome you want. Stay as balanced as you can possibly be and focus on resolution.
- **Say too much** – There's no need to give a big speech. When you're thinking about what you're going to say, keep it as simple as possible. This gives you less chance of being misunderstood and more chance of your friend being on the same page as you.
- **Make it all about you** – It takes two people to make a friendship and two people to start and continue an argument. When trying to resolve it, that means it's not all about you either. Respect the other person's point of view and whilst it's very easy to get wrapped up in how it feels to you and how it hurt you, remember that it probably hurt your friend also. Keep it balanced and appreciate both sides.

DEALING WITH SOMEONE DIFFICULT

As you start to branch out into meeting new people, it's inevitable that you'll meet one or two which test your patience. There are some difficult people out there and whilst we should always give the benefit of the doubt and give everyone a chance, some people are just beyond it!

Difficult people can be thrown into your path in any situation. You might meet someone at the bus stop who just will not stop complaining, you might have to deal with an angry customer at work, or you might befriend someone who seemed great initially but then began to completely rely upon you for emotional support 24 hours a day. It's worth remembering that someone could be just having a bad day but if you experience difficult behavior from the same person on a few occasions, you have to stop and think about whether you really need this in your life.

Let's look at a few examples of difficult people you might encounter and why they're so hard to deal with.

- **Mood Vacuums** – These types of people literally suck the life out of you because they're always so negative and rarely have anything good to say. This type of person can never be pleased and they're often complaining or dragging others down. In the end, you'll feel just as negative and your mood will plummet!
- **Show Offs** – These people always have to go one better and be the best in the room. If you have a new iPhone, they'll

have the brand-new version. If you're feeling good, they're feeling amazing. They do this to some degree because they need the validation to feel good, but the constant comparisons and trying to be better than everyone else is nothing but exhausting.

- **Bossy Types** – The bossy people are often the worst to deal with because they're never wrong (so they think) and they're not going to think twice at stamping over you to get what they want. The best advice with this type of person is to just let them do what they do and walk away. You'll never change them.
- **Doormats** – This type of person is the type you want to grab and shake, try to get some life or emotion out of them. They don't say or do much, they often let other people do their unfair share of work, and they'll just agree to everything you say. Annoying, to say the least.
- **Manipulators** – These people are dangerous, and they're often dressed up as someone you can trust and someone you might like but they end up being worse than the bossy types and can manipulate you into saying or doing anything they want. This category also includes narcissists and it's best to try and avoid them at all costs.

If you feel exhausting dealing with someone on a regular basis and they just don't make you feel good no matter what you try and do, it's probably a very clear sign that this person isn't meant to be in your social circle. If this is someone at work, you're going to just have to tolerate them for your working hours as best you can, perhaps holding them at arm's length. For everyone else, deal with them when you have to and stay the hell away for the rest of the time!

Aside from the types of people you're likely to meet, it's important to know a few techniques you can use to handle these people when they're in front of you. Let's look at that now.

Set boundaries and time limits

If someone makes you feel negative or simply causes you to roll your eyes on a constant basis, you need to set time limits for how long you're going to stay around them and boundaries for what you will and won't tolerate. This is the only way to come out of the situation relatively unscathed and to save your sanity.

For instance, if you have a colleague at work who is always complaining and very negative, you can't just walk away from them because you have to work alongside them and it's rude. However, you can set time limits and boundaries as to how much you'll tolerate before you walk away. You could listen to them for five minutes in the morning around the coffee machine and then make your excuses to leave and go about your day.

Be mindful of your emotions

If someone is really making you feel down and negative, you have the right to walk away from them, politely of course. You need to be aware of your emotions and be mindful of how someone makes you feel. Never ignore your gut, especially when it comes to people and the vibe they give to you.

Smother them in kindness

No matter what type of person you're dealing with, you can't go wrong if you approach the situation with total kindness and compassion. They might hate it secretly, but at least you're doing the right thing! By using this tactic, you're ridding yourself of any bad karma and you're deflecting their negative traits back at them.

Search for some common ground

It's likely that you don't really want to be friends with this type of person, but you still need to have a rapport with the amount of time you need to spend with them. Remember, the best way to build a rapport? By looking for common ground. You might have to search hard and be creative, but there will always be something you can use to build a conversation and steer it away from negativity.

Stay calm

I mentioned being aware of your emotions but if you're dealing with someone who is quite angry and irate, it's vital that you stay calm. If you're dealing with a manipulator, again, stay calm and don't allow them to get into your head. By focusing on your breath, you can keep your own anger in check and your emotions still.

Focus on what you can control

Some people cannot be changed, and you shouldn't ever try. However, you can focus on the things you can control and forget about the rest. For instance, if you're at work and you're dealing with an irate customer, focus on finding a solution and forget the rest. If you're dealing with a friend who is expecting you to be at their beck and call 24 hours a day, set the boundaries we talked about earlier and focus on controlling your emotions and your response. You don't have to answer all the time, not if the person is invading your personal time with family and not being respectful.

CHAPTER THOUGHTS

Most people do not like conflict, myself included. However, conflict is an essential part of life because it allows us to learn and grow. The key is to address conflict in the right and timely manner and to stop problems from festering and becoming infected.

When you have your first conflict with a friend, it's possible that you'll panic and think that the friendship is doomed. It's not. Conflict can be healthy and can help you to become closer over time. All you need to do is be aware of the do's and don'ts that allow you to overcome conflict without making things worse.

As you become more confident in your new social skills, you'll also open yourself up to the chance of more conflict, simply because you're dealing with other people on a regular basis. See this as a positive development in your journey and approach every misunderstanding and conflict as an opportunity to learn more.

15

DEEPENING CURRENT RELATIONSHIPS IN YOUR LIFE

So far, we've talked about using your social skills to meet new people, build a rapport, and then deepen a connection to the point where it may lead to a friendship. At the start of this book you probably never thought that you would be able to do that.

During my earlier years, my shyness held me back from speaking to anyone in this way. If you'd told me back then that I'd be sitting here writing a book, helping others overcome the same thing in the way I have, I'd have laughed at you! However, take my success as motivation and a testimonial into how this whole process can completely revolutionize your life, not just your social skills.

There is one last thing you need to be mindful of – that you don't become so excited about meeting new people and creating new connections that you forget about the ones you already have in your life.

FRIENDSHIPS IN ADULTHOOD

In childhood, friendship is easy. You can bond over the cute color of your sweater and you'll be playing in the sandpit for hours afterward. However, as adulthood takes over, it becomes harder than ever to find the time to dedicate to our friendships. As we've already talked about, one of the most important aspects of any friendship is spending quality time together.

In many ways, this issue is that life becomes busy and takes us in different directions. Friends go traveling, maybe they move to another country, some get married, maybe they have children, and others become so engrossed in their career that they don't have much time for anything else. As we move through life, we also meet a new group of people and it's very easy to feel closer to them because they're reflecting the state of our life right now. Our childhood friends, or the friends we made earlier in our lives, might not provide you with the same common ground anymore.

However, it's important to remember that common ground rarely changes that much, and the longer you've been friends with someone, the more important it is to keep that friendship alive.

Let's look at a few ways you can make time to catch up with your friends, even in today's busy, modern world.

Create a group WhatsApp chat – Even if you don't have the time to catch up regularly, you can do so virtually via messaging apps. If you have a group of childhood friends or friends you've known for a while, create a WhatsApp group and you can stay in touch with each other on a very regular basis, without much trouble whatsoever.

Connect on social media – If you don't want to set up messaging apps, you can simply connect on social media and stay up to date with what the other one is doing. However, do be mindful that your connection should not be simply virtual and that you do need to meet up in person to keep the friendship alive.

Have a day every month/week you arrange to do something – Everyone can spare one day or evening a month, surely! If you can stretch this to a week, try it but if not once every fortnight or once every month for a catch-up is a great idea. You could go out for a meal and some drinks or simply go out for a coffee and a good chat in the afternoon, but do not cancel it!

Make your time together a priority – Maintaining long-term friendships is about making them a priority and not letting life take over. The moment you start to cancel and rearrange meetings, take it as a warning to be more mindful of what you're doing. It's a slippery slope towards growing apart and that's not something you want.

STAYING IN TOUCH

I've already talked about the fact that as we move through life, it simply becomes busier. It's easy to turn all your attention to the new things in your life and before you know it, you're forgetting about everything that was there before, old friends included. Staying in touch isn't difficult, and it takes literally a few seconds to send a quick "I hope you're okay" text.

Start to view staying in touch as less of a burden and more of a positive habit you get into on a regular basis. You probably call home to your parents every week, so why not do the same with your older friends?

A busy life shouldn't stop you from staying in touch with people and failure to do so actually points towards a lack of interest, more than a busy life. Nurturing relationships comes down to keeping the connection alive and even if you can't stop everything and meet up for coffee, you can do a small thing that shows your friend that you're thinking of them and that they're important in your life.

A few ideas include:

- Stopping by for a coffee on your way home from work
- Sending a text to check in with them and see how they are
- Remembering birthdays, anniversaries, children's birthdays, etc.
- Sending funny memes and gifs via WhatsApp, just because
- Tagging friends in things you see on Facebook and commenting "do you remember when … "
- Asking if they have time for a coffee during your lunch break at work.

As you can see, it doesn't have to take a long time, it doesn't even have to be something huge, it's just a point of keeping the connection burning and allowing the friendship to be nurtured over the long-term, no matter how busy life gets.

THE LITTLE THINGS MATTER

Sometimes it's the small things in life which mean the most, don't you agree? It really is the thought that counts more than the grand gestures in life and when it comes to keeping a friendship alive during adulthood, this whole concept is bang on the money.

The knowledge that is needed, you'd be there for your friend is far more comforting and valuable than a huge bunch of flowers. A text at exactly the right time can brighten your day and put a smile on your face more than anything else. A cheeky smile when you both 'get' an in-joke can make you feel completely uplifted. None of these things are huge gestures but they're extremely valuable.

Of course, it would be nice if you had an old friend who regularly sent you huge gifts and offered to whisk you away on a vacation occasionally but what does that even mean? Gifts are pleasant but they don't have the same deep connection beneath them that thought does. A text saying "I know today is the anniversary of your mother's passing. I just wanted to send my love and know that I'm thinking of you". That text on a day like that could be the difference between that person choosing to drown their sorrows in wine when they get home or be able to face the day with some amount of strength. That's the power of friendship.

If you have an old friend who works in the opposite office to you and you simply don't have much time to catch up these days, buying her a coffee and leaving it on her desk as you walk by, with a cheeky smile, is enough to make her feel ten times better. It's about noticing when someone isn't feeling good, it's about remembering special days, and it's just about showing that you're willing to keep putting in the effort.

Small things matter.

BE OPEN TO CHANGE

Friendships change. This is something I've learned a lot over the years. This situation is especially pertinent when you have friends from childhood. My closest friend is someone I've known since I was 2 years old. Our friendship has endured 36 years and counting, through the deaths of both her parents, my moving away, teenage arguments, and ultimately her getting married. That was the biggest change for me because it meant she was in a completely different space in her life compared to me.

At first, I was a little worried about it, because how would it change your friendship? It did change it, but has it changed for the worse? No. Change doesn't have to be bad, and you have to be open to it and embrace it if you want to keep important friendships in your life. You can't force people to stay in the same space their entire lives, it's just not possible, just like you can't be forced to do the same either. What you need to do is adjust and adapt, knowing that if your friendship is strong enough, you've got a great chance at keeping it alive.

Friendships change during adulthood naturally, simply because *we* change. Throughout your life, you might be deeply rooted as the same person, but different facets of your personality and your inner psyche are always shifting and changing. When I was trapped in a cycle of shyness, I was a very unconfident and quiet person, however now I'm entirely different. Am I a different person underneath? No, but the way I do things has changed. That's why friendships change.

Dealing with change is hard for anyone but it's important to see it as a positive thing and not a negative. If you're noticing that your friendships are changing, here are a few tips to help you cope with the overall change.

- **Give things time to settle** – When a change occurs, it's likely to need a little time for the ground to settle. Don't be worried about that and in the meantime, stay in touch with text messages and small touches here and there.
- **Change your viewpoint** – Try to see things from their side and understand that maybe they're going through a stressful time in life, or maybe they're so excited about the big change in their life that they're seeing things through tunnel vision right now. Use your empathy to deal with the moment.
- **Talk it through** – Talk about your feelings with a trusted friend and seek their advice. Often, allowing ourselves to listen to another person's view helps us to reframe the situation more positively.
- **Focus on yourself in the meantime (but don't forget them)** – Whilst the ground is settling focus on yourself and head out to meet new people. That doesn't

mean you're forgetting about your friend, but you're simply giving them the time they need to adjust to their new change.

It can be hard when friendships change but hanging onto the past and wanting things to remain the same is just going to bring you sadness in the end. It's far better to be willing to go with the flow and allow friendships to evolve. Most of the time, you end up with something far more valuable than you began with – a friendship that has endured.

Of course, there may be times when a friendship doesn't endure, when the other person drifts too far away and they don't put in their necessary side of the effort. This is a very hard thing to handle and it can be extremely upsetting, but you must see this as something which is inevitable in life and something you can overcome.

I've had friends come and go and many have left my life because we've just drifted. This wasn't anyone's fault, and it wasn't down to a lack of effort, it's just one of those things. When a friend leaves your life, wish them well, send them love, and focus on the good memories you have. If you allow yourself to become bitter about the fact that your friendship drifted away, you're just going to affect how you interact with people in the future.

In this case, simply hold your current friendships that little bit closer and know that life has an odd way of righting itself in the end.

IT'S THE QUALITY FOR ME

We live in a world dominated by social media. We're all obsessed with getting x number of likes and hitting a certain number of friends. But, do you count these people as real friends? I don't.

For me, I have social media friends, who I would prefer to call followers, and I have real friends. Some of my real friends are also on my social media but it's the time we spend away from our phones and laptops that is most important.

As you build up your social skills, you're probably going to do your best to find as many new friends as possible. You're flexing your new communication muscles and I can't blame you for it – you deserve a huge pat on the back. However, know that in the end, it's quality over quantity that really matters.

How many of your friends would be there if you really needed them? Those are the ones you need to focus on the most. It's nice to have a lot of friends, for sure, but the ones who would be there for you are the ones that are the most precious and count the most.

I would recommend doing a social media inventory every so often. Not everyone on that list may be serving you well. As you strive to hit a certain number of followers or "friends", you might be adding people who using your social media accounts as a surveillance tool, rather than because they're genuinely interested in what you're up to in your life. Toxic friends aren't friends, they're just people you really don't need in your life.

If anyone makes you feel uncomfortable, takes far more than they give, talks behind your back, manipulates you, belittles you, or spreads false rumors about you, delete them and move on. This should be no detriment to you because these people are not real friends. I've lost count of the number of people I thought were my friends only to turn out to be toxic individuals who had another agenda. Don't give them another second of your time and delete them from your life, virtually and realistically.

I'm not suggesting you go having a friendship cull every six months, but just be aware that having real friends you can rely upon is far more important than having a long list of people who might appear to be your friends, but are actually far from it. Quality is far more important!

CHAPTER THOUGHTS

Friendships come and go, but the best ones endure over the long-term. Maintaining friendships into adulthood is hard and nobody should ever try to tell you any differently. My closest friend and I lost touch for a short amount of time in our early 20s and came back together again around 5 years later. We're closer than we've ever been because we learned from our mistakes and we put in the effort to stay in touch, even though there's currently quite a lot of actual distance between us.

It's great to have a lot of friends and when you start flexing your social skills, you'll find that you meet people far more easily than you ever did before. However, within that, make sure you remember your old friends and make time for them. Loyalty counts for a lot and that's what will show you who the real ones are versus the ones who will come into your life, stay for a while, and then drift back out again.

Know that not everyone is meant to stay in your life and as painful as it can be sometimes, you have to allow the flow to do its thing. People often drift apart and there's nothing to pull them back, but you should always try to make that connection once more before you give up.

As friendships change, know that you're changing too and not all of it is bad.

CONCLUSION

And there we have it!

We've reached the end of the book. How do you feel now? I hope you're feeling confident, invigorated, and that you're looking forward to the countless opportunities that are sitting right in front of you.

Maybe you have started on your journey towards communication mastery already, or maybe you have read the book cover to cover before making a start. Whatever route you have taken, know that the next steps are in your hands. Your future does not have to look like the past. You don't have to let barriers stand in your way of having the life you want, and you can change anything you want to change, as long as you put in the work.

Your social skills are a million times more important than you know. They affect every single thing in your life, from how you make friends to how you maintain them, how you find work that fulfills you, to how you learn and grow. They affect how you see yourself and how you interact with others, and they affect how you read people. Social skills also affect how you manage your emotions, because they link so closely to emotional intelligence.

By reading this book and taking the advice I've given you, your emotional intelligence level will rise. It's inevitable because as you take the steps outlined throughout the book, you're improving your social skills, you're becoming a far better communicator, and you're learning about people every single day. I hope you feel excited right now because I feel excited for you. Oh, the possibilities!

Right now, I want you to imagine the life you want for yourself. Go on, allow yourself to dream for a minute. What does it look like? What does it feel like? Are you smiling? You should be, because that image you have in your mind right now could be your life in a relatively short amount of time. You might not believe me completely right now but ask anyone who knew me before I made my own journey.

I was a shy and very quiet person. It's not that I was introverted and it's not that I wasn't confident in myself – I was, I just wasn't confident in speaking to other people and that affected every single part of my life detrimentally. You see, once you make a decision to change something and you really go for it, there is no stopping you. And once that confidence takes hold and you know that you can do the one thing you didn't believe you could ever do before, it's a feeling like no other.

YOUR JOURNEY STARTS WITH ONE STEP

All you need to do is decide to change and do it. It sounds like a huge undertaking but that's because you've built it up in your mind to be that. It's not. It's just small exercises every day that will snowball into this massive change in your life.

We started the book by talking about emotional intelligence (EQ) and what it is. Your level is pretty low right now because you've openly admitted to having low social skills by picking up this book, but that's going to change quite rapidly!

We've talked about what social skills are and why they're important, and you now know that in every aspect of your life, your ability to communicate in the right way makes a huge difference. I've given you plenty of practice help and advice on how to get started, including where you can go to meet new friends. The onus really is on you to do all of this but know that at any point you can go back to this book and find someone who understands you. I do. I get all of this because I was there. I believe in you.

We've talked about the things you might be doing to sabotage your efforts to meet new people and you know exactly what you need to do to make changes. You know everything there is to know about first impressions, body language, non-verbal communication, and how to get your message across and make sure that you're understood.

We finished up the book by talking in detail about friendships and how to handle the trials and tribulations that come alongside them. Whilst friendships take work and they certainly come with a fair amount of drama attached to them occasionally, they are one of the most valuable things you'll ever have in your life. Supportive, genuine, and caring friends will help you through the hardest times and share your joy in the good times. That's exactly what you have to look forward to.

SO, NOW WHAT?

Now the time has come for you to take everything you've learned in this book and put it into firm action. Work in a way that suits you best. Maybe you've started already, but if not, you can start chapter by chapter and work slowly if you want, or you can read all the way through, make notes, and then get to work. Everyone learns in a different way so make sure that you tailor your approach to your own learning needs.

If you forget something or you need clarification, you can simply go back to the chapter you need and find the answers. This book will always be by your side throughout your journey and beyond. You might think that this journey has an end date – it doesn't. My journey still hasn't finished I'm still learning. People are very complicated begins and we have to grow and adjust depending upon the people who come into our lives and their particular personalities. We're constantly kept on our toes and that's what makes it so wonderful!

Start small or start big, work in your own way. However, if you're someone who struggles with social anxiety or shyness, work slowly and know that every small win you have along the way is huge progress. This isn't a race and nobody else even has to know what you're trying to do – the results will become very evident to them when your confidence levels are transformed and you begin to carry yourself naturally in a way that makes you glow from the inside, out.

You might have the odd mishap along the way and know that's normal. You might wake up one day and feel completely off your game. That doesn't mean all the progress you've made so far has gone to waste, it just means that you're having a bad day and you need to be kind to yourself. We all have those days, we're human after all.

All that's left for me to do now is to wish you good luck. The power to change your life is in your hands and you and you alone can make the changes you really want to see. Remember to pat yourself on the back and celebrate every success, whilst also helping other people around you who may need some help with their social skills. Share the knowledge and let's build people up!

Your journey has only just begun.

REFERENCES

A New Layered Model on Emotional Intelligence. (2018, May 1). PubMed Central (PMC). https://www.ncbi.nlm.nih.gov/pmc/articles/PMC5981239/

Advances in the Research of Social Anxiety and Its Disorder (Special Section). (n.d.). PubMed Central (PMC). https://www.ncbi.nlm.nih.gov/pmc/articles/PMC2846378/

Behavioral inhibition system and self-esteem as mediators between shyness and social anxiety. (2018, December 1). ScienceDirect. https://www.sciencedirect.com/science/article/abs/pii/S0165178117323326

Body language in the brain: constructing meaning from expressive movement. (2015). PubMed Central (PMC). https://www.ncbi.nlm.nih.gov/pmc/articles/PMC4543892/

REFERENCES

Everything You Ever Wanted to Know About Shyness in an International Context. (n.d.). American Psychological Association. https://www.apa.org/international/pi/2017/06/shyness

Gibbons, S. (2018, June 20). *You And Your Business Have 7 Seconds To Make A First Impression: Here's How To Succeed.* Forbes. https://www.forbes.com/sites/serenitygibbons/2018/06/19/you-have-7-seconds-to-make-a-first-impression-heres-how-to-succeed/?sh=1897dbf656c2

O'Connor, P. J. (2019). *The Measurement of Emotional Intelligence: A Critical Review of the Literature and Recommendations for Researchers and Practitioners.* Frontiers. https://www.frontiersin.org/articles/10.3389/fpsyg.2019.01116/full

Okten, I. O. (2018, January 31). *Studying First Impressions: What to Consider?* Association for Psychological Science - APS. https://www.psychologicalscience.org/observer/studying-first-impressions-what-to-consider

Social relations and life satisfaction: the role of friends. (2018). PubMed Central (PMC). https://www.ncbi.nlm.nih.gov/pmc/articles/PMC5937874/

Speaking of Psychology: Nonverbal Communication Speaks Volumes. (n.d.). American Psychological Association. https://www.apa.org/research/action/speaking-of-psychology/nonverbal-communication

Tadjer, H., Lafifi, Y., Derindere, M., Gulsecen, S., & Seridi-Bouchelaghem, H. (2018, September 13). *What Are The Important*

Social Skills of Students in Higher Education? ResearchGate. https://www.researchgate.net/publication/329761072_What_Are_The_Important_Social_Skills_of_Students_in_Higher_Education

EMOTIONAL INTELLIGENCE & CRITICAL THINKING SKILLS FOR LEADERSHIP (2 IN 1)

20 MUST KNOW STRATEGIES TO BOOST YOUR EQ, IMPROVE YOUR SOCIAL SKILLS & SELF-AWARENESS AND BECOME A BETTER LEADER

INTRODUCTION

Leadership. It's a prized position, a measure of personal and professional respect. Many strive for it but few achieve it. Some believe it's inborn into a person's personality, that only the naturally charismatic can be true leaders. Others may feel their leadership waning, control over professional and personal aspects of their lives slipping away. Their leadership skills need improving and fast, before it's too late.

Whatever your specific situation, you're reading this now because you want to strengthen your leadership skills, if that's possible. And, of course, it is. Any skillset can be sharpened, and leadership skills are crucial to so many aspects of life; personal, professional, social, familial. The better your leadership skills, the better your life will be and the happier and more fulfilled you and those around you will be.

And this book has the answers you need! You'll learn everything you need to know and more about psychological principles and research-based concepts which are backed up with easy-to-use tests you can take on the spot. We break down leadership skills like clear communication, empathy, reflection (among many others) and what they entail; emotional intelligence, cognitive abilities, critical thinking, and social skills. We'll apply these skills to various arenas and stages of life, demonstrating how certain basic concepts are consistent in any type of development. The latest medical information and industry data is compiled in this easy-to-read handbook for leadership self-improvement.

We publish books designed to improve every part of your personal and professional life, with a staff of dedicated writers and researchers to help you overcome your challenges, achieve your goals, and have a happier, longer, and more fulfilling life. I've personally used these techniques myself and I can vouch for their efficacy. They will make you more emotionally intelligent, more self-aware, more mindful and grateful, more relaxed and stress free. Even a small handful of the principles in this book could turn any life or career around. Using all of them could be revolutionary for you and anyone you know or love.

This book has all you need to get started right away, from home or the office or where ever you are. In fact, if you are paying attention, ready to focus, retain, recall, and apply this information, you've already taken the first step to better leadership skills. Now turn the page and take the next step. The time is now. If you're finally reading this, then you've been thinking about this for a while. There could be problems in your workplace or home even now, and they're likely getting worse. Miscommunication, disorganization, disrespect, and dissatisfaction can (and will) fester in silence, they grow in the shadows. Things in your marriage or career or with your kids or friends or adult siblings could already be approaching a crisis point. Or you may go on languishing on the lower rungs of life for another month, another year, another decade.

Time is the one thing money can't buy, the only thing we cannot afford to waste. So, don't waste another second! Start improving your life now, while there's still time!

Heightened emotional intelligence, sharper cognitive and critical thinking skills, the keys to repairing or creating stronger relationships and superior team results are in your hands, yours for the taking. Enjoy the journey and don't worry, you won't be alone. Now let's move forward to a better career and a better life!

I

SELF-CHECK: WHAT KIND OF LEADER ARE YOU RIGHT NOW?

1

ARE YOU A TRUE LEADER?

We can vaguely define *leadership* as the process of influencing others to accomplish some objective by means of coherent and cohesive organization. But that's a lot easier said than done. What makes a good leader? Are you one, or is there room for improvement? Do you have what it takes to be the leader you aspire to be? The answer, of course, is yes, or we wouldn't have published this book. It's a handy guide to make you the leader you want and need to be.

But what kind of leader is that?

A LEADER IN NAME ONLY

You're a leader, a true leader. Your concern is the efficiency of your staff and the accuracy and efficacy of the results. You know your workers are crucial and you value their humanity as well as their utility. You and your team can be trusted to get the job done. Otherwise, what kind of leader are you?

Sadly, you'd be like most in that position, a leader in name only. This is an easier trap to fall into, and most people who do it don't even realize. It may even have happened to you, despite your best efforts to the contrary.

Scary, right? You could be asleep at the wheel without even knowing it. But it's never too late to snap out of it and take control of your team again. Ask yourself some of these helpful questions to make sure you're not a leader in name only.

What's really more important to you, the results of the project or the benefit to your career? Be honest. A lot of people put their career first because we're trained to do that. Our competitive society, especially in the United States, gears us to base our entire identities on what we do, how much we earn. Status symbols are everywhere, from the cars we drive to the houses we live in. Our success is often the measure of our worth, the measure of our humanity. Furthermore, a person's career will have a lot of projects, just as a doctor's career will have a lot of patients and an accountant's career a lot of taxpayers. What matters more to the accountant or doctor or manager? A doctor may lose a patient, but he or she still has a house to pay for, kids to feed, clothe, and put through school. An accountant has clients who come and go, but only one family, one career to see to that family.

So, it's common and it's not unreasonable. But it's not good leadership. Because a good leader understands that the ultimate success of that singular career is based on the successes of the smaller units, the project or the patient or the taxpayer. Too many losses or failures and the doctor or accountant's careers dry up. Even if the patients and taxpayers keep coming (and they will) there's a matter of professional integrity. The good doctor or accountant does a good job for their patient or taxpayer, they do the best they can do every time. Sometimes mistakes are made, and they can often be corrected. But a leader knows that he or she is not the center of the project. A good doctor doesn't go into the operating room concerned with their reputation; they go in concerned for their patient. The accountant may know he or she will have to stand behind their work, but first and foremost they should be concerned with the accuracy of the tax return they're creating. That's the measure of their professional worth.

It brings us to an important concept, one you must know. Successful people prioritize the end result and not their place in the project. It's a sign of security and self-actualization to put the project above the person. It's an externalizing technique which separates the person from the behavior which allows failures to be seen as stepping stones to success instead of as stains on a person's reputation. Too many failures will have an adverse effect professionally, of course, but that can lead to overthinking and negative self-talk, and they can put anyone, manager or worker, into a destructive downward spiral.

Overthinking, in brief, is the tendency to endlessly ponder what could have been done in the past, or what might be done in the future. Replaying old arguments while inserting rewritten lines or imagining conversations which have yet to occur (and may never) are good ways to waste time and energy and generate anxiety and stress.

Negative self-talk is the tendency to tell one's self that they're worthless, doomed to failure. It's the self-punishment that goes along with overthinking, and it's absolutely toxic. No good leader indulges in this harmful practice.

It comes down to a mindset; either a fixed mindset or a growth mindset. A fixed mindset associates the person with the events around them, the way a leader in name only may do. The fixed mindset believes the results are foretold, because if a person had had a failure, they must be a failure, and they always will be a failure. Overthinking and negative self-talk help to ensure this mindset, and it influences behavior. Lack of self-confidence will either restrict opportunities or create failures through the principle of the self-fulfilling prophecy.

A growth mindset accepts failure as a learning experience and is necessary to ultimate success. This mindset externalizes the events from the person, they believe a person may fail without being a failure, that they can grow through the process of failures. This mindset tends to avoid overthinking about the past or future and focuses more on the present, on getting the job done. They indulge in positive self-talk, supporting themselves with self-sympathy. This gives them the confidence to take on new opportunities and have new successes because of the principle of the self-fulfilling prophecy.

The leader in name only is likely to have a fixed mindset. The true leader is likely to have a growth mindset. Which mindset do you have? Are you a true leader or a leader in name only?

Are you consistent? We mentioned integrity before, and it's time to take a closer look at that. It's an aeronautical term, referring to the wing of a plane. The wing is expected to bend and yield to certain external forces like wind and temperature. But integrity refers to the way in which the wing responds. Given the same external forces, the wing should react in a predictable, reliable fashion. That is known as the integrity of the wing. When this integrity is violated and the wing is reacting in an unreliable, unstable manner, it may tear off and cause the plane to crash.

People are the same way. They react to the forces around them, a supervisor or a puppy dog elicit different reactions. But a person should generally be reliable in their reaction to each. And a wing is still a wing, it doesn't act like an engine or a window. It is what it is and does what it does no matter what the elevation, if the plane is moving or not. People likewise shouldn't become radically different people in one person's company or another. Otherwise, they're not reliable, they could be anything at any time, they have no integrity.

Leaders especially must exhibit this integrity. They must be reliable and stable. Their team relies upon this. They set the example that the team will certainly follow. A stable, reliable team leader, one who shows consistency and reliability, is necessary for any project's success. Lacking this quality, a leader is a leader in name only.

And, like a wing, a good leader is flexible. The leader in name only will say, not without reason, that the system works and shouldn't be changed for every accommodation. This is not an uncommon nor an unrealistic perspective.

The Twentieth Century existentialist Michel Foucault broke down society into two models, a system model and a process model. Those who followed the system model had good reason to believe that society functioned best as a collection of systems; the judicial system, any government, the penal system, the Catholic church; these things prevailed because they did not constantly change. They had integrity and were stable and predictable. To this end, the individual was not integral nor important. The system was dominant and the individual served as part of these systems; a student in the educational system, a prisoner of the judicial system. This created a functional society.

Others, according to Foucault, follow the process model. The process model focuses on the individual and eschews the dominance of any system. In this model, the individual creates their own system based on the process of examining systems but not succumbing to them. In this model, systems fail and only a process can create the ideal individual. The society with the most ideal individuals is the superior society in this model.

And this also makes perfect sense. In the modern world (and throughout recorded history, really) systems do fail. The penal system has been privatized, creating mass incarcerations and terrible mistreatment. The system known as the Catholic Church was so rife with corruption selling indulgences that Martin Luther's Reformation was necessary in the 1500's, creating the Protestant tradition, of which there are now many sects, each predicated on its own system formed by process.

In general, a fixed-minded individual will lean toward a system-oriented world view. One doesn't question the system; the system is fixed. A growth-minded person is more apt to be a process-oriented individual and resist system thinking as rigid and prone to corruption and failure.

Are you a system-oriented thinker, or a process-oriented thinker? Are you willing to modify your approach and accept flexibility as part of the process, or are you convinced that the rigidity of the system must be enforced? Are you a flexible leader, or a rigid leader in name only?

Did you assemble a team based on their ability or your own? Give this one some thought. A leader in name only wants and needs to remain the leader. Because they generally have a fixed mindset and believe that they are personified by their achievements, leaders in name only cling to their position. Therefore, they are apt to assemble teams which will not outshine them. Negative self-talk and overthinking will lead them to be suspicious of and competitive with their own team. Growth-minded managers will know that their own self-worth is not tied to any particular results, certainly not the positive results of anyone on their team. If anything, that reflects well on the leader. But the leader in name only will become fearful of losing their place, competitive with their best team members. This, of course, is a form of self-sabotage in a number of ways.

On one hand, it may encourage workers to hold back and not do their best for fear of upstaging their insecure boss. This contributes to the overall failure of the project. And that's a pity, because it's the success of the project which matters, it's the success of the sum total of everyone's best efforts which creates the leader's success.

Also, it sets a terrible example that everyone will surely follow. If the leader is insecure, they're unreliable and lacking integrity. His or her team won't be on board any more than you would get on a plane if you knew the wing would tear off in midflight. The team will be insecure and unreliable, they'll suspect and be competitive with one another. This will destroy the chances of success, for the project, the team, and their leader.

A good leader with integrity will always choose the best team members, regardless of any sense of insecurity. Think of the pilot of a big commercial jet. Are they concerned about the navigator taking their job? They shouldn't be thinking of that even for an instant. His or her only concern must be the safe delivery of their passengers to their destination. That's all. The good surgeon doesn't put together a team of lesser technicians for fear of his or her own career. The best surgeon has the best support because their only concern is the success of the operation, the life of the patient. Anything less and they're a doctor in name only.

Are you a leader in name only? Did you assemble a team certain not to outshine you or did you get the best possible talent to do the best possible job?

Be decisive. If you are the leader, you must lead. That means being flexible, as we've mentioned. It also means having some grounding in systems as well as processes. Things will happen for which you may not be prepared. Complications arise during surgeries. Unexpected weather patterns can make a flight treacherous. Decisions will have to be made and may have to be adjusted given varying factors. A leader must be ready to act in response to changing influences. A leader may not always be certain of what to do, and a lot may be on the line.

This brings us back to the concept of overthinking. An overthinker may circle around a problem so much that they become unable to act. It's known as *analysis paralysis*, and it's a lot more common than you may realize. A person may spend their entire life not writing that novel, not creating that business, not perfecting that invention, because they couldn't stop thinking and couldn't start acting. This causes negative self-talk, the habit of bludgeoning one's self with reprisals and berating self-loathing which in itself creates an unwillingness to try new things, a fixed mindset, and a series of self-fulfilling prophecies which may cripple any personal or professional life.

The results of such a downward spiral, by the way, include stress and anxiety, poor diet and sleep habits which may result in substance abuse, weight gain, and the ensuing physical repercussions. Heart attacks, stroke, premature death, and suicide are often the results.

The fact is that not every decision will be the right one. Success entails risk, and risk entails failure. Your decision may result in failure, this you must know. But to not proceed for fear of failure is to ensure failure, that is failure; failure to act, failure to decide.

And if your decision results in failure, it can likely be corrected. If not, you'll be able to externalize that and not let it define you as a person. You'll know that the failure will result in a lesson well learned, and that will contribute to your later successes, it's even considered a necessary part of that success.

Are you decisive despite uncertainty, like a real leader, or do you suffer analysis paralysis like a leader in name only?

A good leader considers the input of others. Some people are utterly confident, and confidence is a good thing. But a team is just that, a team, and it thrives when every member's point of view is considered. There could be wisdom from the perspective of a lesser team member, or one higher up on the hierarchy. This goes back to a level of security on the part of the team leader. A confident team leader will welcome contributions from the team without worrying about being outshone by a member of the team. A true leader will value the end result more than his or her appearance as the source of all good ideas. A leader in name believes only he or she knows the correct course of action.

True leaders set the bar high and reach for it. They know this is the way to improve individual and team efficiency, the way to increase the team's abilities. A leader in name only sets the bar low, knowing it will be an easy success. But easy successes are not successes at all, they are the status quo. Success entails risk, and low-bar achievements require little or no risk. That's why they're not really successes, and why they are commonly set by leaders in name only.

Leaders are gentle in their leadership, not overly authoritarian. Some leaders believe a strong hand is important to keep the team members in line. But that kind of leadership only engenders bitterness, insecurity, paranoia, competitiveness, in-fighting, and that makes for an inefficient team and prevents team successes.

THE CHARACTERISTICS OF A TRUE LEADER

We've taken a look at what makes a leader in name only, and by contrast what makes a strong leader. But there's more to being a strong leader than merely not being a poor leader. The true leader has characteristics he or she brings to the job. It's not just a matter of managing, but of strengths of character which allow a true leader to manage wisely and well.

From George Washington to Richard Branson, good leaders are persistent. They accept failure as part of the process of success. They're growth-minded individuals who can separate their own value from the value of their decisions and actions. They know that no outcome is predetermined, and when they do fail, they don't linger on it. They don't let negative self-talk prevent them from trying again, to keep striving toward ultimate success. Harry Potter author J.K. Rowling, Stephen King, Walt Disney, even the Beatles all faced rejection early in their careers, but persistence led them all to be true leaders (Ringo, maybe not so much).

True leaders have insight, especially into themselves. People who achieve are often self-made, and that takes a lot of confidence. But confidence does not mean being deluded into thinking one is a genius at everything and at every turn. Nobody's perfect, and a true leader knows this about themselves first and foremost. In the same way a true leader listens to the members of his or her team, who are the best he or she can find, a strong leader knows that he or she has some strengths and some weaknesses, just like everybody else.

And a true leader takes this into account when putting the team together. A true leader, secure in his or her position and concerned primarily with the success of the project, will hire people who have the skills the leader knows is lacking in themselves. The leader may be a good motivator, but he or she may lack organizational skills or accounting or artistic skills. That's what the team is for, to provide those things. So, the true leader creates a team with skills that are unique to the team, not the leader.

Along these lines, a true leader is an active listener. They digest what they're hearing, they don't just nod and smile. They want new information and they process it, turning it into positive action if possible. The true leader is never condescending to their team either, because they know the information could further the success of the project, and that is what's most important to a true leader. A leader in name only will appear to listen, all the while thinking about themselves or perhaps looking into a mirror, waiting for his or her time to speak without digesting anything which is being said.

Honesty is a crucial trait to any true leader. We spoke of integrity, reliability, but honesty is key to these things. A person whose word of honor is reliable is a person who is reliable. Nobody has integrity without honesty, because they will react in any way which is best for them. Their words and actions come to nothing more but expressions of desire and convenience. Team members will follow the leader's example and be dishonest themselves, with each other and with the team leader. This will almost surely have disastrous results for the project and, thus, for the team. A person who is lacking in honesty has no place on your team or any team, but certainly not leading a team.

A true leader communicates openly and clearly. He or she says what they think without being frank, crass or rude. They know how to say something positive before saying anything negative. They explain their opinions to better educate the team member and so to elicit even better suggestions to come. A leader in name only relies on old-hat empty phrases (*"We're going in a different direction"* or *"I'll know it when I see it"*) or otherwise muddled or confusing instructions or opinions. It may be inspired by a desire to be kind or gentle, but lacking directness is where things go wrong in almost every professional instance. They also reprimand without being degrading or humiliating their team.

A good leader is forward thinking. They don't just rely on old ways of doing things, no matter how reliable or time-tested they maybe. A good leader is up on the latest technologies. Imagine a team manager who doesn't have a mobile phone or can't use PowerPoint or can't open or send email. From Kubla Khan to General George Patton, great leaders have relied upon the newest technologies and the most creative ideas.

A good leader is likewise fixed on the future, of the project and of the team. He or she knows the ramifications of failure or success, of quality work or work that lacks quality. So, a true leader is always looking ahead. Likewise, a good leader does not linger on failure. They learn the lessons from that failure and then they move on, as quickly as possible.

True leaders not only surround themselves with the best and brightest without concern for feelings of insecurity or competitiveness, they guide and develop others, either in their team or not. True leaders know that the strongest team will prevail, that the team can always be made a bit stronger by improving the performance of the individuals in that team. The true leader develops the skills of the individuals on the team, knowing it will make the team's performance better. True leaders also mentor others who are not on their team. This creates professional bonds which can serve the leader well throughout their careers, and serve as good connections for later projects. Mentoring also increases the general quality of work, and while some may see this as helping the competition, others know that when the water level rises, it lifts all boats with it.

True leaders are self-actualized. They have earned their place by fulfilling their own needs, basic, more complex, aesthetic, and even transcendent needs. They have answered the existential questions of their own lives, they know who they are and they have established a strong set of beliefs. These beliefs must include the higher principles of honesty, integrity, humanity, or the leader is a leader in name only. The true leaders share these standards with others and will not tolerate less from members of the team.

A true leader will lead by example. Behavior is always the benchmark of beliefs, and the leader knows that his or her actions are under special scrutiny; from the team, who look to the leader for an example, and to the client, who looks to the leader for results. So, a true leader always behaves in a way which will be a good example and will make a good impression. And, of course, the true leader guides their team to be and do likewise.

A true leader will work alongside the team. True, the manager often has different duties than the members, who have individual creative and administrative duties. The true leader lets them get their tasks done and goes about coordinating and planning. But the true leader is also there with the team, present to answer questions, ready to react to unexpected challenges which may arise. A leader in name only merely appears from time to time to lord over the crew, throw their weight around, then disappear. They see the team as a resource for them, but they overlook the fact the leader is a crucial resource for the team.

Along these lines, a true leader will not micromanage or control their team. Rather, a true leader will inspire their team, encourage, and guide them. The true leader has assembled the best team possible, and they allow that team to flourish. The leader in name only believes only he or she knows best and feels they have to have a hand in every stage, every task. But that leader does not know their own weaknesses or their team members' strengths.

Along these lines, true leaders delegate to the members of their team. They're confident that they've assembled the best team, and they rely on the members of that team.

But true leaders are not afraid to push their team to reach the highest standard. The true leader knows what must be done and is willing to make sure their team gets it done. While not demanding or authoritative, the true leader still has authority and must make demands, not requests. Of course, the true leader balances authority with humanity and knows that demands are made on everyone in the team, the leader included. Everybody must carry their weight, it's the true leader's job to make sure that they do and coordinate those best efforts. After all, if one member isn't doing their best, the overall success of the project is threatened.

A true leader knows how to properly manage time. This will include time off for self-care, of course. It also means watching timelines, requesting time logs from team members if necessary. Because a true leader is responsible for his or her own time, but also the time management of their team members. A true leader knows that time is the most valuable thing in life, as no amount of money can purchase even a tiny fraction of it (save for a medical context, perhaps). Time is the only thing we cannot afford to waste. And, as the old business adage goes, time is money.

A leader in name only is lazy with time, allowing deadlines to go missed or rushing at the last minute to get things done. A leader in name only will allow his or her team to be slovenly with their own time management, to the detriment of their projects' success.

A true leader will hold his team and his- or herself accountable and responsible. Too many people are too ready to blame somebody else for their mistakes. Often others may err, and teammates will judge them harshly, blamefully. But a true leader sets a better example, one which includes taking personal responsibility. A true leader knows that he or she is ultimately responsible for every member of the team, and they set this high example for their team members to follow. The leader in name only will always blame the team for a lack of success and excuse themselves.

A true leader will keep things in perspective. They make measured decisions, neither suffering from analysis paralysis nor rushing into foolish moves. They consider alternatives, they digest the viewpoints of their team or colleagues, and they make their best choices, then take responsibility for them. They're forward thinking, so they know that their choices will have far-reaching ramifications. The leader in name only is impulsive, making uninformed decisions based on their own needs and not on the needs of the project.

BORN LEADERS VERSUS SELF-MADE LEADERS

It really comes down to a question of nature versus nurture, an age-old question which has been the center of philosophical thought and the inspiration for stories from *Pygmalion* to *Trading Places*.

Almost nowhere is the question raised more often than in the arena of leadership. Out of a group of children, all raised more or less the same, a natural leader tends to rise to the fore. This encourages the nature-based perspective. But others would say that children are rarely treated the same way even by the same set of parents, and that some parents may generate more leaders than others based on parenting styles.

The fact is that people are born with different innate skills and talents. Everybody born in the United States may be equal under the law (ideally) but they are not born equal. In fact, since everybody is unique in very specific scientific ways, there can be no true equity. Some are bigger and stronger, others are gifted with genetic attractiveness, some are born with deformities or other physical challenges.

And many would say that leaders are gifted with the qualities they'll use later in life. These qualities might evince themselves as boldness or even youthful aggression, a raw manner of taking control. Leaders are generally intelligent, and intelligence is undoubtedly an inherent quality, genetically gifted to some more than others.

Some are gifted with genius, and their names ring through history; Albert Einstein, Mozart, Stephen Hawking. Though it's interesting to note that these are leaders in their field, though they often worked alone. They were not managers, not leaders of teams. So, following that train of logic, one can argue that inherent intelligence may have nothing at all to do with leadership skills.

Likewise, aggression can become anti-social, which is not the quality of a true leader. Children who are reserved can grow to become adults who can calmy manage others. Many would argue it's a matter of life experience which shapes an individual and prepares them for one role or another in society; a manager or a maker (a specialist member of the team, usually creative in some way) a nurture-based perspective. Though the naturally creative requirements of the maker are generally both inherited and also developed through time and experience.

Most behavioral theories hold that leadership is a skillset which can be acquired, it can be taught and learned. There are countless books, classes, and seminars predicated on that concept, and their success is testimony to their effectiveness. If people are learning these skillsets to become better leaders, then leadership can be learned, and leaders made and not born.

A growth-minded leader knows that leadership is, like most things, a process. It can and should be refined and improved with time, results and efficiency made even better. This also speaks to the nurture-based side of the argument. Every military in the world engages in leadership training, it's both how and why they move up through the ranks.

Leadership is really an art, and like all the arts it must be learned. True, some geniuses like Mozart can do it virtually from birth. But we're not Mozart. We may have some innate skill, but in general we have to learn and develop that skill through years of painful development and instruction.

Leadership may also be a matter of timing. One may find one's self in the position by happenstance. The true leader is prepared to lead when the moment arises. The leader in name only will either panic or become swelled with egotistical power and delusions of grandeur.

Think of the great leaders in history: Mahatma Gandhi, Nelson Mandela, Martin Luther King Jr, Abraham Lincoln. These were leaders who didn't seek fame or wealth. They were selfless, loving of people, and of justice. They had high standards, integrity, and the courage of their convictions.

The truth is more likely to be, like most truths, comprised of various circumstances. Like most contests of nature and nurture, the answer is, frankly, a bit of both. Some people are gifted with the necessary gifts of leadership, and those can always be refined, and other aspects of leadership can and must be learned through instruction.

The Pareto principle is also known as the *80/20 rule*. Named for economist Vilfredo Pareto, the 80/20 rule tells us that about 80% of effects happen as a result of roughly 20% of the causes. It's confusing, but to make it easy, the rule suggests that a true leader is 80% made and 20% born. However, studies conducted out of the University of Illinois support research that leadership is 70% learned and only 30% genetic.

Leaders apply skills and knowledge in what is called *process leadership*. But It's also a fact that traits can affect our actions, known as *trait leadership*. Leaders carry out this process by applying their leadership knowledge and skills. It's a combination of both that makes a true leader.

WHAT KIND OF LEADERSHIP STYLE ARE YOU USING?

Whether or not or to what extent a leader is made or born, they usually adopt a certain style. They can even be generalized, as the patterns seem to come down to seven leadership styles.

The first is the autocratic style of leadership. This is the most authoritative style of leadership, a my-way-or-the-highway arrangement. A lot of people with military backgrounds may assume this style of leadership, as strictly following orders is part of their training.

But this kind of leadership style is generally fixed-minded and not open to the contributions of others. If often fails to take into account the leader's strengths or, in this case, their weaknesses. This old-fashioned way of leading isn't as effective in the modern era, though some people do still swear by it. Not *my* boss, luckily.

Those who lead in the bureaucratic style are similar to autocratic leaders. They expect the team to follow the rules the leader has set. But the autocratic leader emphasizes his or her own place at the head of the team. The bureaucratic leader, you may have guessed, emphasizes the team as a whole and relies more on the team. This *laissez-faire* hands-off approach can be efficient, but it can also lead to inefficiency, the hallmark of any bureaucracy.

The authoritative style, sometimes called the *visionary style*, also sets the pace, but this style engages team members more than the autocratic style, exciting them and gearing them toward greater participation and superior results.

This is a style that emphasizes guidance, not merely leadership.

The pacesetting style is so-called because this leader sets the pace. They set the bar high, they drive their teams hard and fast. This energetic style is effective but can also be tiring and stressful for some employees.

The best management style in these turbulent times may be the agile leadership style. This is similar to the pacesetting style, but has eyes on the long haul. The pacesetting style may be good for quick turnarounds and short-term projects, but the agile style, a bit more laidback, is better for the long-term.

The fourth style, the democratic style of leadership, emphasizes group think a bit more, leaning on the opinions of the team members. Some leaders find this approach to diffuse, but others realize that the leader still has the deciding hand in all matters. That's what the leader is for, after all. But this style allows for more creativity, greater contributions, encouraging a team spirit, and often creating superior results. It makes the work mood a lot lighter than the previous styles as well.

The coaching style puts the most emphasis on the team members, giving them added responsibilities, a higher bar, and actively encouraging, and guiding them. It's a bit like the pacesetter style, though this approach puts even more emphasis on the team members and their contributions. This leadership style lends itself particularly well to mentorship, which has a variety of other benefits.

You may never have heard of the affiliative leadership style. This leader is more than just a coach, even more of a mentor. The affiliative style, which works in conjunction with others such as the democratic style, focuses on the needs of the members outside the strict confines of the project. Emotional needs are considered, for example, not just practical needs to get the project done.

Some feel those things should be left out of the office, that things become too messy. And it's true that an emotional state and a rational state cannot co-exist in the same psyche at the same time, rational thought should always be the focus of the workplace. Emotions, some would say, are for the home. And that would be true but for the fact that humans carry their emotions around all the time, and the workplace can be a stressful experience. That stress often expresses itself as emotion.

But this leadership style can smooth out conflicts and create collaborative relationships in any team. It's an ideal style for a stressful situation.

Ultimately, this style is all about encouraging harmony and forming collaborative relationships within teams. It's particularly useful, for example, in smoothing conflicts among team members or reassuring people during times of stress.

The *laissez-faire* style will be familiar to anybody familiar with history or politics. Born of the French phrase for *leave alone*, this style takes a hands-off approach to leadership. This style delegates more than leads, gives team members the utmost control over their work schedule. The idea is to let the team flourish, though the downside is often disorganization and a scattershot result.

A transformational leadership style is comparable to the coaching style, but it puts more emphasis on the project goal and less on the team member's performance. The transformational leader is more interested in the game than the players.

A transactional leadership style uses incentives to inspire the team; bonuses, prizes, using contests to keep the team fired up. It's a potent tool for mentorship too. It's great for getting the job done, but creative types tend to resist it, and that's a big part of any manager's job.

In situational leadership, the emphasis is put on the situation above the leader, the team, or even the project. Situational theory stresses four styles of leadership. There is telling, which is instructional; there is selling, which seeks to convince; participating, which invites team contribution, and delegating, which de-emphasizes leadership contribution. The situation will determine what kind of leadership is required.

Which leadership style will work the best for you? It depends on you, your team, and the situation. If you're thrown into a crisis and you have to turn things around, a democratic approach will get you the best results from your team. If you're a new manager of a team already in full swing, you might try the *laissez-faire* approach and switch to democratic if things go wrong. You may lead with one style at one stage of the project, maybe pacesetting at the offset to get things off right, then easy back into an affiliative approach as the office runs along from project to project.

Again, know your strengths. Are you an easy-going type? Affiliative may be right for you. Are you more of an outgoing personality? Maybe the coaching style would be more effective than the autocratic style.

Just keep in mind that there are different styles, and know which one you're employing and why. Don't just wing it. Be aware, be strategic, learn to read when one leadership style will be more effective than another. During times of crisis, you may choose the affiliative style, but only in those times.

If your leadership skills aren't as effective as you'd hoped in one style, figure out why and make improvements. Hopefully, you're growth minded enough to know that everything and everyone can and will likely be improved with time and experience.

Like all skills, leadership skills should be practiced. Don't fall into the trap of thinking you've nailed it. Skills can atrophy, they have to be kept loose, fresh in your mind's so-called *muscle memory* (a term athletes, dancers, and musicians use for a repeated muscular movement which becomes second-nature).

Whatever leadership style you employ, be genuine. Let it come from some real part of you. Don't pretend to be an authoritarian if that's not you. Don't try to coach someone if it's just not in you. And it should be. We all have various facets of our personality which we don't often employ. Discover yours.

EVOLVING TO A LEADER YOU WISH TO BECOME

As we've seen, true leadership is a skillset reliant upon certain personality traits and strengths of character. There are different leadership styles, each of which has strengths and drawbacks. Knowing what type of leader you wish to become is central to becoming that leader. So too are the tools and techniques you'll be reading and learning about in this book. Now that we know what a leader is and who can become one, let's take a closer look at the building blocks of a great leader.

2

THE BUILDING BLOCKS OF A GREAT LEADER

BECOMING A TRUE LEADER IS A PROCESS

We've already seen how leaders are not born, they're made (well, they are born, but not as natural born leaders). Desire and willpower can make an effective leader of just about anyone, experts agree. It is an ongoing process of education, study, experience, and training.

As we defined it, leadership is the process of influencing others to accomplish some objective by means of coherent and cohesive organization. We find it in all facets of our lives; professional, social, and familial.

We've looked into the qualities of a true leader, and of a leader in name only. True leadership requires influence, not power. It requires others, it's not a solo practice.

A leader needs followers, one of the building blocks of any leader. And the true leader knows that different people need to be led differently. Some require a bit more pampering; others bristle at it. But followers there must be, and they are crucial to any leadership. Without them, there's no leadership at all. So, a true leader must always keep in mind how important their followers or team really are.

Clear, healthy communication is vital to being a good leader. That only makes good sense, as the team is so critical to the leader, and communication so vital to their interaction. Learn to improve your communication skills to be the best leader you can be.

Situations are critical parts of being a leader. Situations happen, no matter where you are or what you're doing, it's a situation. So, this is part and parcel of leading. The effective leader must take the situation into account when leading. A conference room is a different situation than a burning building and should be treated as such. The latter is no time for the affiliative approach to discuss emotion. That's a good approach for after everyone's made it out alive.

MANAGEMENT OR LEADERSHIP?

There's a subtle but important difference between leadership and management. The main function of management is to produce *consistency* and order through deliberate processes, including organizing, budgeting, planning, staffing, problem solving, and more.

The main function of leadership, on the other hand, is to produce *change* through a series of processes, such as aligning people, inspiring, and motivating. One may lead through change, but manage the status quo.

While leadership's main function is to produce movement and constructive or adaptive change through processes, such as establishing direction through visioning, aligning people, motivating, and inspiring.

LEADER OR BOSS?

The boss has power, that's true (it's also known as *assigned leadership*). But this can be a leader in name only. The true leader makes their followers want to accomplish their goals, not merely to feel that they have to comply with the boss' demands (also called *emergent leadership*).

EMERGENT LEADERSHIP VS. ASSIGNED LEADERSHIP

So, to be a good leader, you must be more than just a boss, more than just a manager. You must be respected for your ethics and integrity; you must inspire others with a strong vision of the future.

THE PRINCIPLES OF LEADERSHIP

In 1983, the US Army presented the eleven principles of leadership. Any true leader knows them, incorporates them, and now you can too!

Some of them we've already covered, including know yourself and seek self-improvement; be well-trained and experienced, take responsibility and develop that same sense in members of your team, act in a timely but reasoned manner, lead by example, know your team, communicate clearly.

But you will also want to train as a team if you can. Let a new member be trained by the team as they go. Develop and maintain a team spirit, remind everyone that the end result is what's important, not the contribution of any single member.

The US Army stresses the three concepts of leadership: *Be, know, do.* They know who they are, they know their job and the people around them, they do what they must to achieve the goal. It's a good thing to keep in the back of your head.

A true leader exerts an influence on the environment, and they do this with three distinct actions. They establish; performance standards and goals for their team, values for their company or organization, concepts of people and the business they do.

Standards apply to strategies, plans, productivity, reliability, quality, leadership. Values apply to the concern the business has for its customers, employees, investors, and the environment. Concepts apply to products and services offered and the processes and methods of conducting business.

The combination of these three things define how a company is seen, by customers and competition alike. It defines roles and relationships, rewards, and rites within the company.

Roles are, basically, positions within the company which have defined expectations of behavior and productivity. Every team has roles; one the writer, another a graphic artist, the other an engineer, yet another an accountant. Every role has its place, every member of the team has a function.

Relationships depend on the task given to a certain role. Some are isolated, some require more interaction. But no matter how isolated a worker may be, they still must be led effectively.

CULTURE AND CLIMATE

Roles and especially relationships on a team or in a company are affected by both culture and climate. Every company has its own culture. Some are more modern, with offices filled with toys and ping pong tables and other things to create a fresh, young, creative feel. Others are more traditional. This will have an effect on relationships between roles.

Think of the climate as the general feeling which arises from the culture. A newer approach may create a fresher, more easy-going climate, but that may not be best for productivity (though it may do wonders for your ping pong game). Traditional cultures in business may produce a stuffier climate, not conducive to creativity.

Know the climate and culture of your situation and you'll be better suited to lead it correctly and effectively.

Climate and culture can both apply to ethical standards, environmental considerations, even stock payouts. But climate may change and culture is a more enduring concept. The climate may change with an economic downturn, though the cultural model of the company will endure.

Leaders are unlikely to be able to sway the culture of the company, which is generally determined by the company's founders. Unless the leader is the founder, there's somebody else's vision to serve here. But managers and true leaders do affect the climate of the office, and that is one of the true leader's primary functions. Put your focus there when managing or leading.

Other researchers have found more building blocks of great leaders. They often challenge the systems they work with. They're process-oriented thinkers. They inspire the idea of a shared vision, and they inspire others to act accordingly.

5 THINGS EVERY NEW & EXPERIENCED LEADER CAN DO TO BUILD ESSENTIAL LEADERSHIP HABITS

Making the most of your possibilities as a leader means making the most of your own skills. A true leader knows that leadership is an ongoing process. As we've discussed, they include active listening, emotional intelligence, a growth mindset, conducting purposeful conversations, asking questions, being a good coach.

Bad habits which prohibit true leadership include unrealistic expectations. Don't expect supersonic results overnight. Don't expect Herculean results from mere mortals. The best results are often neither quick nor linear, there's not a straight path to success. Often enough, it's a twisting path.

Successful leaders focus on who they want to become, not what they want to achieve. I know this is counterintuitive, and I've been asserting the virtues of putting the results of the effort above the qualities of the individual.

But one does not set out to complete one project, save one patient, or to file one tax return. One sets out to do this continuously, and that has to be kept in mind. It's still imperative to keep a project's success in mind, but it's a matter of perspective. Overall success is achieved through a series of smaller successes. If you're going to be a leader, you're best served to set out on a deliberate course to become a leader.

One building block to great leadership is the understanding between the difference between action and motion. That may be something you've never considered, so let's take a closer look. There's much to be revealed.

Understand the difference between action and motion. Motion is a feeling we get from taking action. But motion does not entail the risk of failure, action does. Still, motion requires action. The trick is to know the difference.

Your risks occur when you take action, your rewards occur when you experience motion.

One habit all leaders seem to develop is reading. It excites the mind; it keeps a person forward-thinking. It's an invaluable resource of information which no YouTube video can replace. And with Kindle, reading is faster and cheaper than ever. Gone are the days of musty bookshelves or cardboard boxes full of books. Almost every book ever written is at your fingertips, in just about every language still used on Earth. And with over half the book market devoted to non-fiction, much of which is self-help, there is a plethora of data to absorb, almost all of which will be new to you and a lot of it applicable to your situations in life.

Leadership also means being generous with praise. Morale is crucial to teamwork, and true leaders know this. Not only should a leader not be competitive or insecure about his or her team, the true leader builds up their team and acknowledges their efforts.

Positivity is a key building block of any leadership. All of the leadership styles are predicated on the concept of positivity. Nothing can happen in a climate of negativity.

Rest is one crucial aspect of good leadership which often goes overlooked. It's vital to an individual's mental and physical health, and to the health of any team. A leader must be well-rested, and he should see to it that the members of his or her team are well-rested as well.

True leaders likewise make their physical health a priority. Regular exercise and a good diet have a positive effect on every aspect of a person's life. And a true leader leads by example. Any good leader would want their team to be physically and mentally fit, and so they must also be that, even more so. Also, there's more responsibility on the shoulders of the leader, and so he or she must be physically fit.

One practical things leaders tend to do is plan their next day in advance. They make to-do lists, and know first thing in the morning what they're going to do. It gives them drive, purpose, organization, and it sets a great example for their team, who should all do likewise.

RESPECT

Respect; it can take a lifetime to earn and only seconds to lose. It's the basis of sound leadership. But how does one earn the respect of others? It's easy enough to see that practicing the qualities of a true leader, honesty and integrity, clear communication and selflessness, will earn the respect of others. But there's another way to think about it, the *12 Cs of respect*.

True leaders *care* about the feelings of others. They show *conviction* and they do it with *clarity* and *confidence*.

True leaders show *courage* in the face of risk and uncertainty and *commitment* to their standards and to their clients and also to their team. They're open to *collaboration*. They *communicate* openly and with *candor, courtesy,* and *credibility.*

The most effective managers know that good team members are supported by their own sense of achievement, responsibility, recognition, and advancement. The best leaders also know that they are in a position of power. They know how to wield that power, and where it comes from, or what kind of power it is. We've touched on some different types of power, but let's take a closer look.

THE SIX SOURCES OF POWER

1. Legitimate power, or positional power, is generated from their role in the company. This is a formal authority; branch managers or sports team coaches.
2. Referent power derives from the individual's ability to attract others and to earn their loyalty. Many managers and team members have this power. Referent power often arises from a personal trait, likability, or charm, as these are at the root of interpersonal influence.
3. Expert power draws on a person's knowledge and skills. It's a narrow source of power, but it's particularly potent when their skill sets are especially valuable to the company.
4. Reward power is derived by one's ability to dispense rewards. Common rewards include pay increases, extra time off, or other promotions.
5. Coercive power is the flipside of reward power, given to those who can dispense punishments instead of rewards. Often this power and reward power are imbued in the same individual. Rewards are usually the favored motivator, as this creates a healthier climate in the workplace.
6. Informational power is wielded by those with access to information. The gatekeepers of data in this day and age wield more power than they realize. Information can be used in transactional exchanges of various sorts. Information is power.

We've taken a deeper look at what makes a true leader. Now, in the second section of this book, more skills which are even more highly regarded than IQ (which, honestly, is just about *all* of them).

LEADERSHIP SKILLS TEST

Here is a research-tested test of your leadership skills. Answer on a scale of one through five, where one is the lowest (no) and five is the highest (yes).

- I always try to see another person's point of view or perspective before giving feedback.
- I don't like breaking a big project into smaller portions.
- I don't take the time to evaluate strategies or progress of the past, I'm more interested in my own perspective and solutions.
- I'm an authoritative leader, it's my way or the highway.
- I believe superior performance and hard work should be recognized and rewarded.
- I can't maintain a positive attitude; it feels fake to me.
- People expect me to give them hope when things go wrong, but I'm just not feeling it.
- Long-term goals are important to me, they bring me more happiness than momentary satisfaction.
- I'm a generally positive person, even when the going gets tough.
- I find it hard to deal with stress.

- I'm eager to follow up one success with another, and I'm excited by new projects.
- Disappointments upset me.
- I tend to blame myself when things don't go as I'd hoped.
- A good manager follows their own vision and doesn't need the contributions of others.
- Employees are trustworthy, for the most part.
- The team leader sets the example of behavior for others in the team.
- I often get angry at things other people don't seem so offended by.
- The harder I work, the harder my team members are likely to work.
- I'm confident in my actions and decisions.
- I'm not really sure where my organization is headed. I keep my eyes on the next deadline.
- Managers should lead by example.
- There's no shame in losing.
- I have a positive influence on others, how they perform, and how they approach their performance.
- I know my team pretty well, what each one is good at and what their weaknesses are.
- Even if I know my team, I don't invite their advice. It only causes problems when I don't use them.
- A good leader harnesses the power of the team.
- Ideals are more important to me than profit.
- I can't manage to prioritize things; they all seem equally urgent to me.

- I do not trust anybody.
- People don't seem to follow my lead.
- I try to argue my case, but I'm just not good at swaying others.
- Brainstorming brings out the best in me creatively.
- Sometimes I feel great, then I'm suddenly thrown into a pit of despair.
- When I lead a meeting, everybody leaves psyched and ready to get back to work.
- I'm not easily discouraged.
- I know my company's mission statement and let it guide my decision-making.
- I stay in touch with my company's evolving place in the business world, changes going on at every level.
- I'm comfortable asking for the feedback of others.
- I have no trouble showing my gratitude for positive contributions and good performances of others.
- Details tend to distract me.
- I don't understand the term, *Thinking outside of the box.* What box?

Don't worry about your score. You'll know by your answers where you need to shore things up to improve your leadership skills. Now let's move on to emotional intelligence.

II

EMOTIONAL INTELLIGENCE

3

UNDERSTANDING EMOTIONAL INTELLIGENCE

IS EMOTIONAL INTELLIGENCE REALLY MORE IMPORTANT THAN IQ?

You've heard the term IQ all your life, but you probably don't know that it stands for *intelligence quotient*. It's a measure of your relative intelligence. EQ, on the other hand, stands for *emotional quotient*. It's a measure of your relative emotional security and control, how you manage yours or others imagination.

There's a standardized test to measure a person's IQ, but not one to measure a person's EQ, so they're hard to equate. But they can be compared. An IQ score of 70 or below is considered an intellect with a disability, 145 is near to the genius level, 180 is the top possible score.

But there's no way to measure your EQ.

And research demonstrates those who lead well and perform well have high IQs and also adequate emotional intelligence. Both are necessary to act and react in the fast-paced corporate world of the 21st Century.

Unlike the IQ, the EQ isn't particular merely to the individual. It breaks down into two components; internal and external, how we deal with our own emotions and also how we deal with the emotions of others.

As regards the management of one's own emotions, there are three hallmarks of emotional intelligence. Self-awareness, in which you understand your own moods and emotions and what effect they have on others. Self-regulation is the ability to control those emotions and impulses, to think before you act. Motivation is the third hallmark of self-emotional intelligence. Motivation is a kind of passion which is more internal, based on inherent propensity to achieve, an internal drive, more than external factors like utility, other people, or the influence of your surroundings.

That's all for the internal part of emotional intelligence. What about the external quotient?

Externally, your EQ measures your management of others' emotions and your own emotional expression. We can break our external EQ down. Social awareness, understanding other peoples' emotional makeup and how they react to your emotional expressions. Social regulation, on the other hand, is how you influence the emotions of others.

TalentSmart researchers assessed over 2 million workers and found that just 36% of them could accurately assess their own emotions as they happened.

There are two more components of external emotional intelligence. Empathy, the ability to share the emotions of others, is a crucial part of emotional intelligence in the external. Likewise, basic social skills are necessary. These include communication and listening skills.

One company, selling insurance, found that their sales agents who lacked empathy, self-confidence, and initiative, all evidence of emotional intelligence, averaged less than half the sales of those who demonstrated those qualities.

The lack of emotional intelligence can have devastating effects in the workplace. Stress and anxiety are always lurking in the shadows of any office, and a leader lacking emotional intelligence will miss the signs and may allow those festering challenges to affect productivity and efficiency. Passive/aggressive interaction, jealousies, resentments, and other destructive sentiments are likely to run wild and create a toxic climate in the workplace. It creates disorganization and mayhem and may tear a team apart.

And, unlike the IQ, a person's emotional intelligence can be increased. A leader can adapt emotional intelligence, refine it, by being more self-aware and communicating more clearly. One study found that roughly half of children enrolled in the public-school system's Social and Emotion Learning program (SEL) had higher achievement scores and 40% demonstrated improved grade point averages.

EMOTIONAL INTELLIGENCE IN EVERYDAY LIFE

Emotional intelligence is quite common in everyday life. When a child comes to you with a scraped knee, you use emotional intelligence. If a coworker is scorned or reprimanded by your boss, they require your emotional intelligence. Even watching a soap opera on TV engages one's emotional intelligence.

But it's especially important to keep emotional intelligence in mind in the workplace. There are rarely family bonds there, probably not as many office romances as one would think. That means the connections aren't as strong in the workplace and they can become easily frayed. Competitiveness, insecurity, and other factors make the workplace especially vulnerable to the kind of anxiety and stress that go along with a lack of emotional intelligence. The EQ is especially important in the workplace.

Greater emotional intelligence benefits the leader by increasing internal awareness, empathy, self-regulation, and collaborative communication. Benefits to the company include better team management, reduced stress, improved company climate, more effective planning, and better results.

And it really should go without saying that emotional intelligence is crucial not only to workplace situations, but personal, familial, and romantic; every facet of life requires emotional intelligence.

MORE ON THE FIVE PILLARS OF EMOTIONAL INTELLIGENCE

We've looked at the five pillars of emotional intelligence; self-awareness, self-regulation, motivation, empathy, and basic communication/people skills. But how can these things really improve our lives? We've seen some examples, such as improving the climate and productivity in the workplace. And we know the same emotional intelligence is required in other areas of modern life. So, let's take a closer look at emotional intelligence outside the workplace.

We've mentioned emotional intelligence in the home. Besides the workplace, emotional intelligence is most important in the home. Only the fact that so many daytime hours are spent in the workplace, and that it's a place of frequent action and crisis, make the notion of emotional intelligence so important.

But the home is really no different. Interpersonal conflicts, unexpected crises, matters both urgent (time related) and important (goal related) arise constantly and need to be managed. When children are in the family, this is even more important. Children have less emotional intelligence and it's up to their parents, the team leaders, to manage their emotions well. If not, the damage can be severe and far-reaching. A child who does not learn emotional intelligence may grow to be an adult who lacks it as well. It's up to the parents to raise an emotionally intelligent child, and to do that they must first be emotionally intelligent. A good parent, like any true leader, leads by example.

There's also the very practical matter of running a happy home. A home in which children are fighting with each other, parents are fighting with each other, or parents are fighting with the children is not a happy home. The children will be raised to behave that way as adults and to raise their own children in a like fashion. If this sounds like your family, know that you can break the cycle now by improving your own emotional intelligence and then increasing the emotional intelligence of those around you through guidance and education and, well, emotional intelligence.

Since stress and anxiety have such detrimental effects on one's physical and emotional health, it's important to note the connection between emotional intelligence and physical or emotional wellbeing. Lack of emotional intelligence allows stress and anxiety to flourish, and they have recorded effects on sleep and eating patterns, causing malnutrition and weight gain and depression, which can lead to substance abuse. These are all proven to cause psychological complexes, mortal disease, premature death, and suicide.

So emotional intelligence is crucial to a long and healthy life.

Emotional intelligence also has an existential benefit. The existential questions of identity and purpose are best approached with emotional intelligence. These aren't mathematical equations, after all, but questions about the meaning of life. They plumb the very depths of the mind and soul, and intellectual intelligence is not enough to find a satisfactory resolution.

In fact, the very concept of success itself is predicated on emotional intelligence. Because those who have it enjoy a smoothness, a functionality in life which naturally leads to increased socialization. That leads to opportunities and those are the gateways to success. Emotional intelligence is something others pick up on, especially if they are the sources of the emotional crisis. Emotional intelligence engenders gratitude and respect, and those are the qualities which lead to opportunity and the success which may follow.

ARE YOU EMOTIONALLY INTELLIGENT?

We've already touched on a few of the hallmarks of emotional intelligence; willingness and desire to succeed and to help others succeed, empathy, self-awareness, passion.

But if you are to be truly emotionally intelligent, you also need curiosity. Self-awareness of one's deficits and passion for knowledge and self-improvement create curiosity about new information, better methods. Curiosity is the hallmark of a growth-minded individual, which all true leaders are. True leaders are also emotionally intelligent.

The emotionally intelligent should have an analytical mind too, in order to process the causes of their own emotions and the emotions of others. Remember that emotion is not rational, but reason can undo emotion. Therefore, the true leader and the emotionally intelligent know when to reason, they can analyze cause and effect and better manage their own emotional expressions and how to deal with the emotions of others.

Those with emotional intelligence also have a kind of faith. It's not religious faith necessarily, though that may come into play. It's a matter of having faith in one's own emotional intelligence. Once one is emotionally intelligent, they must utilize that intelligence in a practical fashion, and that takes discipline, mastery, and confidence. The emotionally intelligent have faith that their EQ will serve them and others well, and they have faith in the techniques which are the hallmarks of EQ, and other communication techniques presented in this book. And there's no reason for the true leader not to have faith, as these techniques are research-driven and time-tested.

Needs and wants are imperative to consider when looking at emotional intelligence. Abraham Maslow's hierarchy of needs illustrates which needs are basic (food, drink, shelter) and which are psychological (love and belonging) and some which are related to self-fulfillment (aesthetic or spiritual or other self-actualization needs).

Wants, on the other hand, are indulgences which may bring pleasure but which are not necessary. A bigger house, a fancier car, the latest iPhone are all wants, not needs. The emotionally intelligent know the difference, but the emotionally unintelligent do not and will often confuse the two. They may need a fancier car or the new iPhone, or at least they think they do.

The emotionally intelligent are generally optimistic, because they're confident in their approach and they have a keen understanding of those around them. This leads to a general positivity and is conducive to effective leadership styles such as coaching and democratic styles.

The emotionally intelligent are often adaptable, as they have their core standards well-grounded and they know they can handle any unexpected crisis which may throw their team into emotional disarray. The emotionally intelligent are also agile enough to know when to change course, to admit when something isn't working or when something else could work better. They accept this without regard to their ego or personal insecurities, as any true leader would do. Like everything about emotional intelligence, this is as critical in the home or in social situations as in the workplace.

The emotionally intelligent tend to be shape-shifters, adaptable to different circumstances and situations. Emotions tend to be chaotic and may erupt out of nowhere, and so the emotionally intelligent can quickly adapt to a new situation and accommodate it appropriately.

Emotionally intelligent people are very rarely perfectionists. Generally, growth-minded individuals, those with emotional intelligence realize that perfection is rarely attained, and that to be a perfectionist is to suffer from overthinking and negative self-talk and a fixed mindset which are all antithetical to emotional intelligence.

They're generally grateful. The emotionally intelligent have prioritized what is important (health, strong social ties, self-actualization) and what is not (material wants or ego gratification). So, they're grateful for what they have instead of desirous of what they do not have. This is especially potent in family, social, or workplace situations, but it is also crucial to the individual and their inner peace, though that's not what we're focusing on here.

The emotionally intelligent don't seem to get easily distracted. Once again, it's about priorities. The emotionally intelligent know what's important and they stay focused on that, whether it's the task at hand or the emotional tumult of a coworker or team member.

Emotionally intelligent people generally have well-balanced lives, with fair amounts of work and play, social and private time. This is because they're more confident than most, less insecure, and more capable of achieving their tasks to relieve the need for overwork.

The emotionally intelligent tend to embrace change, they don't fear it. Their confidence allows them to see the opportunity in the perceived crisis. The growth-minded true leader with emotional intelligence knows that change is both necessary and unavoidable and looks forward to the positive results the change may bring.

Do you have these qualities? Are you lacking in some but not in others? The more of these qualities of emotional intelligence you have, the more effective a leader you'll be, and the happier a person too.

MEASURING YOUR EMOTIONAL INTELLIGENCE

As we've said, there's really no standardized test for EQ as there is for IQ. But if we can put a man on the moon, we can measure emotional intelligence. Leave it to some of the cleverest minds in modern psychology to give us just about everything we need to get the job done. So, if you want to know just how emotionally intelligent you are (or aren't) then read on.

There are several institutionalized tests for EQ, but no single standard. The EIQ:M creates a profile of seven emotional competencies. The EI Report is part of the OPQ Expert System. The Bar-On EQ-i is called a *self-report measure* for varying purposes. Others are other-reported (based on Q/A and involving a questioner or tester) or ability measured (tests of skill or knowledge). The MSCEIT measures ability. The EI-360 test is used for career management and development.

We've included some sample questions from some of the leading tests to set you off on a new understanding of yourself, of others, of your world and everyone in it.

Ask yourself and then answer with a simple *yes/no* answer or on a scale of one to five, where one is the least positive (a *no*) and five is the most positive (a *yes*).

- I recognize my own emotions as soon as I experience them.
- I often lose my temper in times of frustration.
- I am told that I am a good listener.
- I can calm myself when I'm feeling upset or anxious.
- I organize groups well.
- My long-term focus is hard to maintain.
- Frustration and unhappiness often inhibit my decision making.
- I know what my strengths and my weaknesses are.
- I try to avoid conflicts and/or negotiations.
- I do not enjoy the work that I do.
- I encourage feedback and digest it reasonably on what I do well.
- I often review my progress on long-term goals.
- I'm often confused by other people's emotions.
- I don't build rapport well and find it hard to bond with others.

- I consider myself an active listener.

Now try these samples from yet another EQ test, using the same answer style. Consistency is key.

- I know when not to talk about my personal problems with others.
- When facing obstacles, I reflect on previous similar experiences and take comfort and renewed passion from them.
- I don't expect to fail, not even on the first try.
- People don't often confide in me.
- I find it easy to understand non-verbal communication, such as body language.
- I'm in control of my own non-verbal communication.
- Major life events have given me pause to reflect and reconsider my priorities.
- My mood effects my perspective.
- I enjoy the emotions I feel as they are generally positive.
- I live in the expectation of good things, not bad things.
- I tend to share my emotions.
- I savor positive emotions and can make them last.
- Others enjoy the events I arrange or organize.
- I'm eager for new activities and seek them out.
- I generally make a good impression.
- I can read people's emotions by looking at their faces.
- I can read people's emotions by the tone of their voice.
- My emotions change, but I'm aware of how, when, and why.

- Being in a good mood sparks my creativity.
- I visualize the results of a possible success.
- I freely compliment others.
- Being emotional tends to inspire me.
- I often retreat from a challenge, knowing I'm certain to fail.
- I enjoy lifting people's spirits.

Here are some from the Profile of Emotional Competence (PEC), other good examples of questions you'll find in almost any good EQ test. Answer these honestly for a clearer picture of your emotional intelligence.

- I can't track my rising emotions.
- I don't understand why I often respond so emotionally.
- I know how to influence people's emotions if I need to.
- I know how to convince people's intellects if I need to.
- I know the difference between satisfaction, happiness, and relaxation.
- I am comfortable describing what I think and feel.
- I can calm myself down after an emotional eruption or trying experience.
- I have little difficulty cheering myself up.
- I find it easy to handle my own emotions.
- Others often take offense to the manner in which I express emotions.
- I'm often sad and I don't know why.

There are right answers and wrong answers, but no winning score. That will be for you to decide. If you're deficient in your emotional intelligence, you'll know it by your answers and you'll know where to work harder. Are you lacking empathy or self-awareness? Are you deficient in motivation? Take a look at your answers to these questions and they'll tell you.

Now that you've got a grip on your emotional intelligence, let's look at different ways you can increase that EQ!

4

THE 20 MUST-KNOW STRATEGIES THAT CAN BOOST YOUR EQ

We know that emotional intelligence, like leadership skills, can be attained and modified and improved. But ... how? Here are some concrete, proven methods you can apply in order to increase your own emotional intelligence. You can do them at no cost, with no professional assistance, and the results can be immediate.

We've already talked about understanding your emotions, but now it's time to name them. It's not enough just to have a temper tantrum and then feel badly about it. In order to be in control of your emotions (necessary for emotional intelligence) you must know what emotions you're feeling in order to be able to deal with them properly. Is jealousy the root of an emotional outburst, or frustrated expectations resulting in disappointment? If it's jealousy, ask yourself what you're jealous of, how that makes you see yourself. Ask yourself what productive qualities, if any, do your emotions have. Some emotions can inspire, others detract. Name these emotions, understand what they are and what inspires them. Then you can learn to manage them properly.

Seeking feedback is crucial. It's a fact that we just don't see ourselves the way others do, we're far too subjective about the subject of our own bodies, skill, talents. Oftentimes we have no sense of our own limitations, but just as often we have no sense of our qualities. We're generally harder on ourselves than on others, a condition which causes overthinking and negative self-talk in a fixed mindset. That's why it's so important to ask others for their more-objective opinions. Ask them to be honest and don't take offense. You're trying to improve yourself and we could all use some improving in one aspect of our lives or another. Feedback could well be the key to unlocking your true emotional intelligence.

Reading remains the best way to increase your emotional intelligence. Of course, self-help books like these are invaluable (check out our complete line!) and Kindle makes reading easier and more affordable than ever. But don't stop at self-help books (check out our complete line!) because novels and poetry are great ways to increase your emotional intelligence. Works which are heavy on romance and pondering the existential truths excite the brain to these emotional aspects of life, making any person more sensitive to such things. Go and read anything by the great Romantic poet John Keats, who pondered love and mortality in the three years during which he was dying of tuberculosis and see if you're not suddenly more emotionally aware.

Pay attention to how you behave. Do you get more emotional and less disciplined when you drink? Be aware of this and change your behavior. If you know one person to be a trigger for your emotional mood swings, and you know that certain alcohols (or any) tend to aggravate our behavior, change your situation. Stay out of the room, forego the liquor, or simply exert some self-control.

Take a moment to question your own opinions. This is the exercise of the growth-minded individual. It's possible that opinions have evolved, or that they were never well-founded to begin with. Opinions are too often the result of emotion and not reason. It could be that the reasons or circumstances surrounding the reasons have changed. Review your opinions to root out their cause. Also, questioning your own opinions proves that you are secure in your identity and your ethics, you know they will withstand any scrutiny and will only be strengthened by open-minded reconsideration.

Set time aside to enjoy the positive aspects of life. It's great to be learning from the past and working toward a better future, but all too often we neglect the present. Positive results from team members shouldn't be overlooked, nor should a warm, sunny day. The emotionally intelligent are sensitive to positive energy and they know the value of celebrating it. So, make sure you're not overlooking the positive elements of your project, your team, your family, your friends, and your life.

At the same time, you don't want to ignore the negative. If corrections have to be made, they can be done with kindness and consideration and will be all the more effective for that effort. But to ignore poor results or bad behavior is to guarantee that they will continue, and that's not true leadership, that's being a leader in name only.

Deliberately take time to relax. You may meditate, which many do as a relaxation technique. You may enjoy a hot cup of coffee or tea at some point in the day, but make sure to do it. It prevents burnout and gives you time to reflect, reconsider, to gather your physical and intellectual energies for the tasks to come. Make it ten minutes, whenever you generally find yourself most stressed. In the workplace, this is often late in the morning after a rush of necessary business, or late in the afternoon as the end of the business day looms. For families, watch for these pitched moments in the early morning before school and the hours during or after dinner. These are the times when a relaxation break may be the most valuable.

Along these lines, stand up and stretch at least once a day. Lean back, raise your arms, stretch your muscles for about ten seconds. This physical action of pro-active relaxation has notable effects on the brain. Try it for yourself.

While you're trying new things, try to see yourself objectively. It won't be easy, as we've discussed. Body dysmorphia disorder and reverse body dysmorphia are only two ways that we tend to distort our visions of ourselves. Narcissism, delusions of grandeur, the God complex, anorexia, bulimia, and a host of other harmful conditions and disorders are associated with our inability to be objective about ourselves.

Nevertheless, you have to try to see yourself as others do. You have faults, know them. Others do. You have qualities of character, and you should know these too. And it's not only what, but how much. You may have some talent at one thing, more talent at another, but still not as much at either as somebody else. Know your limitations. Know your habits and inclinations. Know what situations and what people and things trigger what emotions and use that knowledge to manipulate yourself or your circumstance, as we've just discussed.

Keeping a diary is a great concrete step you can take to increase your emotional intelligence. It helps you become more objective about yourself, because it externalizes your thoughts and emotions from your actual, physical self. It's also a way to express yourself to yourself, which is key to emotional intelligence.

Get into the practice of looking ahead to how you will feel later, in the near future. Use the popular if/then technique to ask yourself something like, *"If I drink when this person is around, then how am I going to feel? If I feel badly, then how am I going to behave?"* If you're honest with yourself, you'll know how to modify your behavior in order to better manage your emotions.

Get in the habit of paying attention to your intuition. A lot of people ignore this, to their detriment. Overthinking tends to drown out the voice of intuition. But intuition is born of instinct, and that can often be more reliable and accurate than an over-rationalized position of analysis paralysis.

If you don't already have a weekly or daily schedule, create one. Organization is central to emotional intelligence and everything that goes along with being a true leader. But before you can manage a team, you have to be able to manage yourself. You'll also want to encourage your team members (or family members) to maintain a strict schedule too, but that requires that you lead by example.

Maintain (or begin) a healthy lifestyle. Substance abuse and malnutrition has all manner of ill-effects on brain function, and that's at the heart of emotional intelligence. Lack of sleep is also antithetical to emotional intelligence and true leadership.

Engender trust. If you win trust doing one thing (repaying a debt, let's say) that trust will likely carry into other aspects of that relationship. When the people around you know they can trust you to be emotionally intelligent, they will surely open up more often and more thoroughly, creating a healthier climate. Without trust, no organization can truly flourish. The stress, anxiety, duplicity, and chicanery a lack of trust engenders can be crippling for any project, team, company, or family.

Exercise self-discipline. You're not subject to your emotions, they are subject to you. Don't give into them and burst into a tantrum. Find something else to do, if you must. Feel compelled to explode? Go to the bedroom and punch your pillow, that's a time-tested trick that a lot of people find convenient and effective.

Set some personal goals. This is a great way to keep your mind alert and functioning on a high level. It's a series of challenges which will result in satisfaction and accomplishment. It almost doesn't matter what those goals are; clean the closet, repaint the bedroom, quit smoking, fix the fence in the backyard, resolve your back tax problem. Whatever it is, just do it. Be pro-active and goal-oriented.

Volunteer in some way. It's like on-the-job-training for emotional intelligence, including so many of the pillars (especially empathy). It's a good way to spend extra time, it will broaden your social circle, it offers personal satisfaction, self-discipline, and self-awareness.

Make sure you're approachable. A true leader with emotional intelligence knows that open, clear communication is key to a successful project, team, or organization. And hopefully he or she has adopted a leadership style which leads them to interact with the team. But you don't want to be intimidating around your team, and you don't want them to feel intimidated. You want them to feel that they can approach you with questions or concerns. Do this by being gentle without being weak, demonstrate concern for others, just about everything we've covered in this book so far. But apply them deliberately, in a measured fashion. Mastering the application of these principles is key to being a true leader with heightened emotional intelligence.

We've talked about perspective, but it bears repeating here. Emotional intelligence requires you to be able to see the world from somebody else's perspective. Without that, you have emotional ignorance.

Don't be afraid to share your own experiences. If somebody opens up to you with an emotional crisis, consider sharing one of your own. It lets the other person know that you understand their perspective and share it, that you're empathetic, that you'll do whatever you can for them as you would for yourself.

Another concrete step you can take to increase your emotional intelligence is to immerse yourself in a new culture. Travel, see how other people live. You may be surprised at how much suffering there is in the world, so much to inspire gratitude, empathy. It's a great way to refresh your perspective, to learn to see life through somebody else's eyes. If you can't travel, consider picking a culture and making a project out of it. Read some books, both fiction and nonfiction, watch some videos, think about learning at least some of the language. There's great wisdom in most of the world's cultural traditions, and as a growth-minded person you know the value of learning and growing in your journey of self-actualization.

Another good exercise is to find somebody and indulge your curiosity about them. Call and old friend and ask them about their life, what they've been doing and thinking and feeling. Don't talk about yourself until they insist. This is an exercise in putting the focus on somebody else. And it's a great way to keep your friendship alive (which needs to be done proactively).

One invaluable exercise in building or refining emotional intelligence is to cut off from social media for a while. Sadly, this ever-more-pervasive medium has only stunted our emotional intelligence due to isolation and lack of personal interaction. So, don't just message your old friend on Facebook, get together for lunch if you can. There's no substitute for personal interaction where emotional intelligence is concerned.

You may want to get out into new situations a bit more. A bar, a festival of some kind, anything that will put you into contact with new people. Then demonstrate curiosity about them. You can see how these techniques work together for even greater effect.

WHAT NOT TO DO

Don't get dramatic. Emotional intelligence engenders patience, consideration, reason, not an emotional outburst. Be rational, not dramatic.

Don't complain. It puts you in a position of being a victim, not a leader. Instead, focus on a solution to the problem.

Don't be negative. True leaders and the emotionally intelligent are positive in their perspective and their behavior.

Don't dwell on the past. The past cannot be changed and the future cannot be known. Overthinking is the destructive habit of focusing on the past (what could have been said or done) or the future (what may or may not happen) to the detriment of the present (what might be happening now). So, let go of old hurts, grudges, feelings of resentment or betrayal. Those emotions are toxic and may lead to all manner of psychological and physical maladies.

Don't give into peer pressure. It sounds strange to take that out of a high-school context, but it is a problem which lingers in adulthood for a lot of people. But true leaders and those with emotional intelligence know who they are and what their ethical standards are, and those are the influences which prevail, not trends or fads.

Be aware of your vocabulary. Words have meaning. Make sure you're using the accurate words, forgoing hyperbole. Do not use expletives or racial slurs. Carry yourself with dignity at all times, be reliable in this and demonstrate integrity. And it's more than what you say but how you say it. Enunciate, don't slur your words. Don't sneer to lend subtext to certain words. Your intent will always be clear, so you should be clear about it first. The way you speak speaks volumes.

Respond, don't react. A response is generally intellectual, based on reason and consideration. A reaction is generally a more emotional behavior, and should be avoided. If nothing else, one should act with deliberation and not react without it. But often enough, action isn't necessary, simply a measured, rational response. But do respond, it's part of clear, effective communication and it's the leader's responsibility to communicate with his or her clients and/or team.

So not only can emotional intelligence be increased, but these are some sure-fire ways to do it. But what about empathy? You can refine what you think and how you behave, but can you control what you feel? Let's find out!

5

GOING BEYOND SYMPATHY

WHEN SYMPATHY IS NOT ENOUGH

Sympathy or Empathy?

Both end with the suffix *-pathy*, which translates from the ancient Greek as *feelings* or *emotion*. *Suffering* and *Calamity* are also associated with the translation.

Sympathy translates roughly as *with feeling.* It's best used to describe a way in which we share another's feelings. We can relate to those feelings, be they good or bad.

But when we actually feel those feelings, we're experiencing empathy, meaning roughly *passion from emotion or feelings."* An empathetic person can feel the emotions not only of a person nearby, but a long-dead artist or playwright or the feelings of a subject in a painting or photograph.

Of the two, empathy is the key to emotional intelligence. Sympathy falls short because it is a rational response, not an emotional reaction. Now that we've got the definition of empathy (and sympathy) straight, let's take a more in-depth look at the concept of empathy. There's a lot more to it than you may have realized!

ELEMENTS OF EMPATHY

First, let's review the elements of empathy, many of which we've already touched upon as empathy relates to emotional intelligence and true leadership.

Understanding others is key, knowing their emotional and reasonable positions, knowing their strengths and their weaknesses, knowing their personality types and how to know which management style will be most effective in managing that type.

Developing others is a hallmark of empathy, the desire to reassure and reconstruct, to help others as much as to help one's self. This includes guidance, mentoring, offering incentives, and rewards for accomplishment.

Having a service orientation is critical. Always keep in mind that any leader's efforts are in some greater cause, and in the modern world that is basically oriented to proficient service. A manager is answerable to their supervisors. The leader's team is answerable to the leader. Everybody's efforts are in the service of the project, of the client. This approach is like going the extra mile and is likely to engender professional respect and fondness.

Empathy leverages diversity. Remember that. Leveraging is about being agile in your interactions. Without violating your integrity, you will be leveraging your behavior a bit with your own supervisor compared to the way you'll behave with your team. The manager is the authority figure in one circumstance, but not in the other. And the true leader and the emotionally intelligent person knows that different situations require different, calibrated responses just as different people require and react better to different leadership styles. So, diversity is an opportunity to the emotionally intelligent true leader.

Political awareness is also key to empathy. If you can feel for the person on the other side of the aisle, especially in this day and age, then you truly are practicing empathy. Hats off!

TYPES OF EMPATHY

Beyond the elements of empathy, psychologists identify distinct types of empathy.

In cognitive empathy, you may understand someone's emotions and thoughts, but that understanding is more rational than emotional. It very much resembles simple sympathy. Emotional empathy is what we think of as empathy in general, though it's also known as *emotional contagion*. It's related to actually feeling the same feelings as the subject, as if the feeling were contagious.

Either cognitive or emotional empathy may lead to compassionate empathy, which goes beyond understanding or sharing and moves onto action to help or reverse the person's suffering.

Affective empathy entails understanding another's emotions and respond appropriately. This is the cornerstone of emotional intelligence.

Somatic empathy goes even deeper, involving a physical reaction. When one person is embarrassed and another blushes, that's somatic empathy.

Let's try another quiz. Answer *yes* or *no* or on a scale from one to five, one being closest to *no* and five being closest to *yes*. Let's find out how empathetic you are. Some may seem familiar, and that's not a coincidence.

- People often tell me their problems, they trust me.
- I'm pretty good at picking up on how people feel.
- I often consider how others feel.
- People tend to come to me for advice.
- I sometimes feel overwhelmed by events in the news or by social situations.
- I try to help those who might be suffering.
- I am good at reading people's honesty.
- I really care about others.
- I find it hard to set boundaries in my relationships.

The ability to empathize seems to be another case of nature versus nurture. And, as we've seen, the true analysis is that both factors contribute. Some people are more prone to emotion, some to reason. For both, life experience takes its toll and creates the sum total, a person either prone to empathy or those not prone to it.

At the most basic level, there appear to be two main factors that contribute to the ability to experience empathy: genetics and socialization. Essentially, it boils down to the age-old relative contributions of nature and nurture. Parenting has as big an influence as genetics where empathy is concerned.

BARRIERS TO EMPATHY

There are things which prevent the proper development of empathy, however. While it can be learned, it may not be and here's why.

Cognitive biases may include blaming others for internal characteristics while considering themselves victims of external factors. This distortion of perspective can be a crucial mistake.

Dehumanization refers to the tendency to let differences of culture lead to a reductive view of a person or culture. The treatment of the Jews in mid-century Europe is an example.

In victim blaming, the victim may be held responsible for the crime, such as the case of a rape victim whom some might claim dressed too seductively for her (or his) own good and was *asking for it.* But nobody buys that.

NEUROSCIENTIFIC AND PROSOCIAL EXPLANATIONS

Though empathy can be learned, much of it does seem physiological and is rooted in the brain. Researchers believe that the anterior insula and the anterior cingulate cortex play a big part in empathetic reactions. There are proven neurobiological components, mirror neurons which mimic emotional responses, to the emotion of empathy.

There's also functional MRI research which indicates that the inferior frontal gyrus (IFG), also a part of the brain, may play a vital role in experiencing empathy. Studies show that brain damage can affect emotional expression.

Sociologist Herbert Spencer suggested that empathy is hardwired into our brains as a way of ensuring social survival, that without it we would be less united and less social, and therefore, less apt to survive. The story of the human race is the story of civilization, after all. Heroism and altruism are also associated with empathy.

DEVELOPING EMPATHY FOR OTHER PEOPLE, EVEN IF YOU DON'T KNOW THEM PERSONALLY

Empathy shouldn't be reserved for friends or pathetic children in late-night commercials to solicit an impulsive donation. In fact, empathy will be beneficial to almost anyone in your life, as empathy affects every strata of your life. Those most affected by your empathy include colleagues and business partners, coworkers and community groups, friends, family, and romantic/intimate relationships.

The famed social psychology researchers Hodges and Myers have described emotional empathy in three parts. They include sharing the felt emotion of the subject as we've described, feeling personal distress in response to that shared pain, and feeling compassion for the person enduring the original pain.

Try attending somebody else's church. That's a good practical way to see a shared experience though somebody else's eyes.

TOO MUCH EMPATHY?

Is it possible to have too much empathy? Surely, one cannot have empathy for everybody all the time, as that would be too draining on any individual's resources. To have one's body endure that kind of constant sensation would rob it of valuable proteins and other physiological resources needed for survival.

Yet the tendency is all too real. Sometimes we care so much that we care too much. This can stifle empathy itself as a matter of simple self-preservation. Those survival instincts are stronger even than our tendency to overthink.

An imbalance of empathy, or a tendency toward sympathy and away from empathy, can be problematic. It's the difference between a leader in name only and a true leader.

DEVELOPING EMPATHY: 5 STAGES AND 5 FACTORS

Stages of empathy development include newborns, infants, toddlers, early childhood, middle childhood to adulthood. Let's take a closer look at both.

1. Newborns are apt to exhibit signs of distress when other

newborns do. One cries, they all cry. It's called reflexive crying or sometimes emotional contagion, which we've already looked at briefly. It's a sign of innate empathy.

2. Infants often have trouble regulating their emotions or managing others' emotions, though they often exhibit great concern for others. Toddlers (14 to 36 months old) begin to evince empathy in behavior such as apologizing. This is also a very emulative phase of growth, where toddlers are experimenting with different modes of behavior based largely on parental or media influences. Fantasy games are common in this stage of development.

3. In early childhood, children experience others' emotional states and also imagine their experiences. This is when, according to *the theory of mind,* children come to understand themselves in the context of other people and society in general. They also get in closer touch with their emotions, thoughts, wants, and desires.

4. From middle childhood and into adulthood, empathy develops significantly (or fails to do so). Perspective taking and empathic concern develop significantly in this last and longest stage of this cycle.

5. Temperament is also a big part of anybody's propensity for empathy. Shy or fearful children appear less likely to engage in empathetic behavior, for example.

6. Parenting is always a major influence on childhood development, but researchers have found a clear link between empathetic parents and empathetic children. This,

like leadership skills and other things covered in this book, is a learned skillset. Most things children learn up to the age of seven years comes from their parents.

EMOTION REGULATION IS ONE OF THE MOST IMPORTANT SKILLS YOU CAN DEVELOP

Emotional regulation, either automatic or controlled or conscious or unconscious, is the controlled governance of one's own emotions. This includes positive and negative emotions.

Emotional regulation generally involves three separate components: enabling actions which are triggered by emotions, inhibiting actions which are triggered by emotions, and modulating responses which are triggered by emotions.

Emotional regulation is a kind of filter to separate important information. In general, people with higher emotional control or emotional intelligence, have better depression management. Those without significant emotional regulatory skills suffer from mood swings and other detrimental behaviors.

Emotional regulation has been proven to delay a fight-or-flight panic response. It allows time for reason to prevail.

3 KINDS OF FUNCTIONALITY

Emotional regulation is important because without it we lackE functionality. There are three kinds of functionality;

1. Emotional
2. Social
3. Executive

Emotional functionality relates to how you internalize emotion. Social functionality relates to how you express your own emotion and interpret the emotions of others. Executive functionality allows for goal-oriented behavior, including planning and execution.

The first two are easy to understand, but what exactly is executive functionality? Here are some hallmarks of executive functionality:

- Flexibility has come up a lot in this book and for good reason. It's central to functionality of all sorts, true leadership and emotional intelligence too.
- Executive functionality engages the theory of mind, or insight into other people's perspectives.
- Anticipation is the result of recognizing recurring patterns in events.
- Problem-solving is crucial to executive functionality, as is decision making.
- Short-term and long-term memory are pillars of executive functionality.
- Sequencing is the practice of breaking down complex tasks

into smaller manageable units and then prioritizing them in a proper right order. This skill is fundamental to executive functionality.

6 MOST USEFUL EMOTIONAL REGULATION SKILLS FOR ADULTS

As we've seen, self-regulation is the art of pausing between emotion and reaction. We know that emotions react and intellect responds, so the idea is to slow down between emotion and reaction, to insert some intellect into the process to create a response instead of a reaction.

But there's also the notion of *value engagement*. Impulsive reaction may detract us from our core values. In the heat of the moment, we may even act in a way which is contrary to those values. Emotional regulation allows time to reconsider those core values and thereby stick closer to them in our behavior.

The same skillset which allows for emotional regulation was also in play in refining emotional intelligence and also leadership skills. Primary among them is self-regulation. Know what you're feeling and govern from within. Name your emotions and deal with them in the appropriate fashion.

Practicing mindful awareness will not only help you emotionally regulate, but it's a powerful tool in improving your emotional intelligence. Mindful awareness is just what it sounds like, a deliberate sense of wonder about the world, yourself, other people, everything. It's about using that positive, optimistic outlook and gratitude we talked about before and being aware of the positive things around you; a sunny day, a pretty girl, a tasty sandwich. It's a stop-and-smell-the-roses outlook which is sure to help you regulate your emotions, become more emotionally intelligent, and be a better true leader.

When you alter the way you think, that's cognitive reappraisal, and it's a pillar of emotional intelligence and emotional regulation. It's also central to various techniques of mental therapy, including anger management. Situational role reversals and thought replacement are common cognitive reappraisal exercises.

Adaptability is key to emotional regulation. Without emotional regulation, flexibility and adaptability are hampered, changes become crises.

Self-compassion is also crucial to emotional regulation. Often neglected in various facets of life and for various reasons, self-compassion is the parallel of compassion for others. It is a cornerstone of empathy, though most people don't realize it. Some even feel that they should be suffering so others can prosper, it's called the martyr complex. But that complex is antithetical to being an emotionally intelligent true leader.

Some popular exercises in self-compassion include gratitude journaling. Every day, write down the things you're grateful for. It's not complicated, but writing things down gives them power and permanence. It takes them out of the ether and makes them concrete. Writing them and then reading them externalizes them and gives them their own life.

Positive self-affirmations are common to those who deliberately practice self-compassion. They may even address themselves in a mirror. The *Saturday Night Live* character Stewart Smalley (Al Franken) practiced self-affirmations this way to hilarious effect ("I'm smart, I'm worthy, and doggonit, people like me!") but it's a powerful tool for a lot of people.

Breath control and relaxation are also common to those who practice emotional regulation. It gives you time to reason and respond instead of just reacting. Meditation is also popular among those who can regulate their own emotions. Meditating simply means to focus on a certain thing, often one's own breath, to the exclusion of everything else. Some concentrate on a mantra, or repeated word or phrase. Some concentrate on a visual focal point, like a crack in the wall. Some meditate for five minutes a day, some for an hour or more.

Emotional support is a big part of emotional regulation, and that only makes sense. Giving emotional support to others can only strengthen your sense of empathy, and that increased emotional intelligence will allow you to improve your self-empathy as well. This advances emotional intelligence and that contributes to emotional regulation. They all work together.

SCIENTIFIC STRATEGIES FOR EMOTION REGULATION

Cognitive reappraisal is a long-term approach to emotional turmoil. It's not about suppressing the negative emotions, it's about eliminating them. With cognitive reappraisal, one embraces negative emotion in order to understand what created it. Cognitive reappraisal sees the emotion as symptomatic of deeper cognitive processes and focuses on those in order to correct the negative emotional response.

Self-soothing reduces the effects of sadness, anger, and agony brought about by negative experiences. It's the opposite of self-confrontation. It's like using positive self-talk instead of the more common negative self-talk. Meditation is a popular method of self-soothing, and so is masturbation. Most people just go with breathing exercises and maybe reminiscence therapy when at the workplace, however. Others enjoy a massage, a hot bath, indulging in a hobby.

Attentional control is a pillar of emotional regulation. After a reappraisal, attention control is a disciplined way of seeing things from a new perspective. What good is a reappraisal if you lack the discipline to adjust your point of view? If you can't change your perspective, why reevaluate?

Unfortunately, some people just can't manage to do these things and they can't regulate their own emotions. These people are said to suffer from emotional regulation disorder, also known as *emotional dysregulation* (ED). Common symptoms include sudden, unexplained and inappropriate outbursts of anger, passive-aggressive traits or practices, inexplicable chronic pain or illness, self-destructive behavior, inhibited social or professional interaction, and inability to focus.

Poor self-control and hypersensitivity are also common to those who lack emotional regulation. Mood swings in the extreme are common as well, as is depression, stress, anxiety and, irritability.

Psychologists often prefer to manage EDD with dialectical behavior therapy (DBT), often combined with other cognitive strategies. But the prognosis for treatment is generally good. Behavior can be corrected, new behaviors learned to replace the old.

FOSTERING EMOTIONAL REGULATION IN CHILDREN

Emotional regulation is crucial for proper childhood development. But how do we teach our kids to do what a lot of adults cannot? It's actually easier, because children are more pliable and learn more quickly than adults and they lack the imprinted behaviors and perspectives which may inhibit adult growth.

First of all, model the behavior you wish the child to emulate. As in all things and especially in parenting, lead by example. It's the best way to lead and the best way to live. It's also the most effective way to teach.

You may want to deliberately delay response time with children. If they're angry, lead them through a moment of self-sympathy, a moment to create an intellectual response to replace their emotional reaction. You had to deliberately do it for yourself, and you will likely have to be the one to do it for your child, who will likely lack the self-awareness and self-discipline to do it. Do it with them and that will teach them to do it for themselves later in life. It's a gift that keeps on giving.

Focus on the emotional vocabulary of the child. Children are often incapable or articulating their feelings, just as adults are. You went out of your way to name your emotions so as to better understand them.

EMOTION REGULATION IS ONE OF THE MOST IMPORTANT... | 289

Do the same with your child, and in so doing you'll teach them to do it for themselves later in life.

You may even make a chart with every emotion along with a facial expression to go along with it. This will help your child visualize and also separate themselves from their emotions. It's also a fun, creative activity that will give you and your child some time together, a shared goal, and the satisfaction of achieving that goal.

Teach your children that actions have consequences. This is key to emotional regulation because the consequences of many actions are emotional responses. An insult may result in hurt feelings, for example. Make sure your children realize that if they punch another kid, that kid may cry and rightfully so. This may create feelings of shame and guilt and will result in punishment.

Make your children aware of things like stress, sadness, anxiety. This will instruct them as to their creation of those feelings in others, and that will help guide them in regulating their own behavior. These are consequences which may derive from your child's actions, after all.

Of course, things with your children may get more complicated than you expect (they often do). Children of different ages react differently to perceived crises. Young children, lacking emotional intelligence, may have meltdowns (so too may adults lacking the same EQ). If these tantrums continue past the age of four, if they become violent, or if they occur often and last longer than 15 minutes, you've got a behavioral problem on your hands. Meltdowns may also be symptomatic of mental illness such as attention deficit/hyperactivity disorder, also known as ADHD.

Meltdowns are caused by so-called *big feelings,* emotions which a child cannot clearly name and identify (much less deal with). But these big feelings can be a problem when a child suppresses their emotions, argues often, makes threats, starts fights, lacks self-control, or has conflicts with authority.

Anger and overexcitement are often associated with mental illnesses and disorders such as ADHD, intermittent explosive disorder, conduct disorder, mood and anxiety disorders, depression, post-traumatic stress disorder (PTSD), and adjustment disorder.

Here are some concrete techniques you may use in dealing with a child who cannot regulate their own emotions:

- To prevent a meltdown, try distracting the child. Move them to a less frustrating situation or activity. Try to meet whatever unexpressed need the child may have. The child can't put a name to it, so it's up to you to know and name their emotions, to know what causes them and to be able to affect it.
- Offer some simple choices to encourage confidence in decision making and lower frustration.
- Actively listen to your child's opinions and concerns. Encourage them to express themselves in this way, as it's key to their own emotional regulation. Validate their feelings too, as they are legitimate whatever those feelings may be.
- Teach your kids what those big feelings are, how to name them and the importance of dealing with them. It's great to

solve your child's frustrating problem on any given day, but you won't always be there to do that for them. What is key is to teach them to do this for themselves, to become emotionally regulated adults.

- But for the moment of crisis, you may want to set aside a safe space where you child can retire for a moment of relaxation and reflection. You do the same thing yourself, hopefully.
- Always communicate clearly with your children, as you would with anyone else. You can't expect them to rise to your expectations if you don't make those expectations clear. A true leader has mastered clear communication and is careful to manage and maintain it.
- Children crave stability, so maintain rituals and routines. Homework after school, brushing teeth before bed, make the bed before school; these are the kind of little exercises in self-discipline that will encourage the bigger tasks of emotional regulation, intelligence, and leadership later on.
- Use schedules and timetables with your kids. It teaches them to do the same and it's a time-tested management tool. All your lives will run more smoothly.

But what do you do during a meltdown, once it's too late to prevent one? The safe place is a good remedy, and there are others. First of all, stay calm. Lead by example here. Speak in a tone which is both gentle and strong, speak from deep in the chest. Declare but do not demand and do not ask. Inquire about the reason for the upset and introduce reason to replace emotion.

After a meltdown, be sure to praise the child for calming down and getting control of themselves; it's a stepping stone to greater emotional regulation, after all. Talk to the child afterward so that you can both digest the details and complexities, the causes and the alternatives. Plumb your child's feelings about the experience, it will help them understand their own feelings and encourages self-sympathy and self-awareness. Talk about problem solving, make a plan to correct things which caused the upset. That's a shared activity with a beneficial goal, a bonding experience for you and your child in which you share positive energy and a positive outcome.

EMOTION REGULATION SKILLS FOR CHILDREN

Here are some time-tested skills any family can work on together:

- First, help your children develop problem-solving skills which use the energy generated by big feelings to create constructive results. These skills fix problems instead of the emotional reaction which only make matters worse.
- Some steps in problem-solving include identifying the problem from the child's point of view, sharing your concerns, working together to make a plan of action, putting that plan into effect, reflecting on the plan's success and modify it for greater future success.
- Teach assertiveness skills, ways a person may declare their needs without being overly aggressive. Teach balanced thinking, to see things realistically and objectively. For kids, books are especially effective ways to teach these skills. There

are mental health professionals who specialize on working with children too. But there are a few more good tips to helping kids with less emotional regulation.

- Make sure they're educated. They can't name their emotions if they don't know the words or what they mean. Teach your children these things, because your local elementary school won't. It's another reason why it's so important that you have a functioning mastery of emotional intelligence; you can't teach what you don't know.
- Resist blameful or shameful language. No person can change how they feel, only how they behave. No emotion should be demonized, merely understood and responded to instead of reacted to.
- As always, be empathetic and an active listener.
- Encourage them toward relaxing activities like exercise and yoga, listening to music, or keeping a journal. Adopt regulating behaviors, such as counting slowly from 10.

DIALECTICAL BEHAVIOR THERAPY (DBT)

Dialectical Behavior Therapy (DBT) focuses on active communication in addressing mental health issues and is particularly useful in treating various personality disorders, such as borderline personality disorder. These are disorders wherein the sufferer may lose control of their emotions.

The idea here is that arousal levels vary with the individual. A child will react differently to a death than a person of middle age, for example. The effects and consequences will vary accordingly. DBT is generally supportive, cognitive (centered on thought over emotion) and mutual (between the client and the therapist).

You may not be a therapist, but you can still do a lot to improve your own emotional management and you can help others do the same. Try the simple techniques you've learned in this book, including identifying emotions, reducing hypersensitivity, and employing stress management.

EMOTIONAL REGULATION EXERCISES & ACTIVITIES

There are several breathing exercises which are perfect for emotional regulation. When you're breath counting, for instance, you're focusing on our breathing, as you would do when you meditate. Breath slowly and deeply.

Slightly different, breath shifting entail putting your hands on your abdomen and over your heart (one each at the same time). You'll be able to feel where your breath is by feeling it. Then shift your breathing downward, from the chest (where it's most likely to be) to your abdomen (where it could and should be).

Breath relaxation is ideal for reducing stress and anxiety and is great for emotional regulation. Not merely focusing on the breath, this practice focuses on the connection of body and mind and visualizes clarity being achieved with every breath. Good stuff.

EMOTIONAL CATHARSIS

We've discussed emotions as being like food; they're necessary for survival, they nourish our lives, but they have to be processed and the residual material ejected or it becomes toxic. One notable thing about EDD is the tendency to hold onto old emotions long past their time. Emotional catharsis allows a client or sufferer to vent suppressed emotions.

But you already have the necessary tools for an emotional catharsis as spelled out in this book. Observe emotions in the raw, unmodified, before you try to change them. Understand them, name them, know them for what they are. Then evaluate your experience and the associated feelings and emotions. Externalize your emotions from yourself. You'll always be yourself, but your emotions will come and go. Name your emotions, seek feedback.

BE MINDFUL OF EMOTIONS

We've already discussed being mindful, or living in the moment with deliberate awareness and gratitude. But there are two types of mindfulness exercises which will definitely help develop proper emotional regulation.

Acknowledgment exercises include observation of behavior and naming thoughts and emotions, as we've discussed. Implementation exercises emphasize non-judgmental thinking and active listening, effective communication and self-expression, and expressions of empathy.

There are also self-awareness techniques which can bring any person greater emotional management. Self-awareness is part and parcel of mindfulness and it's crucial to emotional management.

Every day, ask yourself how you're feeling at any given moment. Be aware of who or what caused it, how you responded. Keep a journal to track your patterns and your progress.

EMOTIONAL REGULATION THERAPY (ERT)

One self-awareness technique is known as *emotion regulation therapy*. This person-centered approach uses mindfulness and parts of DBT, CBT, and other humanitarian approaches to help individuals to identify, acknowledge, and then describe their emotions. It allows for the self-acceptance which results in emotional regulation.

Emotion regulation therapy entail cognitive therapies (thought over emotion) like reappraisal and labeling of emotions. Group therapy may also be effective.

AUTISM AND EMOTIONAL REGULATION

Autism Spectrum Disorders (ASD) is a group of neurodevelopmental conditions which disrupt emotional, social, and executive functionality. Lack of emotional regulation is a hallmark of ASD. Symptoms include communication impairment and impaired social interaction, aggressive or extreme behavior which recurs, low impulse control and poor judgement, involuntary movements and muscular inflexibility or other motor or sensory disturbances.

ASD is often tested with a rating system, listing, visualizing troublesome social factors which serve as triggers for anti-social behavior.

THE RADICAL ACCEPTANCE WORKSHEET

Psychologists often use the Radical Acceptance Worksheet in DBT interventions. It entails seven subjective questions to gage emotional control and reveal cognitive disruptions. It may prove helpful for you or someone you know! Answer these questions for yourself in the interest of self-awareness.

- Describe a single stressful situation. How did it occur and what affect did it have on you or others?
- Did that situation occur as a result of your behavior? How so? Be specific.
- Did others contribute, either positively or negatively, to the situation? How so? Be specific.
- Did you exhibit self-control as that situation unfolded? Be honest.
- How did you react? Did your behavior impact your emotion?
- Did your reaction have an effect on those around you? How so?
- Would you react the same way to a similar situation again?

THE EMOTION REGULATION WORKSHEET

Now try the questions on the *emotion regulation worksheet*. First, consider a circumstance or situation which was emotionally impactful for you. Now ask yourself:

- What caused the situation?
- What was your interpretation of the event?
- Were your emotions intense? Where would they fall on a scale of one to 100?
- Was your emotion impactful on others? How so?
- Were your emotions impactful on your behavior? How so?
- Was your judgement influenced by your emotions? How so?

We talked about the fight-or-flight response, generally a panic-oriented response to crises. This occurs in the parts of the brain called amygdalae, and there's one of each on each side of the brain. It's an instinctive, primitive part of the brain, where the survival instinct is generated.

The prefrontal cortex, on the other hand, handles logic, reason, along with other high-level functions. Albert Einstein's theory of relativity was generated in this part of the brain, for example.

But the prefrontal cortex doesn't operate as quickly as the amygdalae, and that's where, why, and how emotional reaction trumps intellectual response. Normally, this is fine; we have time to reason things out. But when emergencies or crises arise, there's little time for rational thought and emotional reaction kicks in. It's just the way our brains are wired.

But knowing this means anyone can thwart their natural instincts and deliberately pause to let their brain's cognitive powers kick in. It's the concept of relaxation and reflection we've been discussing, and you can see how it all ties in.

Luckily, you can control your brain as much as it controls you. And there are practical ways to do this!

- Identify problematic behavior
- Identify the emotions which precede that behavior
- Identify emotional triggers
- Become a witness to your own behavior
- Deliberately choose your responses instead of letting instinct dictate them.

THE PROCESS MODEL

The process model is the prevailing emotion regulation theory and it specifies a sequence of emotions include (in this order) a situation, attention, an appraisal, and a response. Every emotion is generated by a situation which commands attention. That attention stimulates an appraisal, and that appraisal initiates a response. For example, a racial remark is a situation which may command your attention, generate the appraisal that such a remark is unsuitable, and that may inspire a corrective response.

You can regulate your emotions at any point in the cycle. You can remove yourself from a situation. You can't unhear what you've heard, but you can divert your attention to something else. But you can change your appraisal by seeing things through another person's perspective and practicing empathy. You can consider your response and choose not to respond at all. Not every stimulus requires or even warrants a response.

True emotional regulation is achieved by accepting emotions as honest as reasonable and externalizing them from the person who has them. Anger is anger, jealousy is jealousy, but every individual who experiences those emotions is unique.

True emotional regulation often requires deliberate techniques and their applications, such as relaxation or other behavior changes. True emotional regulation requires impulse control.

OUTBURSTS ARE HAMPERING YOUR LIFE WITHOUT YOU EVEN KNOWING IT

Sometimes something temporary like lack of sleep or low blood sugar can cause an emotional outburst. More often, however, it's a chronic problem often called emotional liability. It's common to those with brain injury or other pre-existing conditions. They're common to sufferers of borderline personality disorder and other serious mental conditions such as adjustment disorder, oppositional defiant disorder, autism, and ADHD (attention deficit hyperactivity disorder).

The emotional outbursts generally feature fits of laughter or crying, sudden irritability, anger without any real cause, loud outbursts or fits of rage or temper.

Common causes of these emotional outbursts include stress.

What are the causes of being unable to control emotions?

These other disorders and conditions are also associated with emotional outbursts: alcohol abuse, antisocial personality, Asperger's syndrome, bipolar, diabetes, delirium, depression, psychosis, PTSD (post-traumatic stress disorder), schizophrenia.

In general, those who cannot control their emotions exhibit common symptoms. These include fearful of expressing emotions, being overwhelmed by emotion, unexplainable anger, misuse of drugs or alcohol.

The condition can become worthy of medical treatment when the suffer feels that life is no longer worth living, wants to hurt themselves or commits self-harm, hears voices or sees hallucinations, loses consciousness.

PSEUDOBULBAR AFFECT (PBA)

The pseudobulbar affect (PBA) affects people with brain injury or neurological conditions and is known for involuntary bouts of laughter, crying, or anger. It happens as the result of a disconnection between the frontal lobe, which controls emotion, and the cerebellum and brain stem. It can often happen as a result of Parkinson's disease, stroke, brain tumors, multiple sclerosis, and dementia.

Other serious symptoms signaling the need for medical attention include emotions without cause, frequent outbursts, difficulty expressing emotions and constant feelings of anger, sadness, or depression.

Treatments depend on the severity of the condition, but cognitive therapies are often effective. For low blood pressure, try glucose tablets, fruit juice, or candy.

Journal keeping is often helpful. Make an emotional journal and write down when and where you have these outbursts, who is around, what is the cause of the upset. This will help you isolate the causes and control the circumstances and avoid the triggers which help cause the outbursts.

EMOTIONAL INTELLIGENCE TEST

Here's a great applicable test to measure your EQ and show you where you can improve yourself right here and now! Pick one of the two possible answers.

1. My emotions generally have …

A1: little to no impact on my behavior.

A2: a strong impact on my behavior.

2. I'm usually guided by …

A1: my values, ethics, and goals.

A2: the values, ethics, and goals of others.

3. Under pressure, I often demonstrate ...

A1: different behaviors than normal.

A2: unchained behaviors.

4. I usually learn most ...

A1: by acting in the present.

A2: by thinking about the past.

5. I usually ...

A1: can laugh at myself.

A2: can't laugh at myself.

6. I usually present myself ...

A1: with power and presence.

A2: with cautious confidence.

7. Facing uncertainty, I'm often ...

A1: decisive and clear-headed.

A2: cautious of making the wrong decision.

8. I express opinions which ...

A1: might be unpopular, but they represent what I think is right.

A2: are popular and widely supported.

9. I generally like to ...

A1: face new challenges.

A2: keep things as they are.

10. I usually ...

A1: inspire confidence.

A2: look to others for confidence.

11. I usually ...

A1: let my moods and emotions influence my behavior.

A2: have control over my impulses and emotional eruptions.

12. Pressure generally ...

A1: causes me to get distracted.

A2: doesn't prevent me from thinking clearly and staying focused.

13. I always ...

A1: do what I say that I will.

A2: do what I must and nothing or little more.

14. The trust of others ...

A1: is usually just handed to me.

A2: has to be earned through honesty and integrity.

15. I am very often ...

A1: flexible in my view of things.

A2: fixed in my vision of events to see them as they are.

16. Facing challenges, I generally ...

A1: work harder and keep up.

A2: manage multiple demands with ease.

17. I always ...

A1: set challenging goals for myself and my team.

A2: achieve lesser goals with less effort.

18. Setback and obstacles generally make me ...

A1: change my expectations or goals.

A2: stay the course and hold my position.

19. Usually, I ...

A1: surpass expectations in achieving my goals.

A2: limit my pursuits to goals I can easily achieve.

20. In the face of opportunities, I am often ...

A1: uncertain about pursuing it.

A2: eager to pursue it.

21. Differences within a group are usually ...

A1: the cause of difficulty.

A2: valued and understood.

22. I consider bias and intolerance ...

A1: a chance to challenge those with the bias.

A2: a thing to ignore so I can get on with my life.

23. I like to help if it's best for ...

A1: completing an important task.

A2: helping others with their thoughts or feelings.

24. I always ...

A1: listen carefully.

A2: listen well enough and read facial cues or body language.

25. The perspectives of others are often ...

A1: clear and well-received.

A2: confusing and unproductive.

26. I typically find social networks ...

A1: a distraction.

A2: a helpful tool.

27. I like to ...

A1: give my customers whatever they ask for.

A2: understand my customer's needs and use my expertise to match the right products or services.

28. I usually …

A1: serve as an advisor.

A2: confirm the customer's opinions or tastes.

29. Customer loyalty and satisfaction …

A1: is central to my work ethic.

A2: is just a cliché and means little to nothing in the final analysis.

30. I always …

A1: inform people of my expectations.

A2: demonstrate the same behavior I expect.

31. I assign projects to workers who …

A1: can do the job well.

A2: will develop and grow with the challenge.

32. I win people over …

A1: with ease.

A2: with difficulty.

32. I always …

A1: follow the changes dictated by others.

A2: suggest changes of my own.

32. I handle difficult people …

A1: with diplomacy.

A2: with frankness.

34. I seek relationships which ...

A1: will help me.

A2: will help us both.

35. My focus is usually ...

A1: stronger on tasks.

A2: stronger on relationships.

Hope you did well. If not, don't fear, as you can always improve your skills and take the test again. That's why it's here, and why *you're* here. Now let's turn our cognitive abilities toward the subject of, well, cognitive abilities.

III

SECTION 3: COGNITIVE ABILITIES

OUR PARENTS HELPED US DEVELOP IT, WE'RE NOW OLD ENOUGH TO DEVELOP IT OURSELVES

We've looked at emotional intelligence, but being truly emotionally intelligent requires cognitive abilities, and being a true leader definitely does. Cognitive abilities occur in the brain; listening, attention, perception. Being attentive to them is crucial for your success.

Cognitive abilities are important in every facet of your life, particularly in the way you interact with others.

Cognitive abilities naturally occur, processing information, recognizing patterns and analyzing problems.

There are different types of cognitive ability. Knowing one from another will be invaluable to your ability to wisely use them all at the proper time and place.

Attention is the way in which you process current information. Paying close attention and retaining what you've learned is perhaps the central cognitive ability. It requires focus and has a direct effect on memory. If you don't absorb it, you won't remember it. On the other hand, the more you absorb, the more you'll retain.

Attention deficit is often a challenge especially in cases of attention deficit/hyperactivity disorder (ADHD). Otherwise, it may strike most people who are multi-tasking or stressed.

There are actually three kinds of attention. Sustained attention is used on a single task over long periods of time. It's central to accomplishing long-term goals. Selective attention is used when there are distractions which are ignored as a matter of discipline. Divided attention is common in this day and age. This is the methodology of the multi-tasker, though it's well-known to be less effective.

Another cognitive ability is memory, the ability to recall information which you have retained. There is short-term memory, things of lesser importance which happened recently, and long-term memory, more important memories from further in the past. Time can often affect the clarity of long-term memories.

Logic and reasoning are cognitive abilities related to problem assessment and solution finding. Memory looks backward, logic and reasoning look to the present and the future.

Auditory and visual processing is all about interpreting information like letters and symbols. It's a useful skill in visualizing goals and outcomes, or for following a map and doing mathematical equations.

Higher cognitive ability generally allows these things to be done quicker. In fact, the higher one's cognitive ability, the faster such mental tasks are generally achieved.

You may not think mathematical skills are as crucial as they once were, and you may be right. But cognitive processing skills may come up in other contexts. Job interviews may require you to assess a hypothetical situation, look ahead to an uncertain and unexpected circumstance, just as will happen in life. Often, you'll be presented with riddles and conundrums which require this cognitive skill set.

Understanding material is important for obvious reasons.

Recognizing patterns of events is central to cognitive ability and one of its most valuable results. If you can see patterns of events, you can predict what will happen. You already know some people may be triggers for others, and you know Mondays are more stressful at the office, so you'll be able to schedule your meetings or manage them accordingly. You'll also be able to gage career opportunities, pitfalls, any number of events others will miss and perhaps fall victim to.

To analyze problems and find options is one of the advanced cognitive abilities. Unexpected things will come up, and options will be necessary. Your job as true leader is to find them, and cognitive ability is the only way you're going to do it.

Brainstorming is hallmark cognitive ability. It's a creative exercise, and it's also often necessary to overcome unexpected obstacles. It's a team activity and good for exciting your team members. It encourages a healthy workplace climate.

Focused attention is key, as we've mentioned. Stay focused and your team will follow your example. This will also help you prioritize and that will make you and your team more efficient and therefor more productive.

IMPROVING YOUR COGNITIVE ABILITY

Like your emotional intelligence, your cognitive ability can be developed and improved. You may not be able to raise your IQ, you can improve your control of this skillset and increase your cognitive ability. Some will be familiar, and with good reason.

Physical activity improves hormone function, and that enhances memory, focus, and retention. It's also good for hand-eye co-ordination and motor skills.

New challenges keep the brain excited and active. Your cognitive ability is like a muscle, and it can atrophy if not worked regularly. New activities almost always include some small failures, which keeps one emotionally aligned not to overthink and to externalize failure from effort. New activities keep brains curious, focused, open to retaining new information, all pillars of cognitive and emotional intelligence.

Brain games are designed specifically to keep your cognitive abilities sharp. They use different abilities, they rely on visual and mathematical patterns, and they can be kind of fun. Just a few minutes a day can vastly improve anyone's cognitive abilities.

Getting enough sleep is crucial to sharpening cognitive abilities. That means less eating and drinking, no cigarettes. Sleep allows your brain to repair and refresh. It may require meditation for some, sleep aids for others.

Keep stress to a minimum in order to maximize cognitive skills. Stress is distractive and reduces focus and hampers attention, retention, and memory. Meditation is great for that.

MEMORY AND MEMORY LOSS

A little more about memory before we move on. We've talked about short-term and long-term memory, but let's look at this a bit more.

The three stages of memory production are:

- *Memory creation* (the result of attention)
- *Memory consolidation* (an organizing and prioritizing of memories)
- *Memory recall* (based on consolidation)

Memory loss can be caused by genetics or personal behavior. Whatever the cause, the brain does have the ability to change in certain ways in a process called *neuroplasticity*. This allows our brains to create new neural pathways to change certain existing connections. The short of it is that memory can be improved, and here's how. They'll be familiar and that's only natural.

Learning something new is the perfect way to improve memory because most things require memory. Languages, artistic skills, just about any new activity will require at least some short-term memory. Using it is the best way to keep from losing it.

Take time for quiet reflection, meditate. It clears away the distractions which challenge memory at just about every stage.

Use your senses in creating memories. The way things smell, touch, and taste makes a big impression on us, so relate events to sensory experiences of that event and this will imprint it on your memory with greater indelibility.

Associate new information with information you already know. One memory will piggie-back on the other.

Summarize what you need to remember from your own perspective. Make it your own and you'll have an easier time remembering it.

Reviewing information is a good way to imprint it on your memory too. Read it and then read it again, then again. Engrain it into your memory.

Mnemonic devices are a great way to increase your memory. Just associate one thing you don't know with something you do know, an exercise we've already visited. For example, if you've never come across the term mnemonic and can't remember it, you might think, *"Use mnemonic or be moronic,"* or something like that.

Seek out challenges, build on your skills, make sure this pursuit has its rewards. It will both inspire and reward your creative mind and stimulate your memory because you'll remember the reward.

Limit screen time to one hour at night. The artificial light isn't good for your sleeping patterns. If you have to read, read from a page with adequate room light. Avoid caffeine at night, as it interrupts healthy sleep patterns.

Relationships are important to brain health too. They encourage brain exercise, empathy, everything we've talked about in this book.

Avoiding stress is good for every part of your life, and your memory will improve for a variety of reasons once you've reduced stress in your life. Stress triggers forgetfulness, for example.

Some ways for managing stress in the workplace may include taking adequate breaks, setting boundaries and expectations, expressing thoughts and feelings, and avoiding multi-tasking.

APPLYING COGNITIVE SKILLS EVERYWHERE

As we've seen, all of these cognitive skills are applicable in every facet of your life. Let's take a look at some concrete examples.

Sustained attention, focusing on single tasks for long periods, is vital in the workplace. You'll use this in the workplace on single task after task, so this cognitive skill is invaluable. But you'll also need it at home, when dealing with long-term tasks like your child's education, home improvements, debt repayment. In social circles, sustained attention is useful in developing and maintaining enduring relationships.

Selective attention, which is trained to avoid distractions, is vital in the workplace, where distractions are everywhere. Every desk has a computer, and that means the internet, one of the greatest sources of distraction in history. There are also phone calls, emergencies, crises of various sorts. Office romances, either coming together or falling apart; the workplace demands selective attention like virtually nowhere else. But the home requires it too. You'll have to muddle through a slew of schoolyard gossip, little conflicts which come and go, and all the same media distractions you get at work. Socially, selective attention allows you to focus on the relationships that matter and ignore the things which don't; loud music, flashing lights, distractions of the social world.

Divided attention is necessary in the workplace, where several projects in different stages of development may need attention at the same time. At home, this can be the needs of a child or more than one, a spouse, perhaps the needs of siblings or the house itself. Electrical, plumbing, foundational issues and more can make homeowning a litany of complex and expensive distractions. You'll often have to keep track of one or more at once, and that's just the house. Throw in the needs of the people in the house and perhaps a few animals and you've got truly divided attention.

Long-term memory is central to the workplace. Lessons from old failures may come into play with new projects, clients from the past may return. At home, long-term memory will keep you from forgetting your wedding anniversary. Socially, long-term memory helps you engage more closely with your long-term friends. Your memories of their lives will be greatly appreciated.

Short-term (or working) memory is vital to organization at the workplace. Deadlines need to be kept in mind. The leader of a team has to have a working knowledge of what each team member is doing, and that requires short-term memory. But household organization is just as vital, and short-term memory will keep you from forgetting the date of your kid's school presentation, your dental appointment. Socially, short-term memory keeps you from missing a lunch date with a friend or the address or directions to the home of a new friend.

Logic and reasoning skills will help you on a daily basis in the workplace. Crises will arise which need quick resolution. Things which were planned can go awry and need to be rethought. A timetable may have to be recalculated due to an unexpected occurrence. At home, logic and reasoning are central to settling disputes (if you have kids, you'll know how valuable this is) and resolving unexpected crises. When somebody drives their car into your living room, you'll know what I mean. Socially, logic and reasoning skills will prevent you from hounding a person who may not be interested in you.

Auditory processing, like visual processing, occur in our lives all day, every day. Even when you're sleeping you may be processing auditory information. At work, this will include important information about ongoing projects, meeting schedules, and unimportant information like office gossip. At home you'll hear a lot of gossip too, but you'll also hear important information about the upkeep of the household and big events in the family's lives. In your social life, you'll hear even more gossip, and that's a good way to tell if you're socializing with the right people. With romances, you'll be hearing details about their lives and tastes and you'll want to remember those. That won't go unnoticed or unrewarded, I promise you.

Visual processing is a bit more interpretive and less direct, which makes proper processing skills even more important. At work, visual processing will be helpful during presentations, which are increasingly relied upon in the corporate world. You'll rely on it to read body language, which tells you a lot about your team, your supervisor, even yourself. While some people learn better from auditory sources and some absorb more from visual stimuli, in the workplace you have to be strong at both. At home, visual processing will tell you how your children are doing. Their body language will tell you if they're happy or stressed. This will be true for your spouse as well. There may be all kinds of visual cues to problems your spouse has never and may never mention. And saying that they never told you there was a problem will not get you off the hook. They shouldn't have had to mention it, and to a large degree they're right. You should have known. Social interaction is much the same. Pay attention to visual cues to ascertain your friends' moods or wellbeing.

Processing speed, which increases along with intelligence, will help you in the workplace by allowing you to solve problems faster and with superior results. This will naturally result in promotion and greater socialization. It will also create better results for the team, and that should create a healthier work climate. At home, decisive problem-solving prevents resentments or other negative feelings to build up among children or spouses. Socially, you'll be able to settle problems between your friends or between them and yourself should they arise. There will be times when quick thinking and measured action are required, perhaps to prevent a bar fight. Friendships can be complicated and may entail all manner of conflicting feelings and hidden resentments.

Cognitive abilities tests generally cover various topics; numerical, verbal, logic, and mechanical reasoning, and spatial awareness.

8

DEEPENING YOUR COGNITIVE ABILITIES

IT STARTS WITH YOUR BODY

We've briefly touched on the effects of diet and sleep on cognitive abilities, and it only makes sense. Garbage in, garbage out, as they say. But is it true that there are so-called *smart foods* which can actually make you smarter?

Strawberries, blackberries, and blueberries contain flavonoids and anthocyanins, powerful antioxidants which can boost your health overall and your brain health in particular. Studies have shown that they slow cognitive decline.

Dark chocolate has a flavanol also found in berries, tea, cocoa, and various fruits and is beneficial to cognitive processing speed.

Nuts are good for brain health overall, and walnuts are high in alpha-linolenic acid (ALA), an omega-3 fatty acid and linked to higher adult cognitive performances.

Broccoli and other cruciferous vegetables contain sulforaphane, which may protect the brain, and vitamin K. Vitamin K deficiency has been linked to Alzheimer's disease.

Concord grapes, available only for a brief season annually, there is concord grape juice readily available. These big, dark grapes have proven beneficial effects on memory function.

The brain is the body's most fatty organ, so it requires good, omega-3 fats found in salmon, trout, mackerel, sardines, herring, and tuna. Omega-3 deficiency has been associated with Alzheimer's Disease.

Eggs provide choline, essential for good metabolism and is associated with better cognitive test scores in controlled studies.

Seeds in general and pumpkin seeds in particular are great brain food due to the abundance of ALA omega-3's. Pumpkin seeds are high in zinc, vital for optimal brain functioning.

Extracts of the herb sage may have a positive effect on mood and memory, attention and even executive function.

Milk provides the nutrient choline, important for optimal brain health. It also has a big effect on brain development in infants. It may also protect against type 2 diabetes and insulin resistance.

Turmeric is all the rage these days, and for good reason. It's great for heartburn, gas, and other digestive issues. It's a great anti-inflammatory too.

Cocoa powder is also packed with flavonoids, particularly epicatechin, which appears to improve cognition and may also treat or even prevent diabetes.

Leafy, green kale has an abundance of the mineral called *manganese*, and also a ton of vitamins A, C, and K.

Beets are high in nitrates, which relax blood vessels and increase circulation, particularly to the brain.

Olive oil is central to the so-called *Mediterranean diet*. It's high in polyphenols, which have been proven to lower risk of Parkinson's and Alzheimer's diseases.

Bone broth is high in protein, which the brain needs to function at its best.

Beans are also high in protein, and ALA omega-3s too. Beans are also rich in carbohydrates, and those are turned into glucose which fuels the brain.

Tea may aid weight loss and help prevent cancer, and it has proven benefits for the brain. It's caffeine boosts energy while amino acid L-theanine helps the brain to relax. Green tea in particular is associated with reduced risk of some cognitive disorders.

Beef is rich in iron, which is central to good overall health, as it carries oxygen from the lungs to bodily tissues. Fatigue is a common sign of iron deficiency.

You may never have heard of yerba mate, but it's common in South America as a hot drink. It has 24 minerals and herbs, 15 different amino acids and a variety of polyphenols, plus theophylline and theobromine.

Whole-grain oats are easily converted to glucose, the brain's favored fuel source. Oats also offer B vitamins, magnesium, and iron. And they won't increase your blood sugar.

Lentils have a lot of folate, one of the B vitamins which is shown to increase cognitive performance in controlled studies. B vitamins decreases homocysteine, an amino acid. Excessive amino acids may reduce cognitive ability.

Flaxseeds high levels of ALA may have a strong impact on suffers of Alzheimer's Disease. Ground flaxseed is often sprinkled over a salad, over cold or hot cereal, or blended into a smoothie.

And there are foods and supplements which are proven to reduce stress and anxiety.

A member of the mint family, lemon balm has been studied for anti-anxiety effects. Omega-3 fatty acids reduced anxiety symptoms by 20% in one study. The herb ashwagandha has likewise been proven effective in reducing stress and anxiety symptoms.

The antioxidants found in green tea increase serotonin levels to lower anxiety and stress. The root called valerian contains valerianic acid, which is a powerful sleep aid and alters the GABA (gamma-aminobutyric acid) receptors. This lowers anxiety.

A member of the pepper family, kava kava is used in the South Pacific to treat mild stress and anxiety.

HAVE YOU BEEN STRESSED LATELY? YOU MUST LEARN HOW TO REDUCE IT

We've looked at stress and its effects on the body and the brain. Stress causes inflammation, poor sleeping and eating habits, substance abuse, ensuing weight gain and ill-health, depression, premature death by stroke or heart disease and suicide.

And we've looked at ways to reduce stress, including meditation. Let's take a closer look at good ways to relieve stress.

Exercise, better sleep habits, better nutrition, avoidance of substance abuse, mindful awareness, adapting a growth mindset, time management; all are critical for a more stress-free life. Clearer communications with others will always reduce or may even prevent stress and anxiety.

Meditation is a popular way to relieve stress, and though we've touched on it briefly, a closer look is probably a good idea here.

When you meditate, you sit quietly and still and focus on just one thing. It might be your breath, the steady in-and-out pattern of inhaling and exhaling deeply and slowly. You might focus on a single focal point or on a repeated phrase or mantra. But there's a lot more to it, as there are lots of ways to meditate.

First, meditation can be grouped into two categories. Calming (*samatha*) meditation cultivates a quiet, peaceful state in the manner I just described, by focusing on breathing or a focal point or a mantra.

Insight (*vipassana*) meditation, on the other hand, develops qualities of character such as wisdom and compassion by focusing on the effects of the breath on the body rather than on the breathing itself. You may start with calming meditation and go on to insight meditation later and them combine the two.

There are eight core techniques from Tibetan and Burmese Buddhist traditions. They combine of both insight and calming meditations.

We've already touched on focused attention, which directs the focus on breath, a focal point, or a mantra. If your mind wanders, return it to whatever you're focusing on.

Body scan meditation directs the attention to the body, starting at the bottom and concentrating on each part of the body and how it feels.

Noting is the practice of being aware of both distractions and recentering focus during meditation. It's a kind of focused awareness of these shifts, how they are caused and then controlled. Use this technique in combination with other techniques when you're ready.

Visualization entails conjuring an image in your mind and focusing on that. It may be a visualization of something or someone you desire, the manifestation of a long-term goal like a home of your own.

Loving kindness meditation focuses specifically on people, even on some we don't like. This technique focuses on directing positive energy toward someone who may be a source of negative energy.

The technique of skillful compassion entails putting the focus on a person you love and then focusing on the effects, the way that positive energy affects your body, comparable to facets of body scan meditation.

With the technique of resting awareness, the mind truly rests. It's an advanced technique, built upon a working knowledge of the other techniques we've looked at.

The reflection technique entails asking a question during meditation, such as, *"How can you help others,"* or, *"What things do you have to be grateful for?"* invites you to ask yourself a question: perhaps something such as, "What are you most grateful for?" Be mindful to use you and not I, or you'll be tempted to answer. The reflection technique focuses on the question.

Transcendental meditation focuses on a greater power, whatever your notion of God or a higher power may be.

Those are all self-monitored techniques, but some of the following techniques require a qualified master.

- Yoga meditation often uses Kundalini yoga among other types of yoga and is most effective in a class.
- Chakra meditation focuses on the body's core centers of energy or chakras to keep them open and aligned, remedying various mental and physical symptoms.
- Comparably, the Chinese practice of Qigong meditation harnesses energy by keeping pathways called *meridians* open and aligned.

- Sound bath meditation uses instruments like gongs and bowls to create calming sound vibrations.

BRAIN EXERCISES ARE NOT ONLY FUN, BUT THEY'RE ALSO GOOD FOR YOU

Remember that your mind is like a muscle and it has to be kept in shape. These exercises will go a long way to making your mind stronger, your brain more efficient, and your life better.

Besides the specific tactics you'll learn here are the most common methods of exciting the brain. Board games, new activities, new languages; these are time-tested ways to improve your cognitive powers. Other than that, here are some specific ways you can increase your cognitive abilities.

Here's one great trick to sharpening your memory and increasing your brainpower. Try to draw a map of your neighborhood entirely from memory. Fill in as many of the street names as you can. You won't get all of them, of course, as the likelihood of your knowing every street in your neighborhood is pretty slim. But you will know some of them, the streets around your house and workplace. It's the exercise that counts, not the results.

Are you righthanded? Try favoring your left hand. If you're a lefty, try living as a righty for a full day. Be deliberate about it. Open doors with the other hand, scratch yourself and sign a credit card receipt with the hand you don't normally use. This challenges your brain and your motor-control skills and keeps both sharp.

Test your recall by making lists from memory. Write down what you bought at the supermarket, what exercises you did at the gym and in what order. You might get more specific if you're ready to challenge yourself. Because your task is to memorize that list. Now tend to that task. Memorize as much as you can. You won't remember it all, but remember that it's the exercise that counts, not the results.

Engage in the practice of doing mathematical equations. It's a powerful technique for a variety of purposes, including erectile stamina (you fellas know what I mean). But just the process of running mathematical equations stimulates the brain and keeps it agile.

Here's a fun and challenging mathematical challenge. Pick any 3-digit number then add 3 to that digit three different times. Then subtract 7 from that new number 7 times. For example, you may start with 100. Then add 3 to that three separate times, for a total of 109. Now subtract 7 from that number, and do that seven times. It reduces 109 to 102, then 95 and so on. Remember that you're not filing your taxes, so the results don't matter. It's the exercise that counts.

Create a word picture. You may be thinking of a vision board, which includes pictures of the things you hope to achieve. With this exercise, you simply visualize a word, then think of other words that begin or end with the same letters. *Clouds* may become *cowards* and *sensations*. The results may surprise you.

Try eating new foods. The same old foods put your body into a rut. But new flavors excite your body and your mind. Remember that culinary is one of the arts, and arts stimulate the brain. The culinary arts are unique, as they bring a kind of nourishment and satisfaction that other arts just can't, not even mixology.

Try mixology. There is a lot of data behind the soft science of cocktail creation. Memory and processing are vital, and there's instant satisfaction to your efforts. Those may actually inhibit your memory later, but nothing's free, right?

Hobbies like drawing, knitting, painting, or puzzles are a great way to keep the mind sharp and even increase cognitive skills. A new sport or physical activity will have the same effect, as we've discussed. Fencing is a good choice, or the martial arts. Both are rooted in philosophy and rules of engagement which may overlap into various other facets of your life. Yoga and meditation are popular and beneficial in any number of ways.

Try showering with your eyes closed. You'll be using your tactile senses of touch to feel the shampoo and soaps and the like. Your memory of the shower will guide your hand to the controls. But be careful with this exercise. Be cautious of slippage or of setting the water temperature!

Change your routine. Feel free to create new routines if you need them to get along, and a lot of people do. But change things up. Variety will keep your mind engaged even in the simplest tasks.

Turn things upside down. No, I don't mean that figuratively. You're used to seeing things a certain way, and this can create mental lethargy. Do you have an alarm clock? Turn it upside down literally. Your brain will be able to understand what numbers it's really looking at, and putting it through that exercise will only strengthen your cognitive ability. Is there a vase on the dining room table, flip it over. It may not seem like a lot, but do it enough and your eye and then your brain will be drawn to it.

Switch seats at the table. If it's a conference room table or the dinner table or even a seat in a classroom, we tend to find a spot and stick to it. But switching things around helps you to see things from a different perspective, from another person's perspective, and that strengthens empathy and a number of other cornerstones of emotional intelligence.

Aroma therapy is a powerful technique. The olfactory senses are closest to the brain and therefore, have the most powerful effects. If you doubt that, consider this; do you remember what your childhood living room smelled like? Your father's cigar tobacco or your mother's favored cleaning products? Think of the smell of bacon. 'Nough said.

Drive with the window down. Well, in this case you'd be better served to be the passenger, but it works while you're driving too. This is a powerful exercise because the hippocampus, which is the area of the brain which processes memories, is also associated with sounds, odors, sights. So, take a drive and try to identify the smells you pass; freshly cut grass, a fish cannery, a chicken ranch. Savor and be grateful and experience those smells, bad or good.

Try this; fill a cup full of change. Then swish the change around in the cup and try to imagine the value of the change. Concentrate on the weight, the sound, the sensory input. Try to guess the value. Again, you may not succeed, but it's not a midway game, it's a brain exercise and it should have terrific benefits.

Read aloud. It may sound silly and childish, but it's really not as easy as it sounds. Literate and intelligent people find it hard to read aloud. The sound of one's voice is distracting, the impression it may make causes insecurity, and the twin chores of reading and speaking can be surprisingly challenging. Try it right now by reading this paragraph. Go ahead, I'll wait. Now, did it sound the same as when you were reading it silently? When it does, your cognitive abilities will have been improved!

Make a list of random words, then see if you can remember them. Make sure they're random; waistcoat, sucker punch, burning man, cucumber. The longer the list, the more challenging and the better your performance and the better your benefits.

Imagine a crossword puzzle. It's a series of squares, some in lines and others up against one another. Not count the squares, but not just the individual squares; include the squares created by four or more squares in a cluster. How many squares are there?

Here's one for the left brain. Take the word WALL and change one letter at a time until you get to the word FIRM. The trick is that every change has to create an actual word. For example, you can change WALL into WILL, then WILL into FILL. Once you've completed this challenge, try it again with the same word and a different word. Turning FIRM back into WALL won't be much of a challenge. Turn FIRM into COAT instead. It can be done. Do it. Then pick other four-word or even five-word challenges. Keep doing it, make it a hobby.

Try this: Arrange three toothpicks into the letter nine. Don't bend or break any of them. Can you do it? Hey, it's not supposed to be easy, it's supposed to be a challenge!

Here's a powerful technique: Write a cluster of letters and numbers on a piece of paper, but allow significant space between them. Start at 1 and draw a line to the nearest letter A. Proceed from there to the number 2 and draw a line from there to the letter B. B leads you to 3 which leads you to C, and so forth.

You might try this exercise: Look at the words below and rearrange the letters of each to create words for common colors. Only one of them is a primary color.

- ENOLYL
- RAIGET
- LEWRE
- OVGOEN

What did you come up with? Keep trying, or observe your results.

The proverb experiment is always challenging and helpful. Below is a proverb with all the vowels removed. Just insert the right vowels to complete the proverb. It's like *Wheel of Fortune* in your own home, and your prize is greater cognitive strength.

- TWH
- DSRB
- TTRT
- HNN

Hey, it's not supposed to be easy!

Here's another fun word scramble challenge. How many words can you create from these letters? OGEUNRY

Here's a riddle to excite your mind and keep your cognitive skills alive:

Frank has eccentric tastes; a fan of football but not of rugby; he loves beer but he hates ale; Frank drives a Ferrari though he won't drive a Lamborghini. Keeping these things in mind, is finicky Frank more likely to prefer cycling or skiing?

Try eating with chopsticks. It involves motor control and creates instant gratification.

Now that we've looked into some practical, applicable ways to boost our emotional and cognitive skills, let's take a closer look at crucial thinking; it's central to both and key to your success as a true leader.

IV

DEVELOP YOUR CRITICAL THINKING SKILLS AND USE THEM

WHY CRITICAL THINKING SKILLS?

Critical thinking emphasizes analysis and interpretation. Roughly put, it's not the facts which truly matter, but their evaluation. It's a disciplined process of conceptualizing, analyzing, applying, synthesizing, and evaluating information. This information is generated by or gathered from experience, observation, reasoning, reflection, and communication.

Put more simply, critical thinking allows you to understand things more clearly and make wiser choices or beliefs.

Critical thinking isn't everyday thinking, which is often automatic. Critical thinking is deliberate. Without critical thinking, a person may fall into bad mental habits such as the ones described below.

Ignorant certainty, for example, is the certainty that every question has a single correct answer. But this is often not the case in day-to-day life. This is a fixed mindset where a growth mindset would better serve everyone involved, the thinker in particular.

Naive relativism is like the flipside of ignorant certainty, the belief that all arguments are equal and that there is no single truth or right answer to any question.

But with adequate critical thinking, one may enjoy several distinct benefits.

Critical thinking allows the formation of opinions and having intelligent conversations. It's crucial for self-evaluation. It's critical for decision-making and exploitation avoidance in every facet of your life.

Those who think critically tend to comprehend the connections between ideas, prioritize ideas and arguments, manage arguments, recognize errors of reasoning, handle problems in a systematic and consistent manner, and reflect on their own assumptions, values, and beliefs.

CRITICAL THINKING SKILLS

Those who have these sharp critical thinking skills are well-prepared to deal with almost any critical thinking challenge. Ask yourself if these aren't areas that you could improve in your own critical thinking.

Critical thinkers gather Information. Do you, or do you just wing it? Critical thinkers are observant, they pay attention to the smallest details. Do you, or do you not gloss over the little stuff? There's a lot of information out there, so don't feel badly if you miss small things, then develop that part of your critical thinking.

Critical thinkers infer, use reason and logic for creative problem-solving. They can rationalize, or apply reason to a situation. Reason generally includes either induction (direct information), deduction (indirect information leading to a conclusion), or analogy (using comparisons and previous experience).

They reflect to recalibrate their perspective and make relaxed decisions. They create even if they're not artistically creative. Critical thinkers create solutions, new approaches, insightful analyses. Do you reflect and let that feed your creativity? Or is it always pedal-to-the-medal.

Critical thinking requires organization enough to classify and sequence, or to group and order ideas or items according to shared characteristics. They compare and contrast to similar situations or circumstances. Are you as quick to organize and compartmentalize? Do you keep past lessons or information in mind?

Critical thinkers consider cause and effect and utilize foresight. Do you, or do you just hope it works out?

Critical thinkers synthesize different approaches and ideas to form new ones. Do you, or do you not just apply the usual remedies? Critical thinkers also brainstorm. Do you, or do you not just go with the first idea that pops into your head. A lot of people will say the first idea is probably the best idea and cite overthinking as a reason to go with the gut. Do you? Remember, think for yourself.

Critical thinkers prioritize to keep crises in perspective. Do you, or is every crisis the end of the world? Drama is not part of critical thinking.

Critical thinkers also summarize to ensure a thorough understanding of the event or situation. Do you keep records of these events, journals? Maybe you should.

These skills work great in combination too, like most of what we're discussing in this book. There's a lot of overlap, and something learned in one field of study connects to another.

We mentioned a critical thinking cycle before, let's take a closer look at that. The stages usually occur in order, one following the other. The cycle begins with observation of information or notes experimental results.

Observation is followed by feeling, an intellectual reaction to the new input. This leads to wondering, plumbing the causes or processes of an event. People wonder about who, what, where, when, why, and how, among other things.

Imagining follows wondering, turning wondering away from the past (the circumstances of the cause) toward the future.

Inference follows imagining and visualizes results. Also looking to the future, imagining adds to wondering the question *What if?*

Knowledge is (hopefully) the result of imagining and inference. Knowledge comes from research into previous data to answer the question *What if?*

Experimenting follows knowledge and represents the application of the knowledge attained.

Consulting on the results of the experiment follows and is crucial to the critical thinking cycle.

Consultations may lead to analyzing and identifying arguments, when consultations may be challenged or alternatives considered. Question and understand the source of the arguments and their purpose in every case.

In the judging stage of the critical thinking cycle, one makes a judgment based on the analysis of the arguments.

The final stage is deciding, wherein a choice is made and a plan of action set about to move forward.

SEVEN WAYS TO THINK CRITICALLY

Here are seven ways you can think more critically, starting right here and now!

In our increasingly complex world, don't be afraid to ask basic questions. The basics are easy to lose track of and it's vital to always have them in the back of your mind. Remember that there are no stupid questions.

You may also try to question some basic assumptions. It's like asking basic questions, but of yourself and your perspective.

Be mindful of what your common mental processes are. Try to avoid the common mental shortcuts a lot of us take and really focus on what you're thinking, when and why. You might want to keep a thought journal to illustrate the patterns in your mental processes. You might have biases and prejudices which are more glaring in an objective light.

Reversing things is a great way to think critically. De-engineer a problem if you have to, or read something from the bottom up to scan for errors. It challenges the mind and prevents lazy mental shortcuts.

Evaluating existing evidence is a good way to think critically. Learn from previous instances, previous mistakes. Know the data which has already been collected. When you do, question that evidence in terms of who gathered it, how they did that, and why they did it.

Think for yourself, always. Research will guide you, but your efforts may advance that collected knowledge.

Accepting fallibility is another way to think critically. Nobody functions at maximum capacity all the time, not even you. Make allowances for this with yourself and others.

Critical thinking and decision making often go hand-in-hand. There are elements of decision-making which go hand-in-hand with critical thinking. Both entail logic, (a direct or indirect connection of causes and events), truth (unbiased data), context (external factors and pressures), and alternatives (potential solutions).

THINKING CRITICALLY IN YOUR PROFESSIONAL & PERSONAL LIFE

Critical thinking in the workplace and the home takes many forms and can improve your career in a number of ways.

Critical thinking brings you to clear goal setting, knowing what you want and how to make it happen. This includes knowing what your team members are capable of and what they're willing to do. This is as true when working on a project like an ad campaign or getting your family through the annual summer season when the kids are off school. If you want the ad campaign done on time, what will be required? To keep the kids active and the house quiet, what should you do?

Foresight is central to critical thinking, and it's often required in the workplace. What if moving a project to a different location would be helpful because the location is more optimal, but the move would sacrifice some of your best team members. Is there some compromise or alternative? It's the same when planning family events or seasons. What if one child is miserable at summer camp? What if one sibling becomes jealous of the birthday gifts given to another? Looking ahead to possible outcomes, or foresight, will lead you to the answer.

Conferring with a mentor is a great way to think critically in the workplace. They should be an authority in your area of specialty and experience which you may lack. This is a prime application of critical thinking and will also strengthen your relationship. For domestic matters, mentorship can be a powerful tool too. Friends who had children before you or have been married longer will have invaluable insights to share.

Team-building games and exercises are a great way to improve a team's ability to think critically. It's helpful for the leader as well, as it gives them a chance to think critically and analyze the team's overall executive functionality and that of its members. Games and exercises are great for the family too, and for the same reasons. You'll also create a healthier climate in both arenas.

CRITICAL THINKING SKILLS WILL REVOLUTIONIZE YOUR DECISION-MAKING ABILITIES WITHIN DAYS...

Critical thinking means asking questions, but that can be an art unto itself. Foresight is required, as are curiosity, noting, mindfulness, a lot of the skills you've already acquired from this book. Here are a few more relating in particular to critical questioning. You'll be asking *who, what, were, when, why, how,* and *what if,* among other things.

Consider these points when you formulate critical questions.

- Good questions are designed with the intent of soliciting specific information. So, it should be stated clearly, concisely, and with direct meaning. Vagueness or subtext should be strictly avoided in critical questioning.
- Frame your questions properly. Put it in the right context, make sure they're not just declarations with question marks.
- Try using open-ended questions *("How does that make you*

feel?") instead of closed-ended questions that will likely end with a *yes* or *no* (*"Do you feel good?"*).
- Use follow-up questions and keep them open-ended too.
- When you're asking these questions, make sure they're the right questions. To know this, answer a few for yourself first and make sure of a few key points.
- Make sure your purpose is clear, as we said, be specific in order to get the proper specific response. Instead of asking *if*, ask *when*. Instead of when, suggest a time and place and have a backup ready.
- Specific questions have specific purposes; definition (*"What does working hard mean to you?"*), comparative (*"How do we excel?"*), causal (*"If we make this move, what are the benefits and drawbacks?"*) and evaluative (*"What's working and what isn't?"*).

PROBLEM-SOLVING MODELS

There are various problem-solving models, each with their own specific construct. Let's take a closer look at some of the most effectual.

The simple *6-Step Problem Solving* includes these easy-to-understand problem-solving steps:

Objective-finding to identify the problem and begin finding the solution. Fact-finding collects data, problem-finding analyzes the data, idea-finding brainstorms based on the problem and the data. Solution-finding settles on a new plan of action, and acceptance-finding moves on from that solution.

Additionally, these six come in three phases of problem solving. These are exploring the challenge (Objective- and fact-finding), generating ideas (problem- and idea-finding) and preparing for action (solution- and accepting finding).

The Yale version of the Soft Stage Management model (SSM), uses six steps of action for problem solving, once again in order (most of these models observe an order to the steps or stages).

First one defines the problem, then determines the root cause, then develops alternative solutions, selects one of those and implements it, then evaluates the outcome.

Large group decisions, long-term restructuring, and comparative decision-making benefit from this model.

The political economic social technological model (PEST) is widely used for decision-making and includes, as you might have guessed, consideration of political, economic, social, and technological influences on any decision-making. It's a powerful tool for evaluating markets or strategies or managing large-scale change.

A SWOT model analysis includes focus on strengths, weaknesses, opportunities, and threats. It's effective for identifying toxic or faulty processes or behaviors fast and it's beneficial to brainstorming and strategy building, as well as gathering and organizing information.

As one of the first systematic techniques for observing organizations' weaknesses, the Failure Mode and Effects Analysis (FMEA) system often is used as a diagnostic tool for companies and other large groups. FMEA analyzes the elements of failure and its effects in order to correct them in the present and prevent them in the future. It's widely used in manufacturing and assembly lines. Henry Ford was an early proponent!

Another anagram-based model is the CATWOE defines six areas where soft system problems arise. They include clients, actors, transformation, worldview, owner, and environment and focuses the discussion of those items in regard to potential actions. It's effective for identifying problems, implementing solutions, as well as organizing and then aligning various goals.

A cause and effect analysis, known as *Fishbone* or *Ishikawa diagrams,* takes four steps into account when assessing a single effect to find potential causes. The four steps include identifying a problem, working out which are the involved factors, identifying potential causes, and analyzing a diagram to get ready for action. Categorization and compartmentalization are key to discover proper causes and to understand their effects.

If you're in manufacturing, you might use the six M model (which includes method, material, man power, measurement, mother nature). Those in the service industry often use the five S model (which includes surroundings, suppliers, systems, skills, safety).

CRITICAL THINKING TEST

Try this critical thinking test and see if you can shore up your critical thinking skills! The answers are included in a second set just below the questions:

1) You have two jugs, one an eight-gallon and the other a three-gallon jug, both unmarked. You need precisely four gallons of water. Assuming there's a nearby faucet, how do you get the water?

2) What amount can be added to 1,000,000 such that the sum will be higher than if you multiplied it by the same amount?

3) Find the two one-word answers to this riddle:

The floor of a boat or ship,

you walk on me when at sea;

Make the C an S,

At school, you may sit on me.

I am which two things?

4) A man tells the press he's quitting his job due to, "Illness and fatigue." It's neither precisely a lie nor the truth. Why did he quit his job?

5) Find the two one-word answers to this riddle.

A pseudonym for sick,

The forehead is hot;

Insert an H in the front,

Still, a mountain, I'm surely not.

I am which two things?

6) Solve this riddle:

A goose, a duck, a horse, and a goat walk into a barn at different times. The first is a mammal. The duck precedes the goose and the goose preceded the horse. Which entered first?

7) A woman goes to bed one summer night and woke up in the middle of winter. How can this be so?

Here are the answers:

1) Fill the three-gallon container three times, dumping each load into the eight-gallon container. On the third time, there will be one gallon left in the three-gallon container. Empty the eight-gallon container and pour the single gallon from the smaller container into the larger. Then fill the three-gallon container, add it to the single gallon in the larger container, for a sum total of four gallons.

2) zero, or any negative or fraction less than one.

3) Deck and desk

4) The coach of a professional ball team, he was "sick and tired" of his team's weak performances.

5) Ill and hill.

6) the first to enter was the goat.

7) She was on a ship which passed the equator line while she was sleeping.

How'd you do? Some were easier than others, right?

Now let's take a look at social skills, at the heart of both critical thinking and emotional intelligence.

V

BUILDING BETTER RELATIONSHIPS, THRIVING IN YOUR CHOSEN PATH, & BECOMING THE BEST LEADER THAT YOU CAN BE

10

SOCIAL SKILLS

We use social skills to interact and communicate, verbally and also non-verbally utilizing body language, gestures, and personal appearance. We're social creatures, after all, so social communication is not only natural but necessary.

When we speak, body language and tone of voice has great effect on how that message comes across Knowing this and managing it properly is at the heart of social skills.

But as it is with all skillsets, such as leadership skills, emotional intelligence, and cognitive ability, social skills can be learned and improved. So, if you feel your social skills need work, let's get to it. There's not a moment to spare.

Advantages to sharper social skills include better relations and more of them, better communications in business and other aspects of your personal life, greater efficiency, better career opportunities and projects, increased happiness overall.

Social skills share a certain set of characteristics. For example, social skills are basically goal-directed. They are usually appropriate to the circumstance, and different social skills are best used in different social situations.

Greater social skills are invaluable in your career. A lot of networking takes place outside of the office, after all. Conferences, lunch meetings, dinners, they all skirt the line between work and social arenas. Some career benefits to stronger social skills include gathering ideas, techniques, information, and perspectives, freely providing perspective, collaborating with others and accomplishing shared goals, providing mutual support, expanding your network, and gaining honest feedback.

In the office, better social skills will also encourage interactivity, creativity, efficiency, and a healthier work climate. And since the workplace is such a communication-heavy environment, with phone calls and emails and meetings and other things, social skills are all the more important.

In addition to the aforementioned effective communication skills, good social skills in the workplace will aid with conflict resolution between team members (or even between you and a team member) and thereby encourage active listening, which is key to conflict resolution. Your good example of social skills will lead your team to adopt the same.

Empathy, another familiar concept to us from previous information in this book, and it's central to any set of social skills. Without it, there can be few real connections in either social, professional, or familial areas of your life. It's as potent in the workplace as anywhere else.

Social skills are strengthened by and also strengthen relationship management, a way to organize the various relationships in your life, and a lot of them may not be yours but between your team members, at home between your children. Still, your social skills will be key to managing those relationships.

Social skills both provide and engender respect, and this is crucial when you're a true leader in the workplace or at home or out with the gang.

The ways to improve your social skills are comparable to the remedies to emotional ignorance or lack of true leadership, which probably won't surprise you. They include getting feedback and mentorship, setting goals and encouraging others to share your commitment, identifying resources and areas for improvement or practice.

Body language is especially potent in the workplace. The way you carry yourself will influence how others carry themselves. Slouching and slumping, pointing and yelling, snarling and looking around with shifting eyes and a dubious manner will have corrosive effects. It tells people more about you than anything you could say.

THE CONSEQUENCE OF LACKING SOCIAL SKILLS

To lack social skills is, frankly, to be awkward. Awkwardness is defined roughly as a sort of feeling of social embarrassment, or it's a situation which is not relaxed but difficult. People who are awkward don't know how to communicate clearly, they're withdrawn and generally are not true leaders. They often lack emotional intelligence, about themselves or others. Are you socially awkward? If you are, there are ways to escape it. Let's take a closer look to the betterment of your life in every way, shape, or form. Those who are or feel awkward often feel out of place in almost any situation.

Signs that you may be socially awkward include being avoided by people in social settings and you avoid others in the same way. Dates go poorly and intimate relationships end fairly quickly. Social circles are small and they have an oversized effect on your self-esteem. Overthinking and worry about others' opinions are common. Being called weird may be common, and hurtful.

Reasons for awkwardness may include childhood influences. An overly aggressive parent or sibling may be the cause, or introverted parents who set the example and were awkward themselves. Poverty may engender adulthood insecurity, or a pattern of romantic rejection. Children who grew up in the last ten years may have spent too much time online, and lacking in personal interaction contributes to their insecurity and awkwardness.

Mental or behavioral disorders may also be to blame. ADHD, various complexes, and autism spectrum disorder are common causes of social awkwardness, as are substance abuse and depression. An outsized admiration for someone can cause it too. Who might not be a little awkward meeting their hero?

But you can correct social awkwardness! You might try developing your confidence, but how do you do that? Well, you can use a lot of techniques we recommend in this and other books. Use the Pomodoro Method to break big tasks down into little tasks with manageable milestones. Try new things to stimulate your brain.

Keep in mind that different situations require different behaviors and be flexible, if you can. Being awkward on a date may come down to simply not knowing what's appropriate. These days, it's hard for almost anyone to tell! Do some research, gather your data and decide on a plan of action.

Accountability has its place too. Those who are awkward often feel that they're more accountable than they are, they can't forgive themselves. They're often of a fixed mindset which tells them they can't change, that they're doomed to lives of isolation.

HABITS THAT WILL IMPROVE NOT ONLY YOUR SOCIAL SKILLS BUT YOUR CURRENT RELATIONSHIPS AS WELL

You have to be mindful of your behavior if you're to improve your social skills, as with any other skill set. Here are some concrete ways you can do just that, and in virtually no time.

We've already talked about being an active listener, so you shouldn't be surprised to see it pop here. Active listening is a potent social skill, to be sure. It gives the other person reason to open up, creates stronger, trust-based bonds, and familiarity will defeat the nervousness of the unknown which contributes to awkwardness.

Some people do better one-on-one, others thrive in a big crowd. Perhaps counterintuitively, those who are awkward are often more comfortable in a crowd, where they can feel lost and invisible. Others are intimidated by big crowds and aren't sure how to react.

Avoid negativity and complaining, two big factors to creating an awkward situation even if you don't consider yourself personally awkward. It's a drag anyway, so stop it.

Remembering people's names not only reduces awkwardness, but forgetting their names creates incredible awkwardness all on its own. Use a mnemonic device to imprint the name in your brain. It's such an impressive and rare skill, anybody would be impressed. It demonstrates focus, active listening, empathy, all hallmarks of cognitive ability, emotional intelligence, and true leadership. Likewise, remember their stories. It will make an even bigger and better impression for all the same reasons.

Resist the urge to talk too much. Don't mind the lull and feel you have to constantly keep a conversation going. It's a sure sign of insecurity, and that is a chief generator of social awkwardness. Let the conversation recharge, there's nothing wrong with that. Maybe the other person will start blathering, and their social awkwardness will make you seem all the more cool and collected.

Following up is a good way to defeat awkwardness. It's often uncomfortable to see someone you never called back, and not knowing their disposition only increases nervousness and awkwardness.

Always know when to make an exit. Don't linger. It's a sign of insecurity. And the more you talk, the greater a chance you'll say the wrong thing and stumble into an awkwardness sand trap which you may not be able to dig yourself out of. You can't really have that much to say anyway. Observe the old showbiz adage and leave 'em wanting more.

Love is the greatest social skill, so show it. Whatever you love, share that. It will give you strength, reasserting and reenforcing your sense of self. It's also a great way to open up, and familiarity defeats awkwardness.

YOUR FACIAL EXPRESSIONS SPEAK FOR YOU

Find your so-called *resting face*. It's not easy, because we're all trained to put on a brave face, to change our behavior, even this article recommends mindful smiling. But you should make efforts to be comfortable behind your own face without smiling, without frowning, without any emotion at all. There will be times when you're not emotional, after all. What do you look like then? Whatever it is, the more comfortable you are with it, the more comfortable you'll be with yourself and others. Teeth-grinding and/or jaw-clenching (called *bruxism*) wrinkles, and other dangerous or unflattering results are likely otherwise.

Research by the National Institute of Dental and Craniofacial Research indicates that over 10 million Americans suffer from TMJ syndrome, or temporomandibular joint dysfunction syndrome. Practice various muscle relaxation techniques, meditate, and be mindful of your body language.

Make eye contact more often, but don't be aggressive about it. Do it until it feels good, then don't be afraid to back off a bit. That will draw their eye contact to you to reconnect, and set the intimate example. Cultural differences will affect eye contact, naturally, as some cultures find it disrespectful and a challenge to authority.

Smiling more often is proven to have beneficial effects on a person's overall outlook. The act itself is associated with dopamine and serotonin, a mood-stabilizing hormone. It's also a proven phone sales and tech support line technique, as the shape of your mouth affects the tone of the voice. You'll also be creating a healthier social climate, and that will alleviate stress and reduce awkwardness.

Be mindful of hand gestures and gesticulation. It can open you up and relax you, but some hand movements, such as tucking hands into pockets or wringing your fingers, are sure signs of insecurity and awkwardness.

Remember that a firm handshake not only engenders respect but it generates confidence. Keep a paper towel in your pocket if you've got clammy palms.

SOCIAL SKILLS & CHARISMA ARE THE KEYS TO BEING SEEN AS MORE THAN JUST THE 'BOSS' OR 'MANAGER' BY THOSE YOU LEAD

Charisma might be thought of as the opposite of awkwardness. It's a certain charm, an attractiveness. People with charisma have an influence over those around them. They're often confident because they're better educated or more skilled than others.

There are two distinct types of charismatic people. Some are quiet but beguiling, relying on glances or physical beauty or sheer mystique for their charisma. Others are passionate communicators, they might be inspirational speakers, comics, singers, or actors.

Affability is a constant in either case. Those who have charisma are approachable, even if they're not extroverted.

Try rating your own charisma on a scale from one to five (five being the most positive) in terms of these statements.

I am a person who...

> *... has a significant presence in a room with others*
> *... can influence people*
> *... can lead a group*
> *... comforts others*
> *... smiles often*
> *... gets along with almost anyone*

Now add up the total and divide by six, and that's your average score. If you rated higher than 4, you're ahead of most.

Certain skills comprise and contribute this affability and influence. Developing influence (through presence, ability to lead and to influence); being confident in a variety of situations, either one-on-one or in a group, either as a leader or team member; they're optimistic and positive; charismatic people are persuasive and influential.

The charismatic will open up emotionally but in a measured fashion, never complaining. They are interest*ing* and interest*ed*.

Charismatic people are often engaging, good storytelling, witty, but they don't seek to dominate any conversation. They know the value of the lull, as it demonstrates security and confidence. They laugh at others' jokes and are free with their compliments.

The charismatic are empathetic and engender trust.

Charismatic people communicate clearly. They don't mumble and mutter. So, take some time to work on your speaking voice. It's your most effective method of communication, after all. Make the most of it. Shift it downward deeper into your chest. It may take some practice or some lessons, but you may find it very worthwhile. From trial lawyers to drill sergeants, the voice is a powerful instrument for charisma and influence, which is a big part of charisma as we've already seen.

CHARISMATIC LEADERS

Charismatic leaders are necessary to our societies all over the world. They lead movements and fight for others, for a better world. They lead with courage and conviction. They also lead with compassion for their team members and for their needs and desires.

Charismatic leaders often arise in times of crisis. They lead their followers with a deep sense of purpose and passion. Some of the great leaders in history have been charismatic leaders, including Winston Churchill, Ronald Reagan, Mahatma Gandhi, Dr. Martin Luther King, Jr, Malcom X, and many others.

On the other hand, some of history's worst and most reviled leaders have been equally charismatic, including Adolph Hitler, Joseph Stalin, and Vladimir Putin.

Charismatic leaders are often inspirational and influential to those around them, they're often growth-minded, companies led by such people are often moving in a clear direction with a clear and manifest purpose. They're often catalysts for positive change.

But before you laud charismatic leaders, give some thought to the drawbacks of being or even having a charismatic leader. They're prone to arrogance and myopia. They tend to dominate corporate identity and make the whole company reliant upon them and them alone. They can become disinterested and unresponsive to others. They tend not to learn from mistakes and consider themselves above others, even the law. Ethical or financial transgressions are common with this type of leader in the corporate world and in the religious world as well. Organizations with rigid structures may not benefit from this kind of leadership.

SOCIAL SKILLS TEST

Take this social skills test to see if you could stand to develop your social skills. Answer on a scale from one (negative, or *no*) to five (positive, or *yes*):

1. I try to see other people's perspectives.
2. In conversation, I sit when the other is sitting and stand when the other is standing.
3. I often do or say things which my co-workers and friends consider inconsiderate or insensitive.
4. I'm told that my behavior is often inappropriate.
5. I rarely think about how others are affected by what I do or say.
6. I always explain all my ideas as clearly as I can.
7. During conversations, people often note how interested I appear.
8. I snap at people in times of stress.
9. Friends and colleagues don't seem to appreciate my unsolicited advice.
10. I don't bother telling my friends how much they mean to me. They already know.
11. I keep up with what's new with my friends, the good and the bad.
12. When I'm criticized, I often get defensive.

13. I withdraw when I don't feel comfortable.
14. I know my friends have faults, but I accept them as they are.

Easy, right? If not, you'll know where you can improve your social skills. Now let's take a look at the impact of leadership in every aspect of your life!

11

THE IMPACT OF A GREAT LEADERSHIP IN ALL AREAS OF YOUR LIFE

Every year, about 9% of Americans who make New Year's resolutions (about 41%) succeed. But that's still less than 4% of the country's populace who are adept at making goals and achieving them. Are you in that exclusive group? If not, wouldn't you like to be? Read on and let's make that happen.

As we've seen, the layers of your life overlap, and things you do in one area interconnect with another thing in the same area, same things in different areas, and different things in different areas. So, we've broken them up into categories to keep things organized.

The first category is health. Being a better leader means being a strong leader, and strength comes from good health. We've discussed the so-called smart foods and touched on the benefits of exercise, stretching, and sound sleeping habits. But physical health is predicated on sound mental and spiritual health as well.

A few tips and tricks to better health include doing yoga, running or walking daily, a weekly cleanse, and a home workout regimen.

A big part of health is sound spirituality. Spirituality or religion has proven ties to a positive outlook and, ultimately, a longer life. It doesn't really matter what religion or philosophy you adopt. A lot of people adopt several different or even divergent religions or philosophies over their lifetimes, and there's nothing wrong with that. It's a sign of a growth mindset, and we've already seen how key that is to so many facets of a happy life.

But spirituality can help us answer the existential questions which so often cause us anxiety. It gives us a sense of self, a perspective of who we are (and who we are not). Someone with a strong spiritual life is less likely to have a God complex, for example.

Spirituality will give you good sense of the difference between happiness and pleasure. Happiness is a long-term concept, usually related to accomplishing worthwhile goals. Happiness supports self-confidence. Your family and home and career may give you happiness. Pleasure is related to short-term rewards, like an orgasm.

If you're developing your spirituality, try these handy techniques. You can start immediately, if you wish (but read the techniques first, of course).

You might try meditating every morning, just after you wake up. Do it again before you go to bed. Just for five minutes per session. I'll bet you'll find that you're more spiritually attuned, your mind and heart and other chakras open. You may even think about joining a meditation circle or yoga meditation class.

Fashion a strong definition for spirituality and keep it in mind. You might have heard someone describe themselves spiritual but not religious. Do they even know what that means? You should.

Keep a spiritual journal of what spiritual thoughts you have, when and where and why. That will draw your attention to those things when they recur and you'll be more mindful of them. Mindfulness and gratitude are also key areas for developing your spirituality.

Environment is key to developing spirituality, as it is in so many things. Environment both mirrors and affects our daily lives. A cluttered or stressful environment creates a cluttered and stressful life. You may want to include some religious or spiritual iconography in your environment, including crosses, pictures of the Buddha, whatever is in line with your spiritual leanings.

You may also consider decluttering and deep-cleaning. That's good for the body and the mind and for the property too. Redecorating can bring a sense of a fresh start and open your creative mind as well. This includes new furniture if you can manage that. New clothes may be a good way to change your most immediate environment. Replace those tight-fitting clothes with something more relaxed and comfortable.

Romance is another big part of most people's lives, and strong leadership is crucial to a happy and healthy romantic life. Critical thinking will help you decide who is worth pursuing and who isn't. Foresight will help you visualize what that coupling might be like. Reflection will give you time to reconsider your approach. Charisma will make you more self-confident, and self-confidence will make you more charismatic. Charisma is a hallmark of romance. Of course, awkward people find each other and fall in love all the time, and that's adorable.

Do you approach your romances with integrity, honesty, and clarity? Those are the elements of true leadership, after all. And isn't any romance a team effort? Of course, it is. Can you lead your team to the long-term goal of marriage and family and happiness (if that is your long-term goal)? Are you in control of your emotions? Is your partner? You may know your partner's strengths and weaknesses, but do you know your own? Do you keep a healthy climate when you're together?

Here are a few tips and techniques you may use to create and sustain a healthy romantic relationship!

Date at least once a week. This is as important to romances later in the relationship as it is in the first movement of a relationship. New lovers can hardly make a significant relationship without seeing each other at least once a week. And longtime relationships often need to keep dating just to keep the romance alive in their lives. It's more than reason enough! It's also good for relaxation, reflection, action planning, conferring, and more.

Don't hesitate to confer with a mentor while you're dating or married as well. That's very constructive and it's a technique of a true leader.

Go on a vacation once a year. If you're dating, get away from your home base for a weekend. Or travel abroad. It's a broadening experience for both as individuals and for the couple as a whole. It gives you memories and stories to share with others and will likely give you an added appreciation of one another. If you're in a family situation, take this vacation without the kids. You need time together to keep your romantic feelings strong and healthy. Most of your homelife is dedicated to the kids, so when you're not in the home it's fair to have that time for yourself.

Don't neglect to say, "I love you," and say it every day. That's clear communication, the hallmark of a true leader. Saying things gives them power. It's also supportive of a team mentality and crucial for a healthy romantic climate.

Cleaning the house together is a good way to bond romantically. It's healthy, it's exercise, it's a positive and shared goal which can be broken down into smaller, rewarding milestones. Finding old things may bring nostalgia, a powerful romantic feeling, and these things may bring you back to happier or more loving times, resurrecting old feelings.

And when you're together, on a date or activity, turn your phones off. You should be focusing on each other. And the whole point is to get away from the rest of the world for a brief time, so why bring the outside world with you?

The second big area of your life is the professional category. It includes growth and learning, among other things, all of which benefit from true leadership skills, emotional intelligence, and cognitive ability.

Here are some handy tips to improve your growth and learning skills.

Read more. There's a ton of information out there on just about every subject (we've got lots more books like this one, on subjects like overcoming overthinking and procrastination, effective communications for couples, and more!). Set a goal to read a certain amount every month.

Go to a personal development seminar. There are lots of them and some are quite impactful. Research them online for testimonials and agendas, so you know what you're paying for. Use your critical thinking skills before, during, and after the seminar.

Growth and learning are achieved by accomplishing goals. So set some goals at the beginning of every month and make sure they're achieved by the end of the month.

Develop your communication skills and express yourself more confidently in the workplace. This area of growth will help in every facet of your life. Practice how to express yourself more confidently through your language.

Music is a growth tool, and new music will open up new cultures to you as well as excite your creativity.

Time management is a critical leadership skill in the workplace. Practice it and influence others to do the same for maximum workplace efficiency. Consider a time log for yourself and encourage your team members to keep them too. You may reserve the right to see them from time to time.

Classes, lessons, and degree programs are also great ways to promote growth and learning in the workplace.

School is a part of life where growth and learning are central. Are you retaining what you're learning, or does the information fall out of your head as soon as you take the test? A true leader will retain the information for use in critical thinking later in life. Retention also inspires curiosity, another hallmark of a true leader.

To improve your leadership skills, emotional intelligence, and cognitive skills in an educational environment, consider these elements. First, building sound relationships with teachers and classmates. They're your mentors, supervisors, and fellow team members and also fellow individuals. It's a great way to invite feedback, encourage and support others, and accomplish shared goals. Study groups are a great example of this when put into concrete application. It's one thing to get along, it's another to join forces! School clubs are great to, for the same reasons.

Don't forget to take breaks, it's crucial for your productivity and mental wellbeing. This is something a lot of students forget as they study and cram and complete one project after the next. A student's life is a hectic one, filled with wants, desires, goals, tasks, and distractions. You have to be self-disciplined enough to give yourself some quiet time for reflection and relaxation.

Time management is also crucial for students, for the same reason. It will reduce stress and anxiety and result in more productive and effective performances. Use a schedular like a daily planner to keep your tasks and time well-organized.

If you're not in college yet, keep that in mind as your goal and set milestones toward achieving that goal. Completing classes, scoring good grades, and extra-curricular activities are the milestones which lead to college acceptance, though you'll also want to consider getting grants and scholarships, saving money, getting rid of things you don't need to allow for light travel.

Financial interests are a big part of any professional life, and the skills of a true leader are crucial to successfully managing those interests. Here's some sound advice to consider:

Try to save money for emergencies. This isn't easy, and a frightening number of Americans have no significant savings at all. This won't just happen on its own. Set a schedule of how much to save monthly, set up a special savings account, make sure you don't withdraw from it or change the deposit amounts. Make a plan and stick to it.

Debts, especially credit card debts, are a real drain. A true leader knows that interest rates keep credit card debt lingering for years, and this can cause stress, anxiety, and hamper other efforts. Bad credit is also a source of stress and anxiety and drastically reduces anyone's chance of success as a true leader.

Jobs are hard to find, but look for one that will pay your way. There are service jobs open to students, and afterward there are sales and management positions, work in engineering. Don't earn your bachelor's degree and then go be an actor, unless that's paying your bills.

The mentorship of a financial advisor is going to be very beneficial to you later, and it's another hallmark of true leadership. An advisor will help you achieve and maintain a positive net worth, and that's not as easy as it seems. Your student loan has probably already put you in the red, as they say.

Analyze and understand your income and outgoings. Watch these things closely. It's not enough just to spend as little as possible while saving whatever you can. Mindfulness and a specific plan are the ways to successfully manage your finances like a true leader.

Manage cash flow with detailed budgeting based on your income and outgo.

Accrue capital, which is the money left over after cash flow.

Keep family security a priority. This the source of a lot of unexpected expense and those are necessary expenses too. Insurance is requisite to maintaining family security, including medical, auto, homeowners, and life insurance policies. Family security requires virtually all of them.

Investing is a pillar of financial management. Stocks, bonds and precious metals are popular ways to invest, each with its strong points and downfalls. Stocks are easy to buy and sell, but volatile. Bonds are stable but don't do much to increase capital. Precious metals are costly to buy and store and can be unstable. Digital currencies like Bitcoin are popular investments these days. A home is generally the biggest investment a person will ever make, but some question the value of home ownership. There are large associated costs (fees, insurance, maintenance), it's a hard commodity to liquidate and is largely non-liquid. A house pays no dividends and is subject to the fluxes in the market. However, a house can be refinanced and is a sound asset, which is also important to good financial planning. Cars and boats are also assets, as are life insurance policies.

The true leader keeps a standard of living in mind when financial planning. This is associated with income and outgo and budgeting, but it has to do with doing more than saving every penny. It's about making the most of every penny.

A true leader has a financial understanding of the home and the workplace and makes better decisions based on that information. That includes tracing project budgets, the company's annual performance, monitoring or completing and filing household tax returns, and so on. A financial plan for both is recommended to asses and prepare for long-term goals.

In the workplace, teamwork and true leadership are essential. Here's a good exercise to promote teamwork, self-awareness, and other elements of a healthy workplace. Call your team together and give each a piece of paper. Have them write their greatest strength within the team at the top of the piece of paper. Keep in mind that a good team is comprised of different talents which serve different purposes. One person may write *analytical* on their piece of paper, for example.

Now tape these pieces of paper to the backs of the team members who filled them out. Then have the other team members write things which express or explain the person's proclaimed characteristic. The person who wrote analytical may find that others have added detail-oriented or thoughtful or reflects a lot. Those are all behaviors associated with the characteristic of behind analytical.

It's a good team exercise, it provides some objectivity, it inspires empathy as it encourages you to consider other people's perspectives. It supports a sense of self and a sense of acceptance. Try it!

The third significant area of your life is the personal and it includes family and friends.

A true leader maintains strong relationships with family and friends. First, let's consider the similarities between being a true leader at home and being a true leader at the workplace. We've touched on this, but let's put a finer point on it here. The parallels between leading a workplace team and a family (also a team) are striking, and they require virtually the same skillset.

Discipline is crucial to running both a work team and a family properly. Not that this should be an authoritarian approach, though it may be. Remember that different situations may require different leadership styles. And there'll be times in each where a democratic approach is best, sometimes when laissez-faire is the wiser approach in each arena. But you don't want to let either your team members or your children misbehave without being disciplined. Corrections should come with explanation, clarity, and empathy, but rules must be enforced. In each instance, this may mean dress codes and codes of acceptable conduct and language.

Accountability is also central to both workplace and family. Punctuality, deadlines, behavior; all things for which anybody in the workplace or home should be held accountable. That goes for the leader too.

Praise is invaluable in both areas as well, for your team members, coworkers, supervisors, spouses, and children. It's supportive, empathetic, encourages open communication, shows emotional intelligence, and has many more benefits.

Respect is also crucial to running a family or a workplace. Authorities must be respected, but they must respect the humanity of those under them. Deadlines and protocols must be respected, whether that's at the conference table or the dinner table. Respect your co-workers and respect your spouse. Even if you don't harbor respect, it's critical that you show respect. Being outwardly disrespectful to anyone is a sign of lack of self-discipline and is a trait of a leader in name only, not a true leader.

Restraint is also key to true leaders and to the teams they lead. Be it a workplace team or a family, emotional outbursts must be curtailed, body language must be well-governed, one must be mindful of their own weaknesses, triggers must be avoided, behavior modified. True leaders teach this by example. Likewise, a lack of restraint will rub off on either team or family and create a host of negative and counter-productive behaviors like bickering, gossip, backstabbing, and resentment.

Vision and strategy are key for successful leadership in the workplace and the home. Know what your goals are and how to achieve them, in the short- and the long-term. Clearly express specific goals and follow timelines in both cases.

Be participative and directive. It's not enough to give directions. As we've seen it's important to work with your team, to be visible and approachable. The same is true for the home. Help your kids with their homework and projects, mentor your spouse or work with him or her in problem-solving. Use critical thinking and other cognitive skills.

Motivation and inspiration are central to both team projects and family matters, so are a positive attitude and flexibility. Both arenas can be chaotic and may need quick thinking and measured response.

The trust you build by being a person of integrity is critical to both family and workplace.

Determination and commitment are common to both the workplace and the home. Both will present challenges, but you can no sooner walk out on your job than you can tell your wife you're going out for cigarettes and never come back. First of all, true leaders shouldn't smoke for all the right reasons; its unhealthy and sets a bad example. But mostly, your team, your clients, your spouse, and your children are relying on you. A true leader holds his or her ground and advances, they do not retreat or abandon the field and desert their troops.

As to your family and friends in particular, ask yourself; are you reaching out to communicate with them? Are you showing empathy to their challenges and difficulties? These days families are more disjointed and desperate than ever, and a concerted effort is required to bridge the gap.

Here are a few tips and tricks to keep the bonds strong between you and your friends and family:

Call them, or visit if you can. Forget texts and email, nothing beats the personal touch in these instances. What, you never call your mother?

Listen actively, show empathy, don't interrupt.

Take extra time with your kids, teach them self-defense skills if you know them, or how to deal with bullies. That's constructive, positive, and will be a bonding experience.

Fun and recreation are big parts of the personal sphere of your life. Yet they're often neglected in most people's lives with all the hard work and efforts to succeed. So, take time to have some fun, to get away from the grind. It's good for your body and your mind and even your soul.

If you're looking for some handy tips and techniques, you've come to the right place. Consider learning a craft; how to paint, work with clay, something fun and tactile. Remember that you don't have to be good at it, certainly not at first. You'll want to develop your skills like all true leaders will, but the most important thing is to enjoy the process and reap the benefits of relaxation, cognitive stimulation, and personal satisfaction.

We've touched on vacations, and it bears repeating here. Vacations are designed to be fun and only fun. You don't have to be productive all the time and shouldn't have to be. Cultures all over the world include vacation time (the United States is one of the few countries which does not mandate paid vacation time). And there's a lot out there to see; the Grand Canyon, New York City, the Amazon rainforest.

Sports are a great way to have fun. It also has a number of other benefits, including improved physical health, improved hand/eye co-ordination, improved teamwork skills, and personal satisfaction. Studies show that children who participate in team sports are more successful as adults.

A random road trip is great for a good time. Spontaneity excites the brain and breaks a rut. It stimulates curiosity, it introduces new people and new things, new ideas and new information to be used later. It's great for reflection and evaluation, all true leadership skills.

Learning to cook is a great way to have fun like a true leader. It's healthier than eating prepared food, it entails focus and attention on new information, retention, analysis, planning. It's creative, requires curiosity, provides immediate gratification, stimulates further growth. It's like painting, but with food!

Community is also a bit part of your personal life. Besides just your family, friends, or partners, you have a whole support network of medical and legal professionals, advisors, service providers, familiar faces, and others who make up your community. It also includes people you don't know, like the children at the local elementary school, the homeless on the streets. A true leader is mindful of his or her community and knows how to maintain a healthy climate and clear communication.

Consider paying for someone's groceries, if you're capable and they're in need. You'll be showing empathy and enjoying the satisfaction of having helped somebody. If a friend is having trouble, help them in the same way. They'll never forget it. And who knows? You may need the same kind of help at some point.

Always bring a gift. It doesn't have to be big or expensive, a bottle of wine or a houseplant, a bouquet of flowers, a CD of music you think they'd enjoy.

Volunteer work is mentioned often in this book, and it's a great way to exercise your true leadership skills as well as your emotional intelligence and cognitive abilities, including critical thinking. It allows you to practice compassion, utilizes analytical skills, physical activity, social interaction, active listening.

It's easy to see how these areas overlap, how skills in one area are useful in another. Life is complex and hectic, but knowing the consistency of these approaches in various parts of your life will make each one less complicated and easier to manage. Mastery of these concepts in one area will help you master them in another. And you'll be a better example to more people, creating healthier climates and more productive teams, in the home or in the workplace.

Now let's take a deeper look at leadership skills in the delicate (and sometimes not so delicate) area of romance.

LEADERSHIP AND ROMANCE

In today's #metoo world, it almost seems offensive to think about leadership in romance. It has echoes of outmoded macho perspectives. And that's reasonable. We don't enter into relationships to lead and we generally are looking for those who are our betters or at least our equals and not some follower. We want to be encouraged as much as we want to encourage. We want to grow as much as help someone else grow. Generally, we seek a strong partner, physically and intellectually, and that is independent of gender. Men are instinctively primed to look for women who can raise strong, healthy and intelligent children, and that takes strong genes and intelligence from both parents. Each needs the other to be capable, with strong cognitive abilities and emotional intelligence. Those things are crucial to a romantic relationship, as we have seen.

Now let's take a serious look at how leadership is involved in relationships, how it can affect them for good or ill, and how to use your leadership skills in the arena of romance.

Remember that a romantic couple is a team, with (hopefully) shared long-term goals, short-term challenges, which may face unexpected difficulties. So, a couple really does need leadership just like any other team does. One key difference is that, in a healthy couple, there's no one clear leader. In a good couple, the couple leads.

Leadership still includes the same things, like attention and evaluation, feedback and brainstorming, planning and taking action and so on. But a good couple do these things together. Both partners are both the leaders and the team.

It's hard to stress this enough. Any couple with a power imbalance will eventually succumb to resentments, rebellions, miscommunication, dishonesty, perhaps cheating. When the power is severely imbalanced, the results can be abuse, depression, substance abuse, premature death, and suicide.

But the secrets to a healthy, happy, and long-lasting relationships are basically the same qualities which make a good leader (or, in this case, a pair of co-leaders).

Some experts disagree that the most important facets of a successful relationship are financial wellbeing, shared values, ethnicity or religion. But good communication skills trump all of those, and that's the bedrock of true leadership.

Of course, gender will have some influence on various facets of any intimate relationship. Experts tell us that, in general, a lot of women enjoy feeling cherished. It makes them feel respected. Men, they find, prefer to be respected, which makes them feel cherished.

Even so, everybody wants to be treated well, and that's what true leadership is all about. It starts with clear communication. Be able to express your needs and wants in a way that is concise and eschews vagueness. Listen actively and show empathy when dating. Be able to evaluate, analyze, and take feedback. Make measured choices in a timely fashion.

One leadership technique that works perfectly for relationship building is to keep a journal. Chronicle your dates, your experiences, see if you can identify patterns in your or your new partner's behavior. How can you keep triggering good behavior and avoid the negative responses? What about them triggers you?

Another critical step is to consider your leadership technique, as we discussed earlier in this book. You can go back and reread that if you like, I'll wait.

Welcome back. Of all the leadership styles, the servant leader is probably best suited to a romance. The leader who seeks to bring out the best in his or her team and project and company is also the partner who wants to bring out the best in his or her partner and relationship and life. This style infers trust and confidence in your partner's abilities, and that will win their trust and inspire their confidence. They'll mirror that behavior and treat you the same way, offering their respect and confidence in you. With this trust, leadership can be shared by two partners equally. It may also be shifted from one partner to the other depending on the situation. Some circumstances may require the strengths or experiences of one partner, other circumstances may require the unique perspective of the other partner. Once again, it's vital to assess your own strengths and acknowledge your weaknesses while acknowledging the strengths of your team member. That's another hallmark of true leadership.

One leadership technique which may not work so well in dating is a time log. Time management is essential for productive workplace management and goal achievement. But relationships can't really be put on a time clock. A good relationship should develop on its own time, in its own way.

Let's take a look at a few myths of romantic timetables.

Never call back the next day. What a terrible rule this is! The idea is that you don't want to come off as needy or clingy. But not calling also sends the message that you're not interested. It's careless of the other person's feelings and focused instead on your own. That kind of selfishness and lack of empathy are leading in name only; that's not true leadership. Waiting is also gamesmanship of the lowest order. If you like the person or had a good time, call them.

Texting may or may not suffice. If you had a fun date and would like to meet up again, a text may suffice. It's considerate of another person's time and attention, after all. If you had sex for the first time, a text may likely come off as cold and dismissive. Remember that texts and emails lack the nuance of the human voice, and that can make all the difference. Speaking is a much clearer form of communication as long as you're direct with what you're saying. Once you've had sex more than once, a cute text or even a sex-text (or *sext*) can be fun and perfectly appropriate.

You Should Have Sex on the Third Date. Here could be some practical wisdom here. If you wait too long to make a move, your partner might get the idea that you're not interested or that you lack self-confidence. This creates awkwardness which shatters charisma, and that may be what attracted your partner in the first place. Since it's the first thing people notice, this is quite likely. And your charisma hinges on a lack of awkwardness. A lack of intimacy can quickly become the elephant in the room, and that elephant may not leave room enough for both partners. One is certain to go.

On the other hand, some people have trust issues or painful pasts which make three dates feel rushed. Enter leadership skills like asking questions without blame or shame or judgment, actively listening, welcoming and offering feedback, noting how you feel, reflecting, deciding on an action plan. It means responding intellectually and not reacting emotionally.

Some people will have post-traumatic stress disorder (PTSD) or psychological blocks which need to be seen to by a trained therapist. You can use your leadership skills here too. Pay attention to the problem, analyze the information, encourage feedback about getting therapy, solve the problems of what type, consult a mentor, and make a plan of action to go into therapy if that's what's required. Either way, leadership skills will see you through to a constructive resolution.

But the fact is that not everybody is going to be ready to fall into bed, for whatever other reasons. If that's the case, leadership skills will be just the right skillset to help. Use them, along with these techniques, to introduce intimacy while still accommodating a hesitant partner.

Take a shower together. Not to have sex, just to stand naked in front of the other. A lot of stifled intimacy results from embarrassment about body shape and size, various imperfections. A person may have body dysmorphia disorder (BDD) or reverse-body dysmorphia, which distorts their vision of their body. A simple, soothing shower reveals all in a comfortable setting (which is also quite sensual). Caress one another, soap each other up. Don't worry about having intercourse (that's a lot harder in a shower than you may have been led to believe).

Because another source of intimate awkwardness is performance anxiety. This can happen to men for any number of reasons, both physiological and psychological. Showering isn't about intercourse, so performance shouldn't be a problem. This is just a physical, intimate introduction to one another. We'll come back to this, but let's move forward to other ways to ease your hesitant partner into deeper intimacy.

Sensual massage, or even a nice deep tissue massage, are great ways to introduce physical intimacy in a measured manner. There are all kinds of physical benefits to massage therapy besides introducing physical intimacy:

- Relieved stress
- Relieved postoperative pain
- Reduced anxiety
- Reduced low-back pain
- Reduced fibromyalgia pain
- Reduced muscle tension
- Enhanced exercise performance
- Relief of tension headaches
- Better sleep
- Eased depression symptoms

- Improved cardiovascular health
- Reduced pain from osteoarthritis
- Decreased stress among cancer patients
- Improved balance in aging adults
- Decreased pain from rheumatoid arthritis
- Help with effects of dementia
- Increased relaxation
- Lowered blood pressure
- Decreased symptoms of Carpal Tunnel Syndrome
- Help with chronic neck pain
- Reduced joint pain
- Decreased frequency of migraines
- Improved quality of life during hospice care
- Reduced nausea due to chemotherapy.

It's also great for that physical intimacy. It gives your partner a feel for your sensitivities, your instincts. It's positive time you're spending together with a shared goal, and may even increase your spiritual senses as well. Also, it feels great. Who doesn't like to give or get a nice massage?

Dirty talk is a powerful technique too. Verbalizing things gives them power, and doing this gives the speaker a certain power as well. It demonstrates interest and confidence and will instill confidence too. It excites the senses and the imagination. It's something only intimates do, and that helps identify your emotions (remember that?) and to express them. And if you want clear and direct communication of your desires and expectations, another leadership hallmark, you won't find much better than dirty talk.

Some people are reticent to try this, and of course it isn't always entirely appropriate. I wouldn't blurt it out at the Thanksgiving table with the family all around you, but you might whisper it in the hallway when nobody else is around!

Try it ... they'll never know!

Flirting is a critical element to dating, and it's something you should keep doing, especially if there are intimacy issues. Body language says more than your words do, after all. Demonstrate your interest instead of just expressing it.

Oddly, a romantic getaway may not be the best choice for an intimate breakthrough. The pressure may be too great, and a person may feel more comfortable on familiar ground.

You may want to take a commanding approach, play the role of an authoritarian leader. Direct your partner to comply to your desires. Or you may insist that your partner do it and then be compliant. Power is a powerful aphrodisiac, after all.

Meditating together is a good way to relax and reduce anxiety, and it will have all the mental and physical benefits. If you choose the other person as the focal point, that will utilize attention and empathy, two hallmarks of true leadership.

Share your fantasies. A lot of sexual awkwardness is born of fetishism. But a lot of people are nervous about sharing this information. It's something only our intimates generally know. But we're more vulnerable with our intimates than with anyone else. This is the person we're naked in front of, this is the measure of ability and worth as a lover and companion. That's a lot of pressure as it is. But if a person is unsure of the acceptability or compatibility of their fetish, they're not likely to express it for fear of being judged and rejected. However, fetishists often require that fetish in order to function sexually. This lack of communication creates presumptions, assumptions, a downward spiral of awkwardness and distance which can destroy a budding romance.

The tragic thing is that most fetishes are fairly common, and a fetish match may appear to be a mismatch if this subject never comes up.

So, don't be afraid to either ask or declare (both true leadership qualities). Be honest, have integrity. Know who you are and be confident in your standards and ethics. If your partner cannot abide your fetish (or the other way around) then there's probably a sexual incompatibility that cannot be overcome. But you can still be friends. It's another instance of your leadership skills of clear communication and self-awareness being invaluable in your romances.

Now let's go back and take a quick look at erectile disfunction disorder. It can be caused by nervousness, and a nice, hot shower can get both partners over that initial hump. But what about the other causes and effects?

Erectile dysfunction (ED), the inability to achieve or maintain an erection, may be caused by a variety of neurological factors, including problems in the endocrine, vascular, and nervous systems.

ED may be symptomatic of aging, but it is not a necessary result of aging. ED is treated at every age.

Certain diseases and conditions which may cause ED include blood vessel and heart disease, type 2 diabetes, atherosclerosis, chronic kidney disease, high blood pressure, Peyronie's disease, multiple sclerosis (MS), prostate cancer and treatment, injury to he spinal cord, bladder, prostate, penis, or pelvis, and bladder surgery.

Some medications may cause ED, including blood pressure medicines, antidepressants, antiandrogens (used in prostate cancer therapy), tranquilizers and prescription sedatives, ulcer medications, and appetite suppressants.

As we touched on, emotional or psychological factors may also be working in conjunction with one of the previous factors and include performance anxiety, depression, anxiety, stress, and sexual guilt.

Certain factors related to health management may also contribute to erectile dysfunction, including alcohol and drug abuse and cigarette smoking, obesity and lack of exercise.

12

LEADERSHIP AND OTHER SKILLS DURING A BREAKUP

Unfortunately, not every relationship can be saved, and this goes for romantic and professional relationships, social and even familial relationships. You may have to leave your work due to unresolvable conflicts with superiors or supervisors, or you may be faced with losing a valued team member. Romances end, so do marriages and old friendships. Even siblings sometimes must have to part ways for a variety of reasons. It's sad, but it happens.

And when one of these relationships do end, it's vital that you recall everything you've learned here, as almost all of it will be helpful, sometimes even necessary. So, lets take a closer look at how leadership skills, emotional intelligence, cognitive skills, critical thinking, and social skills to get through a breakup with a minimum of upset or inconvenience for any involved party.

Your leadership skills will be central to the peaceful resolution of a breakup of any sort.

For example, patience is a must. If you're breaking up a romance (or on the receiving end) you'll have to be patient. Let the event happen in its own time. Let the person say what they want to say or process what you had to say. In the workplace, social situation, or in the home, that patience will express your legitimate concern for the other person and your vested interest in their wants and desires and goals, which likely do not correlate to yours any longer, for whatever reason. If you're clashing with an adult sibling or spouse, patience is even more important because these people are much closer to you. And there are external ties, such as children or other siblings, which make some kind of long-term communication necessary if not desirable.

Another hallmark of true leadership, empathy, will be well appreciated by the person on the sour end of any breakup or firing. Express your understanding of their feelings, recognize them as important and legitimate. Be careful not to overdo this during a breakup, however, as it can be confusing. Guilt may inspire you to be compassionate, and you should be. But you may also be unwittingly sending mixed signals which will only antagonize emotional feelings of anger and confusion. If you're ending a long-term friendship, it's likely to be a mutual feeling, so less empathy may be required. You may just drift apart and let the friendship end that way, but it's not always possible. Making things complicated are that coworkers can become good friends and good friends can become coworkers. Any number of things can destroy the friendship but leave the work situation intact.

Active listening, key to empathy, will help you get through any breakup situation, professional or romantic. If your boss is letting you go, really pay attention to the explanation. It could be an invaluable chance to see yourself from a more objective point of view, to better understand your shortcomings, ways you can improve your performance in the next job. It could be that you're not cut out for the job you have, and this may be the only way for you to come to understand this. It's the same thing in relationships. If you're getting dumped, you might have done something wrong. A former friend may have insight into changes in your behavior you hadn't noticed. Or you could be perfect. Either way, the other person has a right to be heard.

Reliability is a leadership skill which is central to navigating a breakup. Maintain your integrity even in that stressful time. It's a crisis, and true leaders are reliable in time of crisis. Don't compromise your standards or ethics for any job or intimate partner. It won't work, as you're sure to return to your innate standards and practices. And you'll resent having to change, perhaps changing those things about yourself you liked best. Just because they're traits a boss or coworker or partner doesn't like, doesn't mean other people won't like them. Sometimes incompatibility comes down to different energies which just don't vibe.

Likewise, dependability during a breakup sends the message to your former partner and to others that your integrity is in tact and that you know who you are. Don't prove your boss correct by throwing a tantrum and destroying the office. Don't prove your spouse or partner right by throwing their stuff out onto the lawn. Don't watch your old friends walk away with their heads shaking while you rave in a drunken stupor.

You'll be leaning heavily on another true leadership skill, creativity, during breakups like these too. You'll need to find new ways to get over the hurt, ways to express yourself. You'll need it to find new relationships, better or different jobs. You'll have to find a way of interacting as adult siblings when necessary while still not compromising the other, new ways of communicating which won't trigger emotional reactions.

Positivity during a breakup will make the difference between a healthy climate and a toxic climate during and after the event. Breakups generally happen as the result of negative feelings and energies, after all. It's a rare breakup which begins and ends with smiles and reason and a friendly hug. Otherwise, you're looking at loads of collected negativity. Feelings of rejection, refusal, anger, betrayal, oppression, depression, and others are likely to surface either during or after a breakup. Keeping things positive is always a good idea. Don't be ridiculous about it, of course. You won't say, "We're over … isn't that great?" But you might make suggestions about the positive aspects of the breakup, that it frees up the parties to move on to greener pastures, for instance. The end of the lingering stresses and the prospects of healing are other positive results of a breakup. Also, looking back with gratitude can't hurt.

Effective feedback may not save the professional or personal relationship, but it's information that could prove invaluable later, giving you an opportunity to see things through somebody else's point of view.

Timely communication is a delicate matter during and after breakups. If you have to break up, do it quickly or they may resent the delay. Don't do it at a family event, but there's little need to wait out the holidays either, as they will only ring false after the breakup and those events will seem dishonest. If you have to do it, just get it done with. Forget the so-called *breakup seasons*. It may be smart not to communicate with a lover after a breakup, as this may impede healing and create false hopes of a reunion. In the workplace, if a team member has to be let go, do it without delay. They may be missing opportunities while you wait to pull the trigger. If an old friend is no longer fitting into your social circle, bring it up sooner rather than later. The problem is only likely to get worse. If this is a divorce or a family feud, there likewise won't be much benefit to waiting. If you're ready to end a relationship, it's probably because you've been waiting long enough.

Team building seems like one leadership skill that wouldn't apply to a breakup, but think again! A loss of a workplace team member will require a replacement, and the team will have to be rebuilt. Other team members may have to be calmed or reevaluated. Keep the team strong despite the breakup by using your team building skills. This is especially crucial dealing with divorce when children are involved. The kids still need their parents, so the team still has to be kept together despite the drastic change in living arrangements. This is a very trying time for everyone involved, but it is especially tough on children. Introducing new spouses also entails team building, and of a most sensitive kind. Here some members of the team (the children, in general) will not necessarily be willing to participate. They'll need all of your empathy, self-awareness, flexibility, and other leadership skills, particularly your team building skills. Losing your friends will require you to build a new team of friends too!

Flexibility is a crucial leadership skill too, especially during breakups. You'll want to avoid being flexible in your position. If you've come to this, backing down will not correct the things which inspired the breakup in the first place. And it may only be delaying the inevitable and offering false hope. But consequences may be many and far-reaching and you'll need to be flexible about how to deal with them. In a romantic breakup, there could be mutual friends involved. Divorcing parents will have property and custody issues to deal with.

Risk-taking is inherent in any breakup, during and after. Just breaking up with somebody is a risk. Will you be able to find another job or a better companion? If I stay, what will I be missing out on? If I walk out on this old friend, what will he or she resort to? If you can't handle risk, breakups of any sort could be torturous for you.

Breakups will also test your abilities to teach and to mentor. How will you teach your children that family is the most important thing if you won't talk to your own brother or sister, or if you're also trying to explain to them why Mommy and Daddy can't live together anymore. Divorce makes teaching kids more difficult because they're only in your company for a limited time. But the skills are crucial to navigate your children through the complexities of a divorce or separation. Chances are your ex-romantic partner or friend or team member won't have much time or interest in your mentoring at that point. But if you are the one being let go or cut loose; the lessons you learn could help you mentor others. It could and it should.

The skills of emotional intelligence will also be invaluable in navigating a breakup of just about any sort, some more than others.

Self-awareness is central to any aspect of anyone's happier and better life, almost nowhere and at no other time than during or after a breakup. If you're being fired, its your responsibility to know why, to know what you've done to warrant firing. It's your legal right in many cases. And it can only aid in developing your self-awareness. In looking for a new job, knowing your skills and weaknesses will help you chose a different career path, if that's what is necessary. If you're losing old friendships, you owe it to yourself to understand both them and yourself. Some cases of feuds between parents and their adult children or between adult siblings often comes down to a certain incompatibility, and understanding that can help us better understand each other and ourselves.

Self-regulation is also crucial during the breakup period and afterward. Not only do you want to regulate your behavior during a firing or other parting of ways, it's just as important after the fact. The days, weeks, months, even years after a breakup can be devastating and inspire feelings of uselessness, helplessness, depression, substance abuse, mental and physical ill-health, premature death, even suicide. A quick recovery for all involved is often the best way, but that required regulating one's thoughts and behaviors. Overthinking and negative self-talk are to be avoided at all costs. Positive activities and energies must consciously replace the negative. If you lost a job, don't languish in unemployment and the downward spiral that creates. If you've had to abandon an old friendship, make a new one.

Social skills will be essential to navigate a personal, professional, or familial breakup. You'll need to show respect, to observe protocols, not undercut the other with their friends. More on this below.

Empathy is one of those skills common to the different skill sets of true leadership, emotional intelligence, and social skills. It's crucial during and after a breakup, though as we said it should be delivered in moderation under these circumstances.

Motivation will really come into play during breakups of all sorts. Professionally, you'll want to send your former team member off with eyes toward a better future, not feeling crushed and desperate. It's part of keeping things positive, one of the leadership skills we discussed above.

Cognitive abilities are also invaluable when navigating just about any kind of breakup and the period which follows.

Sustained attention will keep you focused on the task at hand; retiring one person and finding another, managing what remains of your team, a long-haul project which will have lots of milestones. This is true for social, professional, and intimate relationships.

And because there will be a variety of complex elements to any breakup, selective attention is also crucial. You'll have to pay attention to their feelings and your own, their beliefs and perspectives and your own, other complexities of life. You'll have to stay focused in either a professional or personal arena.

And you'll have to give all these things your divided attention as well. If you're divorcing parents, you have to give the kids your attention, and your spouse, and your job, and your friends. You'll have to use other leadership skills like prioritizing in order to see to all the little crises which are likely to arise.

Long-term memory will be important too. If you're losing a team member, you'll want to use that long-term memory to present a pattern of poor or negative behavior. If you're cutting an old friend lose, your long-term memory of their extended bad behavior will give you cause. It's the same for an intimate partner. This skill will remind you of why you're doing what you're doing even when presented with possibly desperate arguments to the contrary. Long-term memory is what gives you true perspective and it's crucial to your cognitive ability skillset.

Short-term or working memory will be helpful, but it's not crucial to these circumstances. Hey, you can't have everything!

Logic and reasoning, on the other hand, will come into play at virtually every turn of any sort of breakup. You have to stay logical and unemotional. Breakups are often intellectually based. It's usually the result of deliberation, consideration, reflection, and those are intellectual pursuits. By the time the person doing the firing or the breaking up is ready to do it, there's less emotion for them. The person on the receiving end, it's a different story. Without having time to intellectually process their emotions, the emotions are likely to rise to the fore. The emotive side of the brain is the faster to act, after all. So, you can use this cognitive skill to counter emotion, lean toward your better self and keep emotions out of the picture. Emotion and reason cannot co-exist in the same psyche at the same time, remember. Remain reasonable and you can't become emotional. Remain emotional and you can't be reasonable. This principle holds true no matter what kind of breakup we're applying it to.

Auditory processing should be constant. Actively listen, attention and retention and recall. Note changes in vocal tone, speed of delivery, the manner and the matter of what is being said, the subtext (or what isn't being said but is nevertheless true). Never stop listening during a breakup or after, when you're seeking feedback and conference with mentors.

It's the same thing with visual processing. Never do anything without it, especially not during any kind of breakup. Pay attention to little visual cues, body language, turns of a facial expression which reveal what the person you're talking to is really thinking despite what they might be saying. Watch your own auditory and visual signals too, you may learn more about yourself than you care to know!

Processing speed is the last cognitive ability you'll use to navigate a breakup. This is especially true in the period immediately after the breakup. Process the painful information, make whatever adjustments your analysis and reflection and feedback suggest, make a plan and then put it into action. Get a new job, find a new partner, find new friends, change your behavior, move to South America. But it's very important not to languish, to overthink, to get locked into the infamous *analysis paralysis* which prevents further action in favor of constant deliberation.

We move on then, to critical thinking and its applications for a breakup situation, the end of a professional, intimate, familial, or social relationship.

The first element of critical thinking is identification, and you'll lean heavily on this skill. You'll have to identify your emotions at being fired, or you'll be identifying the reasons a person isn't a good fit in your team. You'll be identifying why you want to leave your intimate partner and what you plan to do afterward. If you're the one being left behind, you'll have to identify your emotions and deal with them. You'll have to identify the remedy or remedies as well.

Research is an element of critical thinking you'll find invaluable here. You're doing it right now. But you'll want to ask your mentors how to best get through it based on the particulars of the situation, the behaviors and the personalities involved. This is true no matter what kind of relationship is ending.

Identifying biases is crucial. If you're making your workplace firing based on biases, you're taking a legal risk of a civil lawsuit for discrimination. At best, you're not upholding the best standards, which is what a true leader does. If biases are affecting your romantic life, or your friendships, that's your business legally. There's no law against having biases. And you can't help a bias either. A bias is basically how you feel. Bigotry is essentially how you act based on your biases. So, while you may have biases, you should not ever allow bigoted behavior reflect those biases. That's being a leader in name only, and probably not for long.

Inference will be your best friend in times of a relationship's end. Clear communication will almost certainly be compromised by emotion at some point. People are simply not that forthcoming in such situations (or in any). Politeness and protocol train us not to be completely forthcoming even under the best of circumstances. So, you'll have to do a lot of inferring, no matter what side of any kind of breakup you find yourself on. Be it the true reason for the breakup or the true feeling behind the mask the other wear, you'll do more than your share of inferring during a breakup.

Prioritizing will also be more than handy, but necessary. If you've been fired, you know there's no time to waste. Prioritize getting back on your feet. Did you have to let somebody go? Replacing them with a better team member is your priority and that's easy to see. Heartbroken, abandoned by an old friend? Ask yourself how much that old friend or ex-partner really mattered.

Curiosity is the last element of critical thinking and it must remain alive in your heart and mind during times of a breakup. Be interested in what is coming next. Be interested in what your new team member will bring to the project, or how the climate will be improved. Be curious about your new friends and new partners. You may even want to stay curious about alienated siblings or parents. They're still your family, and a growth-minded person knows that circumstances can change. Just because you can't be in the same room with a person for whatever reason doesn't mean you don't wish them well and want to hear how they are progressing.

Social skills are essentially goal-directed and can vary upon the situation, as we have seen.

Our old friend empathy is central to social skills, because understanding how people feel, being able to share their perspective and even their pains and emotions, is key to social interaction. We've already looked at *The Mighty E* and how it's crucial to our interactions at this stage. Let's move on.

One social skill that will be handy in navigating a breakup of a professional or intimate or social or even a familial relationship; maintaining eye contact. It shows respect, consideration, that you're actively listening. It shows that you're not afraid to reveal yourself, even at that time.

Body language will go far not only during your breakup but afterward. Don't snarl and snap during the unpleasant experience. Afterward, watch your posture and your facial expressions. Don't let the event take over your body. Moving on will mean the self-discipline to control your own movements.

Be mindful (always, but in this case) of being either assertive or aggressive. This is a delicate line that may make all the difference in navigating a breakup of any sort. Assertiveness is about declaring what you want or need. Assertiveness is about standing your ground. Aggressiveness is more about demanding, challenging, attacking. Always favor the former and eschew the latter in any negotiation, be it a contract or a breakup, professional or intimate, social or familial.

Having good social skills includes selecting the best communication channels. Don't break up with somebody via text, don't fire somebody using a bullhorn. Don't end a friendship at the guy or girl's wedding. Don't confront your hostile sibling at your mother's funeral (in that case, you might text … kidding!)

Flexibility and cooperation will be essential in navigating a breakup, especially in the case of co-workers or divorcing parents, as we've seen.

Accepting criticism without defensiveness is another key to handling these situations with skill. You'll wind up getting some criticism somewhere along the line, from a judgmental boss or spiteful team member, from an angry scorned partner or in the form of romantic refusal, from an angry friend or sibling or child or parent. Defensiveness will close your mind when it should be open. It won't be easy, but this is a social skill everybody would benefit from mastering. It's surprising how many people can't handle it even in the most minute increments. The slightest criticism sets some people off into a rage, but these are emotionally ignorant leaders in name only.

Remaining positive is another skill which overlaps from one skillset to the others, but it's a good reminder how important it is in these and other times. In any crisis, positivity is a plus. As are showing respect and being a good learner and teacher. Show respect for the person you're leaving and, even harder, for the person who's leaving you. You may not be able to tolerate your adult sister's company or political views, but you can still retain your good attitude and learn from that experience and share that lesson with others.

Above all, retain your humanity. You're a human being, not a collection of habits and notions. Retaining a sense of your own humanity and the humanity of others will make getting through these trying times easier; professional or personal, intimate or familial. This is the core principle to all the others, the central notion that will guide you in true leadership, emotional intelligence, cognitive skills, critical thinking, and social skills. Respect humanity. After all, it's one thing we all have in common.

CONCLUSION

And that brings us to the end of this particular stage of your life's journey, in search of greater leadership skills. You're now more self-aware of your leadership style, your empathy, and your mindfulness. You're more attuned to your emotional intelligence and have greater control over your behavior and a greater influence over the behavior of others. You've probably sharpened your cognitive abilities, and come to know a little better just what those are. Your new critical thinking skills will serve you in your professional, personal, social and intimate circles, and you'll be able to pass those along to others. That will strengthen your family, your team, and your friendships.

You know how to apply this information to relationships of all sorts and at all stages; at the beginning, the middle, even at the end.

But the journey's not over. Part of being a true leader is to always be curious, always be learning and keeping up with the latest data, techniques, and technology. This book has likely excited you to go on learning in a continuous process of discovery and self-realization. You'll want to take that curiosity and desire for achievement and improvement into other aspects of your life. Better communications in relationships, overcoming overthinking and procrastination and being a more productive worker or manager; there's a lot to learn. We've got the books on these very subjects and many more, delivering the latest information clearly, with practical exercises and just a bit of humor.

Most importantly, you've learned that skills like these can always be learned and improved upon. Your new growth mindset allows you to see life as a process of development. Nobody has to be limited by what seems to be a lack of natural talent. These things are learned, honed, developed, evolved with time and experience. You must have had hope when you started this book, but now you have certainty. And you should have the self-confidence to use this invaluable information to get the job done, for yourself and for those around you. Well done on mastering your leadership skills, now go and master other skills. That is the way to becoming a truly self-actualized person and living a longer, happier, more fulfilling life.

www.ingramcontent.com/pod-product-compliance
Lightning Source LLC
Chambersburg PA
CBHW021952160426
43209CB00001B/18